Righting Our Ship

Re-creating a Nouveau New Brunswick

**With 21st Century
Direction
Expectations
& Governance**

By C F Steeves

cfsteeves™
@cfsteeves™

Steeves, Charles F., 1955-

ISBN-13: 978-1530287161

ISBN-10: 1530287162

Contents

Foreword

Hope Was Restored

(Spem Reduxit)

Restaurons l'espoir

**We have restored hope,
in harmony, community and opportunity**

Introduction

Governing must be in the best interest of the people. Governing should be from a deep seated purpose based on our mission as a people, with motives aligned with our principles, and decisions and commitments that are values based. Good governance in a modern democracy is as tenable a precept of good government as it is with any organization, even more so. While governments ought to be run with modern principles of governance, sound management practices and business-like processes, they cannot be run like a business.

Frequently, we are faced with more questions than answers. We wonder, why it is that politicians and civil servants are adverse to transparency. Or, how it can be that a policy is 'wrong' by the governing party only to be 'correct' once the opposition becomes the government. Or, the same civil servants the politicians criticized while in opposition they defend immediately upon taking power.

No longer is it acceptable to permit the political ego, or a shallow defensiveness because it was "not on my watch". Nor the falsehood that we need a "made in our province approach" (because we are unique). Politicians are elected to represent the people, not represent (i.e., defend) their staff; politicians are elected to abide by what is best and proper by leveraging their professional staff, not choosing political (i.e., electable) options.

There are many questions, but also answers, as there are best practice ways to decide, execute, and deliver. In a province, there are also competencies required by a Premier and Ministers, and by Deputy Ministers and their Directors and staff. This premise is the essence of how we can and should be re-creating what I term a Nouveau New Brunswick, with 21st century direction, expectations and governance.

In nearly thirty years of working with leaders of government, elected officials as well as their senior management and departmental staff, I have appreciated the paradox of the senior civil servant to the elected official. Likewise the seeming ambiguity of senior/middle management professionals as well as the similarity of knowledge workers in any workplace, public sector civil servant or private and publicly traded corporation employee.

Establishing strategic direction at the provincial, regional, or municipal level of government, is as dependent on a fundamental understanding of values and mission as it is in a business. Accountability for actions and results, while subject to judgment at the time of elections, nearly always is lacking in authentic transparency and good governance. While publicly traded corporations are fighting the battle of activist shareholders challenging their boards and management, similarly, taxpayers and voters are in a battle of frustrating proportions with their elected officials who apparently oversee their senior civil servants.

In strategic projects with many Atlantic Canada federal regional directors general and their management teams, several provincial departments in the Maritimes, and with municipalities, I have witnessed the positive and the not so positive. The degree of success covers a wide range from a sound and proper strategy which transformed the direction of a department to two departments laying aside their silos to focus on joint outcomes for their sector of the province. From political meddling at the time of government change casting aside sound decisions without so much as a review to a disjoint of government directions, priorities and actions with those of the civil service and administrations.

During continuous improvement and quality process implementation, I facilitated a major government group in establishing best practice benchmarking, manage by measurable criteria, and strategically influence tactical decision making. As a contrast, in other instances meetings with senior civil servants were incredulous in the incumbents postulating as to why a (proven) outsourcing approach by governments and corporations alike was 'not the same here' and would cost more if not kept within the department.

At the tactical and daily workload management levels, I have seen department staff, hospital employees and teachers alike frustrated in working alongside peers who are unable or unwilling to make the contribution appropriate to what needs be done, should be done, and has to be done.

Frankly it is frightening to see the level of acquiescence, lack of knowledge and apparent recalcitrance, to move us forward—by politicians and senior civil servants. It is the time to transcend the pointing of fingers, hand wringing or wishful thinking, or resigning to perpetual complacency.

For the past few years, it has been a privilege serving my community, three times elected as Chair of the Advisory Committee to the Minister for the Local Service District of Pointe-du-Chêne; elected by my peers to represent the Westmorland County and Albert County Local Service Districts on the Board of the Regional Service Commission for Southeast N.B.; as well as participate as an appointee to the Provincial Local

Government Modernization External Advisory Committee. First hand, I know that we have what it takes to do what we must do.

We are a resourceful people, citizens of a province with political titans like Charles Fisher, Samuel Leonard Tilley, Louis J Robichaud and Francis Joseph McKenna, with economic growth due to our early shipbuilding and lumber magnates to business titans such as K. C. Irving, Wallace and Harrison McCain, and Gilbert Finn; the blended strengths of our English and Acadian heritages, and those of Scottish, Irish, German and other peoples, as well as our Mi'kmaq and Maliseet peoples. We have at various times created and invented and innovated an impressive list of accomplishments.

New Brunswickers, living here and living away, treasure and know of the value of our little corner of the world, the picture province with the wonderful life style, at work and play. We have a prosperity of nature and resources and heritage, with social, education and health systems for all, and people with wide ranging talents and resourcefulness. It is time for us to remove ourselves from the fiscal mire of decades long, overcome the threat, and add financial self-sufficiency and renewed government to our prosperity.

My maternal heritage of 350 years of original Acadian families of Comeau and Arseneau is my innate foundation of belonging and pride of persistence in surviving and thriving. The 250 years of history in my paternal heritage of German original settlers Stieff (Steeves) to The Bend and Father of Confederation William Henry Steeves, and 1800s homesteading Scottish MacFarlane, resounds within me the obligation of contribution and conviction to the destiny of our province.

More than a personal passion for my home province, this book is about my belief that we can, if willing, re-create our destiny as it should be and re-create a nouveau New Brunswick. It is predicated by my experience and a continuously improving personality, which I transformed into a lifetime avocation of contribution to business and community, to share what we can do if we set ourselves to transform into a 21st century people of Direction, Expectations and Governance for self-determining self-fulfillment, by righting our ship in New Brunswick.

> Prosperity is about enriching our lives and others;
> it is a wealth that is more than money.
> cfs

Chapter 1

Righting Our Ship

Righting our ship is the first stage to take control and have a self-determined destiny in New Brunswick. Re-creating a Nouveau New Brunswick is about New Brunswickers pressing for and supporting a transformation, without delay, to a province of self-control, with a renewed sense of destiny and a self-sufficiency—something not seen for far too many decades.

We are at a point where re-creation is what will launch us to 'righting our ship' as a province. It is not, and cannot be, about incrementalism, nor hapless actions, nor timid strokes forward, nor uninformed, inexperienced decisions behind those strokes. We have to stop the unabating 'have not' partner, outward and inward, references within our confederation, beginning by righting our ship. Once afloat, we can transition from righting our ship to sailing our ship.

We can make this happen with a collective understanding of what our reason for being, our raison d'être, our mission, is as a province. We have lost our way, and lost sight of what we ought to do for ourselves as we lulled into a complacency with federal transfers and politically motivated decisions. We are, in many ways, lost in the waves as we wander one or two strokes back, one stroke forward, fighting off condescending criticism and treatment by some of our federal and other provincial leader types.

Further, we must be clear on a mandated mission that we will give to a governing party, confidently entrusting them to govern. From the leaders and parties we need to make this choice, and follow through with nothing less than a 21st century governance between our government and our civil service, including full and respectful transparency with measurable results, to fulfil our reason for being and as a people who are this province.

We are on the cusp, should we choose to act with the right leaders in place and an informed electorate, of proving that we are not the poor cousin province, as we experienced in our 1960s transition. Complacency, from our dependency on federal equalization grants, transfer monies, and regionally favored Employment Insurance, must be converted to an absolute discontent of our current situation.

It has been half a century since Premier Louis Robichaud pulled New Brunswick into the Canadian 20th century with significant reform legislation, touching our social, education, health care and judicial systems, as well as governance structural changes that impacted counties, municipalities, civil service, and even liquor laws. His was a government of action based on well-defined strategic themes—and driven be a vision.

With equal passion and drive, the Premier Frank McKenna decade attracted a whole new industry based on the telecommunications advances of NB Tel and an educated bilingual workforce. To move full stream into the 21st century we require a significant thrust that is a combination of both eras.

Nothing short of a tectonic shift in setting our direction, awakening to the true outcomes to clarify our expectations, and establishing the way we are to be governed, will result in success now and for our longer term benefit. Possibly, in addition to a bold move to righting our ship and correcting our course, we may discover the way and create a model for our confederation and others as to how a provincial or state partner should govern in a 21st century democratic federation.

Perhaps the single biggest obstacle is understanding the underlying constraint preventing our Province from succeeding. We are in the bottom quartile of provinces in our confederation in too many areas, or vying for the bottom depending on the metrics. Yet the top quartile provinces of Alberta and British Columbia and until recently Ontario, have the same constraint.

Modern democracies, including those with a social-mindedness, have grown too large bureaucratically and directive managerially by taking on ill-suited and unsuitable roles to meet obligations to their citizens. **A modern society needs to be steered by a government that exists for a certain set of outcomes, not weighed down with the delivery of programs**.

It has been said that an ant proportioned to the size of an elephant is not possible as the force of gravity will have it collapse within its own weight. Likewise, the modern democracy is collapsing on its own weight of bureaucracy and role-playing. It is being challenged by its people on a lack of transparency, wastefulness, incompetence and disappointments.

Successive electorates have complained, for far too long, in one way or another, of our series of governments along with their civil service leaders, as to a less than stellar level of government and one in which we generally are disappointed. The 'we' is collective; for *we,* as the electorate, are responsible for this, and *we* need to be held accountable to ourselves for what *we* expect and whom *we* elect to fulfill our expectations. Until we accept this accountability and responsibility, we will continue to be ineffectual with our expectations regarding what we want, and whom we want to represent us, govern for us, and do what is right by us.

Can we handle the truth? We cannot expect the politicians that we continue to elect to do things different than the past if we continue to elect politicians who do not know otherwise.

With a small population, resources base, and manufacturing significance, do we have the fortitude to focus on the outcomes we want, making the realistic decisions that will actually effect the change we say we need? Can we not see that the only way, without putting our value of dignity of person and of universal health, education and social services at risk, is by making the right decisions?

We as a people cannot turn blindly away, avoiding the truth that is our reality. As well, we cannot allow a growing cynicism of politicians and what they say and promise to thwart electing the right people to get the right job done right. To accept the status quo, or be blind to it, is to wring our hands, hoping that the economy will get better and everything will be all right.

Even a positive upturn in our economic situation no longer is sufficient to right our ship. Besides which the current indicators are that any upturn could be years away. And that is if we avoid some dark waters now lurking.

Only foundational and transformational decisions and changes in how we are governed, how we allocate resources, how we manage programs, and how we are honest and transparent as a province, will find us living up to our values as a people. Otherwise, it is we who allow our politicians, as we allow ourselves, not to 'talk the talk' and nor 'walk the talk'. In other words, we breach our own values. And, that can only sink our ship, not right our ship.

> "We have met the enemy and he is us"
>
> Pogo, American comic strip

We will right our ship with a leader at the helm, knowledgeable and skillful as a chair of a cabinet of ministers, who is also willing and confident in setting the direction for our Province. In the absence of sufficient cabinet ministers with the requisite capabilities, we may require an appropriate person to be an appointed, non-elected vice-minister to a minister.

Political leadership of a 21st century democracy requires an inherent understanding of the values of the people, and the ability to articulate those into goals and actions necessary to deliver the programs and services to fulfill those values. And the capability. Competency is not over-rated.

Aspiring leaders should have a track record proving their worthiness of meaningful contribution, the parties trusted to elect competent, skills ready nominees to the position of leader, and electors need to be provided a choice from credible options, then be prepared to choose and support. The number one competency of our party leaders must be the capability factor.

When expectations without precedent are met by obstacles without precedent, the 'what' and 'why' must be clear, the 'way' without doubt is transformational, and the 'how' is different than before. Simply, we are not electing enough leaders of sufficient competence from which to make a choice to be our Premier. And so, re-creation continues to escape us.

Likewise, the 'who' must contribute positively and successfully to 21st century priorities while balancing the 'values' of our citizens. Universal accessibility to optimum health and education and social support systems is not possible with 19th century models of solo professionals and silo bureaucracies with 20th century skillsets in the realities of the 21st century. Supporting guidelines and skills updating, with attitudes and aptitudes aligned to the new realities, will take commitment and persistence.

Health care executives, school superintendents and social service professionals should focus on the delivery of services within their expertise areas, not bricks & mortar and vehicles & maintenance. This can be accomplished in each of these areas with an appropriate 'partnering' model, or contractor/service model, with properly established, learned governance. The latter can be ensured through a re-tooling of the civil service mandate guided by a 21st century governance with responsibility delegated to them, and capable of quality in oversight of operations and outcomes success.

Our government must choose outcomes and services so that the most effective, appropriate and efficient choices are made for delivery and bureaucracy. We can focus on the highest quality within our reach with respect to education, safe roadways, support services, health care, and lifelong social support services, without the debt of owning every piece of equipment or building or road that is situated on provincial land. With proper oversight we can own the land below the infrastructure without the burden of the operational costs or debt, just as major financial and other corporations.

Lack of transparency may have been to the benefit of political leaders and civil servants in the past, but clearly it was self-serving in the removal of hassles and obstacles that got in their way, as well as the bypassing of accountability. Today, a political leader, confident and capable, can turn transparency into the greatest release from a bondage of secrecy. Once an area of fear and defensiveness, **transparency in a 21st century society can be a pragmatic and empowering asset**, to the willing.

On a macro level, we need to ramp up results, without procrastination, and with sensitivity; without disruption of vital services but with transformation of provision; without a positive current cash flow but with an about turn of net revenues and expenses. Paramount is how we will balance this cognitive dissonance that continues to grow and continues to reach new levels without precedence.

Our situation has to be approached differently than we have been willing or capable, forging ahead, pulling the people and pushing forward that which is necessary. Most effective would be beginning with affirming what is really important to us, having a collective sense of what we ultimately want, focusing on our reason for being as a province and that of our government's mandate. Most efficient would be a full restructuring of the provincial Cabinet and senior civil service. This is easily enough done by an experienced capably confident Premier. More challenging will be a full and complete overhaul of program delivery to meet our 21st century needs.

With confidence and competence, lest we chop and cut in middle-of-the-road and desperate mediocrity, we need to set our broader objectives for ten years, but with clear, measurable goals and action for the current four year government term, and into the next term. With grit, we task the best people accessible given our situation, make the changes necessary with resources and people, and forge ahead. We turn aside actions which politically and effectively may appear sensitive in the short-run but compromise us dearly.

There will be pain, and misunderstanding, and disagreement, and posturing, through this. But it will be there regardless. In a constant headwind due to less than satisfactory results where has that taken us? Like nearly everywhere in the western democratic world, cynicism and frustration has been growing close to a bursting point. Provided we are focused, while nimble, prepared to meet disappointments while riding the waves of opportunities, and honest and transparent, our horizon will be in sight.

New Brunswick has benefited from leadership inspired by vision and followed up with fulfillment with a circa Confederation duo of leaders, and in the latter half of the 20th century with two visionary Premiers. Although there now may be an absence of such stature of a leader, we need to coalesce in our determination to make our success.

Surely, **it is abundantly clear that a 21st century New Brunswick cannot be successful with a 19th century model albeit modified with a 20th century upgrade**, but now left to only incrementally adjusted leadership and structure. Else, we will remain forever unsatisfied and unfulfilled, and sooner than later bankrupt if not financially then in our capability. And, still cynical.

We can be successful in righting our ship only by throwing overboard the incremental adding here and chipping away there, personal preference of particular non-issues or pet aversions, instead preparing without haste to set the sail overseeing all oars in the water thrusting us into the 21st century. Already a decade and a half into this century, we have no time to waste.

In my New Brunswick, rather than chopping in the water of despair and rudderless movement, or asking for a lifebuoy to be thrown our way, we are taking control and thriving in our sailing forward.

Our Leaders

As citizens, we need to ask ourselves what we want as a province: of ourselves, of our leaders whom we elect, and their governments and civil servants. Single mindedness issues such as anti-toll booths, anti-privatization, anti-shale gas, and other 'anti' decisions, won elections, but have resulted in general dissatisfaction with successive governments. Since the late 1990s only one of our recent governments was re-elected, arguably due to some competence in continuing the predecessor's policies.

This is not to be critical of the people who have, for the most part, sought and attained elected office for the 'right' reasons of making a difference, contributing what they can, and participating in public service. These are people who frequently after years of contributing to our communities in many other ways, then step up and out for elected office. To our loss, not nearly enough of such men and women put themselves forward for the rigors of public life.

The lone exception to this generalized statement of lack of stellar results of the last near half century of premiers, arguably, is the Premier with a singular talent that outshone other similarities with his contemporaries. That was Frank McKenna, and the government he led. His was a talent for attracting and growing business and jobs in this province that continue to echo today significantly. His was a talent that augmented his passion for our people and province. His was a passion driven by vision.

This huge tangible benefit, from one leader, which can be felt through three successive governments, five elections, and over a decade and a half after his retirement, far outweighed some shortcomings his government had in common with most of his successors, and half the mandates of each of his immediate predecessors.

Premier McKenna, more than anything, left a legacy in two areas— attracting private sector jobs by leveraging our telecommunications and information technology infrastructure created by NB Tel, and the modernizing of our highway transportation system. He was a leader who surely knew his capabilities, who knew how to use his talents, communicate with the people of his province, and have the courage to make things happen.

Quite simply, a game changer for New Brunswick—and one with the talent which was desperately needed at the time.

Along with the handful of key Minister and Deputy Minister appointees with appropriate competencies, as well as the succession of visionary CEOs at NB Tel, and the business community driven strategic push of Greater Moncton, this province capitalized on the new telecommunications customer service world. Mr. McKenna remains the most dynamic speaker, of vision and substance with a charisma and obvious far reaching influence, from New Brunswick of our generation.

The McKenna administration requires little explanation regarding the personality of the leader and the personality of his administration. The Premier worked hard, effective and efficient in his efforts and results. The tone of optimism, of building the foundations of a diversified economy on the resources of our people–knowledge, skills and language—rather than just the resources of our land, permeated his Cabinet and caucus, and the primary Deputy Ministers and their civil service staff. This personality was the ambition and the person of its leader.

As the provincial economy diversified and grew, creating jobs with mostly good salaries and benefits, New Brunswickers' self-esteem grew as well. Wherever Premier McKenna may have faltered, it was overshadowed by his talent and passion for his province. His was a decade of significant success in moving our province forward, in partnering with business, community and municipal leaders in the common understanding of stimulating jobs based on what we have and can do. Frank, as he is known to all, was never giving up until a modern twinned TransCanada highway that links the Maritimes to central Canada was complete. With his leadership businesses locally and from afar created jobs that leveraged the foresightedness of NB Tel, and his own 'can-do/will-do' was instilled in his fellow citizens.

> "The noblest question in the world is,
> 'What good may I do in it?' "
>
> Benjamin Franklin

Also game changing in its own way, at least from a perspective as to how our citizens expect our Premiers to behave, is the example of David Alward. While it could be said that he tripped on one or two issues, bold on resources, perhaps not bold enough to act on his Finance Minister's initiatives, he was humble and honest in his work as Premier. Here was a Premier, above simply promising and speaking of consultation, who actually consulted widely. The handful of ministers in his government, who were the most successful during the term of his government—with difficult and demanding portfolios—were also those who consulted more than their colleagues and their predecessors. The remaining ministers, with minimal to nil or too-little-too-late consultation, created the problems for which his government failed to win its second term, leaving it vulnerable to criticism.

The creation of Regional Service Commissions, the groundwork for modernization of government, the beginnings of internal adjustments toward justice process productivity, and the financial budgetary process and decisions—all were done in the planning stages—with less conflict, and more results, than the portfolios of those ministers who failed to consult as their Premier had requested and directed. The initial regionalization concept was created by the Liberal party, shelved in fear of its own appointee's proposed forced amalgamation, but an authoritative guide to a willing government.

Most citizens, if one asks, consider Premier David Alward as a decent, compassionate, down-to-earth, and honest man who was willing to promote what he thought was right for his Province. These all are qualities we say we want in a Premier; and qualities the opposing parties also choose to describe this person.

Most, if not all, people go into politics for noble reasons of contributing and serving their community, province or nation. And, yet, we are a cynical electorate. The multi term re-election of premiers and their governments was stopped at Premier Shawn Graham, not due to a lack of boldness, which is requisite for the times and was shown as is rarely seen in our leaders, but from a failure to communicate, being sufficiently transparent, and informed enough to instill confidence in a significant outcome which New Brunswickers would have to live for generations.

Why is that? Perhaps it is because the history of politics, here and everywhere for that matter, has particularly over the past few decades seen us evolve into this cynical electorate. And no wonder. **Politicians and their civil services have failed to evolve at the same time and speed as the voters**.

While the expectations of the voters could be considered unrealistic in the reality of our financial weakness, empathy is with all who want to preserve the social and health support systems to which our modern nation has become accustomed. Without significant reform and transformation, those expectations will remain unrealistic.

Rounds of consultation by successive senior Cabinet Ministers, inclusive and wide-ranging, revealed **a populace with all kinds of ideas—as long as it did not negatively impact them particularly**. When a rare idea did address inside our system deficiencies or legitimate outside the box thinking, one can expect that if it meant challenging the 'sacred cow' of a government operated public service, then it withered on the white board, or in the clatter of discontent.

Our Decisions

True, it can be said that New Brunswick is a province more complex than most. It is Canada's only official bilingual province, with both majority linguistic communities rights entrenched in the Constitution. It remains the most rural of provinces with three major centers, lacking in a significant densely populated city with the typical inherent exponential economies of scale. It is an inclusive society on its streets and in its classrooms, with a belief in the dignity of persons, but the weight of complexity. And, New Brunswick now is the 'oldest' demographically in the nation.

With Canada's leading equal status recognition of the major linguistic founding communities, there is an enrichment of language and culture. At roughly one third Francophone and two third Anglophone, it was from the migration of Acadians and the influx of United Empire Loyalists, followed by Scottish and Irish and German immigrants, and the earlier Mi'kmaq and Maliseet that became what is called New Brunswick.

Along with a population balanced between rural and urban dwellers, we have three 'major' cities that share the infrastructure and clout that commonly goes to a capital city and largest metropolitan area, like our three sister Atlantic Canada provinces. Authentically, there is a complexity, politically and financially, to lead and manage such an intricacy of interests.

In many ways, politically, it is in the balancing of this diversity that seems to trap our politicians into making the wrong decisions. Only occasionally are we blessed with a Premier who can transcend the scrapping and move us forward on one front or another. Election platforms designed to please, language friction, north versus south, urban over rural, create debates that pull us down rather than thrust us forward.

Reflecting back a half century to the 1960s of Louis J Robichaud, this was a time of transformation of our 19th century county system to a more responsive governing of the mid-20th century, and reforms of significance to our rural and Acadian populations. This was not a time of incremental changes, and the successes would not have occurred if it had been.

Thirty years later the Frank McKenna era ushered in a new wave of optimism in the wake of lost railroads, manufacturing plants and wholesale warehousing. Premier McKenna grasped the immensity of the industry leading vision and technology of our NB Tel Presidents, embracing the 'resurgo' of Southeast New Brunswick, fully engaging his personal skill sets to advance our province, and citizens everywhere.

The decade following "Little Louis" saw a continuity of those reforms. Likewise, "Frank" was followed by a decade of continuity by the succeeding government. Premier Bernard Lord's election may have been won by an aforementioned 'anti-topic' of the day, but the government did provide leadership in continuity of purpose from its predecessor, and its own balanced budgets.

Single term premiers followed who either failed to recognize a modern electorate's demand for transparency or sufficiently demonstrated their policies in a way that resonated with voters. Those were the underpinning shortcomings, although one would not be too far of the mark in pointing out that more effective communications would have assisted their cause. Regardless, not significant enough nor sufficient enough movement was made on the major underlying challenges within our Province.

Now, in the mid-2010s we must make the transformation, one that is well overdue, and be governed by a system and style responsive to the 21st century. All the more difficult will this be because we have waited, and procrastinated, and did not recognize what was necessary. We need to restructure our provincial government and governance; deal with the funding and inadequacies of unincorporated areas; get out of running businesses; create transparent and accountable Ministries and civil service; so that we can attain outcomes while we reduce deficits, debt and delays in service.

During the past decades there was some forced amalgamation, and some situations where governments were frightened to move further, either with amalgamation or by applying creativity in the models necessary. There was the Liberal government sponsored Finn Report that dealt with the problem of 100s of more communities than is even fathomable for a population as small as ours, but because it included forced 'municipalization' it was tabled. Fortunately, the reforms were put on the track forward with the Conservative government move to Regional Service Commissions—the beginning of the emancipation of our unincorporated areas through collaboration.

This province has to stop considering programs as values, as does the rest of Canada federally and provincially. **New Brunswick governments have to begin making progressively improving policies to achieve outcomes consistent with our values and priorities.** This province has to put an end to falling short because it is stuck in the never-ending rut of operating via the civil service practically everything in which it funds.

> "The problems we are facing today
> can't be solved at the
> same level of thinking we were at
> when we created them."
>
> Albert Einstein, great physicist and thinker

We are in the 21st century. The government needs to change its purpose and role as does the civil service. Transformational change needs to be implemented by a visionary with the capacity to communicate, establish a new way of governing, and facilitate effective and efficient delivery of programs. The waves are coming upon us with the ways we now govern.

In New Brunswick, we have both a structural deficit and a cyclical deficit. Our structure of doing things is crumbling within its weight (like the elephant sized ant) because it neither is sufficiently effective nor efficient, hence the structural deficit. Our failure to operate and manage effectively along with inefficient systems creates an anchor from which we have not shown the capacity nor the nimbleness to weather cycles.

Yet, we continue to balk at changing the way we do things or deliver services. We, tax payers and politicians, point to previous failures and criticize some attempts because of a particular perspective or bias. The misplaced bias can be directed at private enterprise, such as it cannot be trusted with confidential information, or safety, or security. Or the bias can be critical of the capability of civil servants, when it is the system within which they work that ought to be changed, and then reassess the employees with metrics that contribute to that new system.

Several private public partnerships (P3) with schools and highways are likely successful; and yet the contracts—public sector, taxpayer funded contracts—are locked in the vaults of secrecy so we really don't know. While salaries once were hidden from the public, the Provincial website now shows the ranges of all management and executive employees. At least some hints of transparency are showing, while all around opaqueness abounds.

Just because certain P3 contracts may be deemed 'failures' does not mean that P3 as a method of program delivery is a failure, nor does it mean that all is being revealed. Firstly, what was the bias inherent in the study and subsequent report? Secondly, what oversight was provided? Ineptitude of oversight is more than likely the problem, not the use of a P3 approach. Thirdly, maybe there is not a failure, but a political bias to frame it thus.

When a Premier and Cabinet of one party creates 'FacilicorpNB' to centralize some non-medical services of hospitals, for economies of scale and savings, the Minister and the successor Minister of another party were each managed by senior bureaucrats, who in these sorts of matters are almost always more skilled than most elected leaders. One result was that laundry now is out-sourced to a single (one, monopoly) not-for-profit corporation for the entire province, and therefore without comparative or competitive benchmarks available.

> "There are many roads to prosperity,
> but one must be taken.
> Inaction leads nowhere."
>
> Robert Zoellick, former president of the World Bank

Another result was our healthcare sector Information Technology, considered to be a 'no-brainer' for outsourcing and corresponding savings and expertise, was "surprisingly" 'proven' to be a better value if it is maintained in-house. It seems that an all government parties committee, benefiting from certain MLAs with expertise as was available at the time, along with an outside consulting expert, armed with financials and competitive bids (none of the latter so far as anyone would know in the public) may have ascertained another recommendation to the government.

Decisions regarding provincial tax payer direct financial support or bank loan guarantees to business are considered confidential. The unincorporated Local Service Districts are without financial statement 'actuals', left with year to year budget comparisons. The real cost of road maintenance and snow clearing is not known, street by road let alone area, so decisions to reduce or eliminate levels of service are suppositional, line item reductions at best.

Where once opaqueness was the 'friend' and the 'strength' of politicians and their senior civil servants, this is no longer the case. This is not to say that either of these groups was deceitful or dishonest, in our colonial days or since Confederation. But, they could get away with governing this way, and it was easier for them to manage portfolios and make changes without the time it took to communicate, explain, debate, consult, and otherwise engage their voting public.

Lack of transparency, and lack of suitable capability for the strategic tasks at hand, are failures in respect of the citizenry. **Transparency and capability are critical to gaining the trust and respect of the electorate in the 21st century.** It was Premier Alward whose attribute was the appropriate consultation mix to make decisions to begin peeling back the lack of transparency. It was Premier McKenna with an unprecedented capability to leverage what NB Tel built to attract investment and jobs.

Our Province ardently needs leadership with both attributes. Moreover, we need both the party in power as well as the party in opposition to have in their ranks members reflective of both skill sets so that first, we can benefit from collaboration, and later so that we have alternatives for provincial leadership from which to choose. The significant decisions which must be made, with informed and measured risk, require also the advice and the capacity of their civil service in a more modern governance role.

A citizenry that is the most educated and knowledgeable and informed in our history, including a large segment of professionals and business owners, cannot be assumed to blindly follow. Today's electorate no longer will tolerate the 'pick the party and its leader' then 'trust us/me' to do the job of governing. Yet, puzzling as it is, that seemingly is what transpires each Election Day. (An exception being the extreme of this occurring in the 2015 Alberta provincial election, where in exasperation the shift was significant.)

A leader who wins their party's leadership, with the expectation to then win at the polls, should not be tolerated with an absence of a strategy and executable action plans of which they are capable, but they are for other 'electable' reasons. The strategy and action plans ought to be well articulated without grandiose innuendo, and the leader does need to have the proven capability and skill set to make it happen. There are no excuses, no reasons to feign lack of access and/or information upon election. In those situations where lack of transparency prevents otherwise, then it must be corrected.

In a political party system, it should be incumbent on the party to elect a leader with these traits, and the failure to do so an abdication of responsibility by constituents. Unfortunately, and to our peril, the level of talent necessary for this province to succeed is rarely presented by the parties to the people.

It is an indication of our times as to the dearth of choice in our political parties of talent at the leader level and leadership team to steer our nation and our provinces. The political parties themselves are as much to blame for their lack of capacity to attract better talent, as it is for the electorate not to become involved at the ground level in the nominations of their riding candidates, as it is for not enough of the capable amongst us to stand for political office.

Politicians seem out of sync with their citizens, as do their political parties. Often is it said that young girls and women need to be educated on the reigns of political power, but that falls short of what is needed. Our political parties need to do a better job to encourage a lot more people to join their ranks, see what is happening at the ground level of our democracy, and be a part of what creates the electoral choices that we have in each riding.

As an electorate we are making too many weak decisions, from the time of selection and nomination of candidates to parties, to the election day when we choose our local MLA, and in turn the party and leader for the subsequent four years. Our political parties are not showing enough wisdom to choose competency and substance over other attributes. Our premiers are not being wise enough to choose a smaller, competent cabinet over the politically expedient spreading around the spoils of electoral victory.

These are our decisions to make, and although we may not know what the solutions to our most troubling problems are, we do need to open our minds and think about what is presented to us. **We need to be more active in the nominations of those whom we choose from at the voting booth**. We need to be willing to consider significant leadership for the significant change necessary for our significant expectations.

Our Electoral Responsibility

As an electorate, can we be mature enough, can we be adult enough, to expect of our leaders to do what is right for us? We realize we cannot afford big mistakes in the decisions, the planning or the execution of what is required. Nor can we afford for our governing leadership to learn on the job, or pretend what they know or what they can do or what they are capable of doing.

There is a courage required, an emotional acuteness and competency awareness, to find the best we can afford to work with for our Cabinet and the key Assistant Deputy Ministers. **There are models of best practice operations that we can, within a modern governance model, adopt and apply to the services and operations of the province**. But, we need to know the truth and accept the truth if we are going to have progress.

"You can't handle the truth!"

Col. Jessup in *A Few Good Men*

Col. Jessup's vehement declaration comes to mind with regard to most of the recent provincial elections in Canada. Nearly everywhere, blinkers on with regard to the realities of deficit and debt, provincial citizens are showing that they cannot handle the truth. New Brunswick, too, is painfully slow in discarding the blinkers.

True, it could be argued that, intentionally or otherwise, party nominees aspiring to be premier inadequately articulate their plan to a populace that is increasingly dissatisfied. Broad policies can be written to sound positive when details are absent, and these are more of the variety of what we want to hear. Yet, this is the same electorate while considering itself educated and well-informed, vote on what it is they like to hear and not what has to be done. **Raise taxes, but not mine. Decrease unnecessary services, but mine are necessary to leave in place. People like the facts that they like**.

The rating agencies, somewhat consistent with their pre-election warnings, seem regularly, in quick fashion, ready to comment on a province's fiscal situation post-election at 'negative' due to their election choice. The Globe & Mail's columnist Jeffrey Simpson wrote in 2014 that "Ms. Wynne [the Ontario Premier] and her government face the difficult task of beginning to tell the truth."

Many in New Brunswick were thinking that the same could be written later in the year about New Brunswick. In short order, during the 2014-15 winter that is exactly what occurred. Editorials in Calgary and other cities, in essence, admonished New Brunswick for keeping our handout for transfer payments while voting against resource development. While we don't like it when central Canadians tell us what we ought to do, there is a truth in much of what is said. As recently as 2015Mar21, John Ibbitson wrote in his Globe and Mail column:

"Who will pay for the health care of a population with so many seniors and so few workers? Who will purchase the houses going up for sale? Who will buy the new cars, the appliances, the children's clothing – all the things that families need when starting out? How far will children have to be bused to the few remaining schools?"

Ibbitson continues, "Such a future can have only one outcome: slashed health care, education and other social services; ever greater departures by anyone able to escape the vortex; rural towns that become ghost towns; growing provincial deficits and debts, along with steadily reduced credit ratings that will increase borrowing costs. Disaster looms unless Maritimers work together to reverse the slide – and, in some respects, adjust their thinking."

We do need to work together. There are trans-Maritimes initiatives that need to be completed in professional designation association acts, bulk pharmaceutical purchases, complete removal of trade inhibitors and opening of free trade inter-provincially, and so on. These are areas of which all Maritimers would benefit, and should demand of our provincial governments. In the absence of material movement forward, we in New Brunswick at least can open our minds toward the possibilities.

And let us agree to stop the blame game. It serves no purpose and those who repeat it should be shushed. We all are well past the time of the self-blaming or generational finger pointing. It is tiring and trying to listen to boomer generation (and now younger) politicians and others with their incessant boomer generation blaming. Blaming to what avail? **The deficit, infrastructure and governance-lacking is an ongoing 20th century multi-generational creation.**

Laying it on with we-shouldn't-be-putting-it-on-our-grandchildren exasperation is disingenuous at best. Ironically, the 'greatest' generation pre-boomers (of whom I love and respect and admire) actually took the biggest losses but also reaped the biggest gains from 1980s unprecedented early retirement, pension benefits and severance packages; and were the very ones in power in the late-1960s to mid-1980s who put us on this path of higher expectations without financial sustainability. But we continue the dream.

Nothing short of a complete governing and structural change of how we view and do things can right our situation. This is more than criticizing or saying what we don't like or what is wrong. It is about knowledge and ability with willingness and doing, and we need to find and elect those people.

Compared to our small province of New Brunswick, the larger provinces of our confederation have significant critical mass of population, industry and natural resources to correct fiscal fate. The proverbial jury is out on if any can do this without the hard decisions, the ones that mean gain even if pain is unavoidable, honesty and clear actions with measurable criteria, which provide the transformational change for its course of events to succeed.

We need to be bold in our expectations of ourselves and our government. We need to be bold to hold them fully accountable, in ways perhaps that we have not shown before, quarterly and annually. **We cannot wait, grumbling and bemoaning, for the next four years until we can vote again. We need to mobilize, collect our thoughts, establish our direction and communicate our mandate to the current government to set the course and stop the sinking.**

Transitioning between governments has to take a priority over political party self-preservation and self-interest at the expense of our province. As many have stated in one way or another, we need each provincial government to provide a non-partisan hand-off of key files to its successor. This could have begun, if even in a moderate way, starting with this incoming government accepting the offer made by the very capable former Finance Minister.

Time should not be wasted in 'studying' and 'learning' for the first six or twelve months of a new government. We cannot afford months of lingering while ministers are learning their roles, or Cabinet is deciding what they really will do now that they are the government. Nor can we afford to wait for the 'best time' politically to enact legislative change to enable real change that is necessary.

Of course, it would be best if a suitable number of MLAs elected were competent in portfolios and management experience that are a part of ministerial responsibility. This is a joint responsibility of the parties themselves, and the electorate involving themselves at the riding level to nominate persons of qualification.

The provincial Cabinet has returned to smallish size, particularly with that of Brian Gallant which was even smaller than the reduction by David Alward. As I advised or suggested more than once, rarely does a Premier have more than a handful of legitimately competent Cabinet ministers. Therefore, it is a mistake to further water down capability and leadership with a large Cabinet.

We are a small population in a not overly large geography, ample in space and diversity off culture while also aware of our roots and commonality amongst those who dwell here. Therefore, other than pure politics, there no longer is a need to have Cabinet representation from every corner of this province. Only competent ministers need be considered—and that must be the key criteria for selection.

As an electorate, we cannot expect competent leadership, reduction of waste and expenses, without allowing the Premier to select accordingly. We cannot, on the one hand, complain and harp about overpaid politicians with their office budgets, while on the other hand expect our MLA or the next riding's MLA to be of a capability to be in Cabinet. If we desire Cabinet representation, **we should elect competent persons who can be eligible and competent for the position**.

Richard Saillant writes in 'Over the Cliff?' we "need to stop rewarding politicians who make lofty promises without explaining where the money will come from." [1] Add to this and stop punishing politicians who do things that are right for us. We complain about waiting times and medical staff salaries; road repairs undone and budget overruns; moose and deer licenses and environmental over-protection or under-protection; and on and on. This, all of it, is as disingenuous and unrealistic as we try to pin it on our politicians.

From the 'Over the Cliff?' book and editorials and pundits commentaries, and economists, and former Premiers, the truth is we have to more than continue on the course of cost containment and continuous improvement, even augmented with major changes, to prevent our ship from sinking. We have to right our ship—now. To pretend otherwise, to ignore the facts, is to be dishonest with ourselves because we want to stay in a dream.

Disregard the 'colour' of government in Ottawa, matching or not with the 'colour' in Fredericton. **We have to stop the dangerously high over-reliance on federal transfers. It keeps us self-reliant on others, vulnerable to policies changing.** And, forever denying the hand-out province (spoken or unspoken) derisions.

> Oh, hear us when we cry to Thee,
> For those in peril on the sea!

The Navy Hymn by William Whiting 1860

It is as if the 'cliff' we are on is a waterfall that if the line was cut even slightly to our buoy of funds our ship would be pulled over by the rushing waters. The inevitable rise of interest rates will add to the pull down.

For our near future avoidance of the brink, as well as our future self-control, we need to come clean with ourselves, ask our government to come clean with us, and not wait. Should a lack of the competencies necessary for success, in any given four year term, not be within the caucus currently governing then recruitment outside of political circles is necessary to special elevated roles of one or two 'Executive' Vice-Ministers reporting directly to Cabinet, or a Deputy Premier who has the competencies and capability to work with these special roles.

It is up to the citizens of voting age to expect and work to ensure that never again can we be told "You can't handle the truth'. Truly, it is despair that we cannot allow and complacent that we must not be.

Any leader, at any level in this province, to not face the truth is a leader in title only, and will contribute to the problems at hand—but not the solutions. Any leader, including a Premier, a Cabinet Minister, a Mayor of a municipality and a Chair of a Local Service District, who does not get on deck is in essence abdicating that leadership—and is allowed by those who elected them.

Bigger than our provincial leaders, the Premier and their governing party, the Leader of the Opposition and their party, this task also will require the collective and independent municipal mayors and their councils, and the Regional Service Commission Boards, to work together for a common vision to right this ship we call New Brunswick.

We *have* to collectively set the course, gather the right crew with the right competencies, upgrade our governing and rehabilitate our services, and pump out the weight of waste, to right our ship.

Times&Transcript 2014-10-11

This will mean a lot of change, a lot of doing things differently, communicating both within and to government, and from government. Consultation and collaboration. Adopting best practices, from other provinces best practices, perhaps other countries' states and provinces, rather than having to invent it ourselves. Believing in our principles and our constitutional rights, so we can leave divisive issues behind, living up to our values, and get to work on what will make things better for all of us.

New Brunswick citizens, politicians and civil servants, and those amongst us as the electorate, have to be fully on deck.

Chapter 2

Setting Our Direction

in the 21ˢᵗ Century

As engaged and enlightened citizens, now is the time to start asking the right questions, the smart questions. Otherwise, we are not setting our direction. Instead, we are subjugating ourselves to elected officials, who may or may not be altruistic, grasping whatever wind is available (which will also not harm their re-election).

Rather than ask why you are cutting the budget for education (even though we know student enrolment continues to decline), we should ask what are the measurable outcomes that you are setting for our high school graduates, the benchmarks for their teachers, and why are we not meeting global standards so that we may be competitive? And, what is the investment being made with our tax dollars providing us as a return on education?

Instead of asking how it is someone can spend $13 on a glass of orange juice (which any traveler knows is an easy item to be bilked on at a major city or airport hotel restaurant) we should ask for transparency on the government website for expense allotments and subsequent net +/- on budget by each elected official.

It seems that if it is not NIMBY (Not In My Back Yard) for resources development, it is Leave In My Back Yard (LIMBY?) when it comes to shifting education and health services to larger centers for quality of facilities and service levels, as well as cost control; or, oil & gas exploration to which one might be environmentally opposed.

We ought to expect, respect and listen to sound and reasonable, non-politically worded, justifications. And, we ought to expect and give due consideration to innovative ways of achieving appropriate levels of services including education and health and social services from new born to senior.

At the same time, we need to expect and demand of our politicians to answer questions honestly and in a forthcoming manner, in a public forum or in the Legislature. We should expect the media to politely and assertively pursue answers from politicians, not aggressively or disrespectfully, and certainly without concern as to whether or not they get that next interview.

We cannot set our direction without knowing what is important to us. It is difficult to confirm and reach consensus as to what is important to us without dialogue, or without leaders who know how to organize and lead such discussions. While we may not have consensus as to the most effective path to achieve certain objectives, we ought to know that our leaders understand what is important to us as a people in this province, so that we can make our choice at the ballot box.

What is important to us is important to us. We may have different ways to express the important things, and we may even have some disagreement as to the way to reconcile the range of perspectives we have, and each of us has the right to our opinions. Our leaders need to understand and articulate these important things, use common threads to bring us together stronger, and transcend the politics and special interests to lead.

So, what is *really important* to us as New Brunswickers? Anyone who has lived elsewhere across Canada knows that much of what we value in New Brunswick is essentially the same or quite similar to other provinces and communities, perhaps a little more like some than others. It is the variation on the theme which makes our province unique. Likewise, it is similarity of heritage, history and economies within the Maritimes which have Nova Scotia and Prince Edward Island sharing much of what is unique here.

Values are like that. **Values are those things that are most important to us.** A country's make up, even a confederation, is held together by provinces whose values are essentially the same. The way in which the provinces and communities define those values is where the differences, if any, may lie.

Likewise, each of us has our values. Individual values may include family, and yet each of us in this 21st century may define what we mean by family a little different than others. Similarly, our commonality of values likely includes areas including physical, work, social, spiritual and financial. Yet, each of us would define what and how these are important to us in a manner in which we have come to believe to be important to us.

At the collective level, we could all have 'Safety and Security' as a value, and yet a Prairie Province community, a large urban area city, and a small Maritimes town, may each establish a different place for guns. Of course, each community wants the highest possible safety and security for its citizens; for that there is little disagreement, and politicians are wrong to manipulate words for votes.

By extension, some of our province's legislation, policies and programs may have differences compared to other jurisdictions, because of what we believe is important to us. We would hope that our values are understood by us, and by those whom we elect to govern for us and on our behalf, but that is not always the case. **Those who come to elected office by way of deep** and **broad local community involvement are most likely those who also best understand who we are and what is important to us**.

It is with too little respect, and too much casualness, that we hear politicians in opposition and in government, scorn their political competitors' sense of what our values are. Unintentionally, but with equal lack of understanding, politicians are too quick in their attempt to educate the electorate, or appear to agree with the citizens, as to what the 'real' values are.

So it is, with an unbelievable frequency, that there are those things called values that are not. Nothing more could be wrong than when a politician refers to Medicare as a value. **Medicare is not a value; it is program, and not the only but one of many, to fulfill a value.** The value may be that each person, in our province and country, has the right and access to modern healthcare. Medicare as a program, seniors care as an obligation, childhood immunization as a policy, are each part of a larger set of criteria that fulfills a value.

Almost as incredulous is the frequency with which politicians, and organizational executives, so quick to compliment people, make sure they show their appreciation to all the people, by using such a displaced word such as 'resources'. As in, "Our people are our most valuable resource". **People are *not* resources, and resources are *not* people**.

More to the point, which likely they wish to emphasize, is that people are what is most important about this province. Our beautiful landscapes, rivers and heritage are awesome, and even more wonderful are our people. It is our people which are most important, is what they mean.

People are not resources. People are people, who ought not to be denigrated to being resources along with our natural resources, financial resources, infrastructure resources, and so forth.

On the other hand, our people do who have a diverse portfolio of resources. These resources include education, various skills, physical capability, intellectual acumen, linguistic skills, artistic and musical talent; a combination we endeavor to leverage for self-fulfillment, satisfaction and economic benefit. People also have traits, many of which may be positive, such as perseverance, tenacity, creativity, intellectual capacity, resourcefulness, even friendliness and neighborliness.

It is the pool of resources and traits that each person has that manifests the competencies to contribute to their personal, family, workplace, volunteer group, community and province— important areas of their life.

People are what make New Brunswick, and what we determine to be important to us is how and what we should base our decisions. Like much of the western world, our freedom of democratic determination, generally free market economy, and confidence in our society, are being challenged.

During the shifting tides of the past half century we have seen the demise of buildings that encapsulated our post World War II values system.

Consider that only a generation or two ago, every city sub-community, town and village, had a post office, a church or two, a school, a hospital and a government building (transportation department garage, or county office, federal edifice, or the like), and frequently a passenger rail stop. During the growth period to those constructions, we also experienced a 'connectivity' unlike ever experienced before in our world.

Schools and hospitals, historically, began as church or community supported structures and services. While the level of construction and service may have been inconsistent across the province, most were staffed with volunteers, church workers and for-fee professionals, or low paying vocation teachers. Then social government relative to these essential services entered as the economy was growing exponentially each decade.

We witnessed, experienced, and came to expect programs such as universal education and healthcare in nearly every community; the introduction of policies such as overnight postal delivery; and local government workers jobs in every community, as well as more accessible services.

Consciously, but far more frequently sub-consciously, we related these policies and programs to our 'values'. More tangibly, we began the incremental move to relate these policies and programs which formed our criteria of our values in those buildings. Consequently, as the years have gone by, as many of these buildings, these institutions that represent our post-war progress, are emptied and either torn down or sold to new owners, we feel that our values, too, have eroded. **Since we have externalized our values to these institutions, we feel abandoned as the buildings disappear.**

It is understood, in a heartfelt way, that our communities, where people are experiencing the loss of young people to centers of work; the loss of small and lowly populated schools as these are abandoned for busing to larger centers; the loss of the small community or rural hospital; and, the loss of the local post office; are grieving. Aside from the obvious services moved to another locale, these buildings as they are emptied, sold or bulldozed are tearing at our sense of community, and consequently what our community values.

Empathy is plentiful, even when not explicitly evident, amongst those making the 'hard' decisions for residents living in these communities. While sincere, the empathy is not accompanied with a replacing of the removed criteria recognition of buildings (the external 'values' indicator). In some cases, due to urban sprawl, quality roads and other access, the quality of service compensates for the additional travel and distance. In most rural decision making situations, our leaders' lack of creativity, and awareness of innovation available today that could and should be a significant part of the new values indicator, is less than stellar.

Top of the tier leaders, of which by definition there are not many in commerce or government, **understand the essence of values and lead by those values as a base, their mission as a mandate, and their vision as an inspiration**. [2] If a company is values-based, customer-centric, and sales-driven, there is very likely a leader at the helm who also is top tier, and quite likely the organization is faster, more nimble and more successful than its contemporaries.

Companies built to be, and grown into, global leaders have leaders who are the top of the top tier. Such companies are either started from the ground up or taken from lack luster status to their full potential by leadership icons, or a leading succession plan that continues exemplary leadership. Jack Welsh and Lee Iacocca, along with a few others, transcended their contemporaries of their half-century, with Jack Welsh considered the top manager (that is top of the top tier) of the last half of the twentieth century. Bill Gates and Steve Jobs, and their contemporaries, led us into the 21st century with products and services beyond our imaginations.

Other top tier leaders also are recognized by their organization's vision and values, in the corporate world, not-for-profit, and politics. When this is real, and the people are of like mind, decisions and implementation are effected to heights of success that others only can admire.

Canada's greatest Primer Minister, Sir John A MacDonald, was a 19th century icon whom many acknowledge as the greatest of the great contemporaries of his day. Sir John A was also our first and our last true visionary leader. Who doesn't know of the railway that literally tied our country from sea to sea, based on a values set of a Canadian identity from the two founding European nations that settled here that did not want to be swallowed up by the expanding USA. It was our founding leader's mission to make it happen.

So it is possible to have a top tier government leader, even a top of the top tier as Sir John A surely was. And of course **it is possible to have a top-tier government leader today—if we could find one, and elect them**. A small province could do well if it had a top-tier leader for the times we are in.

This inspirational and sky-high achieving leader's sense of values is not to be confused with those clearly not of the same level and capability. A person in a leadership role may invoke the words of values, but without a depth of understanding, and may provide inspirational (to some) speeches, but lack breadth of knowledge and capability to achieve that of the top tier leader.

"We've tried nothing,
and we're all out of ideas."

From the Simpsons

It is nothing short of a failure of our politicians and community leaders to allow the erosion of indicators and metrics of our values to also melt away some of our self-sufficiency as a people, and our self-esteem. But, then how could they when it appears that they, too, seem unaware of what really is happening. They are not unaware of the pain, tribulation and loss to the affected community. They are unaware of what to do.

It also is disrespectful by politicians when they sugar coat or politicize or demonize the largesse of the federal transfers of payments system, a requirement of huge proportions for equity to our confederation's small economies such as New Brunswick. While not everything can be 'accounted' by financial metrics, our nation needs a renewed sense of defining what is equity, how to measure it, and timeframes to keep things in perspective. As do we need to in our province. It always comes down to our values and our cognizance of what they mean to us.

The Maritimes, when Saint John was a major center of the British Empire, by accounts had a reasonable prosperity during the pre-confederation north-south trade that was gradually eroded partly due to being subjugated to the east-west trade mandated by central Canada nation-protecting anti-reciprocity legislation and the reality of American aggression. The Prairies were recipients of support from the original provinces of Ontario, Quebec, New Brunswick and Nova Scotia. Then, the Maritimes were recipients as the 'have provinces' as they became known. Now, even Ontario is a recipient.

There has been a moving of funds via federal transfer payments or direct investment across the country for the right reasons, and for the wrong (political) reasons. Of the latter, one could say when this occurs it violates principles of integrity and trust. Regardless, it seems that **New Brunswick needs to do what it can to rely far less than the necessity of which federal transfer payments has become our lifeline. This full circles back to our values.**

Disrespect also surfaces in discussions on income and income class, and contribution to insurance plans and use of social services. There is no positive purpose served when groups are pitted against each other during debates or for scoring political points. The self-appointing as standard bearers for middle class and the derogation of welfare or EI recipients come to mind.

Our direction forward is thwarted by negativisms and old century thinking. More constructive dialogue would begin with transparency of the facts by and to all citizens, as well as a wider advisory group to the Premier and Ministers to ensure their education and grasp of situations. *Strategic* decisions consider impact of actions taken beyond any specific area of focus, extending to the cause and effect within the full breadth of the Province's various systems.

We have within our province a wide range of income, by individuals and by businesses. We have some businesses within certain big profit industries that provide higher than average salaries and benefits, due in part to their proximity to the realities of the global economy. We have other businesses that rely on lower wages to lower skilled employees to compete locally as well as be in line with out of province businesses. Some of these businesses are small, and some are large. We need economic environment positive policies for all of these businesses to thrive as well as for workers to live and thrive. But do we need to use tax payer monies directly?

As the closest microcosm of the wider Canada, New Brunswick has opportunities to collaborate with our federal government. From developing and piloting newly refined programs for an aging population, to innovative application of payroll funded EI funds, we can leverage our limited resources to the eventual benefit of the nation.

These actions should be abiding by a principle of integrity and living up to a value of Governance that includes openness and transparency, tossing aside old words and dogma.

> "The dogmas of the quiet past are
> inadequate to the stormy present.
> The occasion is piled high with difficulty,
> and we must rise to the occasion.
> As our case in new,
> so we must think anew and act anew."
>
> Abraham Lincoln,
> Second annual message to Congress, 1862-12-01

In New Brunswick we cannot, nor do we have to, wait for national definitions such as 'middle class'. We can decide what these criteria are within our province to best establish efficacious methods and means of taxation, and appropriate allocation of social support systems. Can we not ask: What is fair to all concerned? It will always come down to our values.

We have a huge challenge, in a sea change of global competition, a mobile society, a rising senior citizens population, a slower growing younger workers population, all the while with increasing expectations of health, education and other services. Our values as a people need to be respected, the balancing of these values is ever challenging (as it is in our personal lives), and once clearly expressed then responded to so that voters can decide as to whom they will entrust oversight and management.

A top-tier leader will speak to what we know to be our values, lead with vision and inspiration, and know and respect the mission granted by the people for their term at the helm so that we can make a choice as to whom we will entrust the next term of government.

New Brunswick is well into a new period in our history which is without precedent, for which we cannot rely on the customary operative skills or and old century leadership capacity of elected and public service officials, so we need to renew our way of thinking and acting, to re-create this province. As a people we can rise to the occasion by demanding nothing less of our government.

Assuming our principles are agreed, protected and abided by, it always comes down to our values. As it should.

Our Principles
as a Province

Principles seem to be a lost reference point in our vocabulary, lost in the corporate use of values, political espousing of values—i.e., "Canadian Values" or "American Values"—and lack of knowledge of principles as compared to values. The two words, principles and values, are so often interchanged in usage, that to most they are the same. They are not, and we need to use these correctly to transcend disagreements of core conduct and move forward collectively.

From the Canadian Bill of Rights of 1960, we read: "It is hereby recognized and declared that in Canada there have existed and shall continue to exist without discrimination by reason of race, national origin, colour, religion or sex, the following human rights and fundamental freedoms, namely: a. the right of the individual to life, liberty, security of the person and enjoyment of property, and the right not be deprived thereof except by due process of law; b. the right of the individual to equality before the law and the protection of the law; c. freedom of religion; d. freedom of speech; e. freedom of assembly and association; f. freedom of the press."

The Canadian Charter of Rights and Freedoms, which among other things was an entrenching of our bill of rights in the 1982 Constitution Act, outlines key principles for our nation. Although subject to the "limitations clause" or the "notwithstanding clause" (together distinguishing our constitution significantly from the United States Bill of Rights) it does extend the 1960 version to legal rights. These include: right to life, liberty and the security of the person; freedom from unreasonable search and seizure; freedom from arbitrary detention or imprisonment; right to legal counsel and the guarantee of habeas corpus; rights in criminal and penal matters such as the right to be presumed innocent until proven guilty; right not to be subject to cruel and unusual punishment; rights against self-incrimination; rights to an interpreter in a court proceeding.

Further, as the Charter of Rights and Freedoms was intended as a way to describe our national identity and define our values, therein lies a wrangling of phrases and words that keep our justice system busy. This also causes confusion in our nation at large, and within our communities, as to principles vis-à-vis values. This is more than semantics, it is expression, and it is communication, and understanding, and efficacy in our dealings and decisions.

Aside from the legal words and manipulation thereof in too many speeches to the public, the erosion of principles in our national lexicon may have begun with the 1960s-70s decline of church attendance and religious centric 'rule making' (and, politically, some would say with the 1960s Liberal Party of Canada ensuring the flag was all red so as to make it Canada's naturally governing political party's flag; rather than options with blue favoured by some Conservatives). It was not helped by the co-mingling of these phrases.

As with many of all parties, my personal preference is the flag design and colour as chosen, irrespective of political party colors, for its simplicity and strength of image. It is with this flag, leading up to the pride swelling of centennial celebrations, that we experienced a self-branding of ourselves as a people. This brand began its crescendo in the 1700s as an emblem, in 1860s on Ontario's coat of arms and the patriotic song of 'Maple Leaf Forever'. In the 21st century the maple leaf is the brand, internally and externally, to which Canadians and other peoples recognize this country.

Metaphorically, within the embroidery of the Maple Leaf imagery are what we as Canadians feel as the principles and values, and the vision and mission of our federated nation. While not always expressible by all citizens, and too often appropriated for partisan purposes by politicians, we 'know' what we mean by our Maple Leaf and our Canada.

Like most other provinces, in New Brunswick the Maple Leaf is our significant key identifier, with the provincial flag a secondary representation, and the l'Acadie star honoured as well. While our flag of a ship in full sail with oars in the water may harken a bygone era, the modern stylized version of the ship used in advertising and on government communications, is indicative of our intended new sailings. It is representative of a people with hard working tendencies, self-setting direction, and buoyancy through trials. Principles and values intertwined.

When a principle is cited, even in an appropriate context and with honesty, it sometimes becomes a touch point of bias, prejudice, or sometimes racism. This is unfortunate as we then devolve into disagreements, platitudes, misunderstood statements and unintended reactions. Frequently, either in error or as an appropriation taken, the principle is defined by personal perspective, circumstance or for purpose of argument.

> "A people that values its privileges above its principles soon loses both."
>
> Dwight D Eisenhower
> American President and decorated General

Principles are universal truths, developed over millennia by ever evolving societies, that become the standard bearers of how we live, regard each other, and live together. While the justice system may deal with the abstract of legal definition, or with conflict, or with individual or collective application, citizens should expect our political and civic leaders to understand and act upon our society's principles while sharing their perspective of our values.

One principle, as it is imbedded in our Constitution, is the language rights of Canadians, including English and French as the official languages of Canada—and New Brunswick. This and the related rights are enshrined in the Charter of Rights and Freedoms, and therefore as a principle of our nation. Too often 'bilingualism' (as it is in our Canadian context, referring to French and English) is misplaced in its usage and termed a value. This always has the danger of falling down a slippery slope, thereby morphing the term away from its purist intent to a subjective topic; which it is not.

Likewise, certain aspects of bilingualism, including situations relative to everyday living and interaction with others, are within our values. It is this area in which those at both extremes either manipulate or react for their own agenda. When this occurs, feelings are hurt, editorials are written, and long series of personal comments are appended to the online newspapers.

In New Brunswick, a listing of principles would include:

Respect;
Integrity;
Bilingualism;
Rights entrenched in our Constitution
(by the Canadian Charter of Rights and Freedoms)

Apropos is this review from the Government of Canada 'Canadian Heritage' website: "The Charter is founded on the rule of law and entrenches in the Constitution of Canada the rights and freedoms Canadians believe are necessary in a free and democratic society. It recognizes primary fundamental freedoms (e.g. freedom of expression and of association), democratic rights (e.g. the right to vote), mobility rights (e.g. the right to live anywhere in Canada), legal rights (e.g. the right to life, liberty and security of the person) and equality rights, and recognizes the multicultural heritage of Canadians. It also protects official language and minority language education rights. In addition, the provisions of section 25 guarantee the rights of the Aboriginal peoples of Canada."

This also is presented, "There are many other laws that protect human rights in Canada. The *Canadian Bill of Rights* was enacted by Parliament in 1960. It applies to legislation and policies of the federal government and guarantees rights and freedoms similar to those found in the Charter (e.g. equality rights, legal rights, and freedom of religion, of speech and of association). The Bill is not, however, part of the Constitution of Canada."

All of these rights, founded by the rule of law, along with the imbedding of bilingualism as is the case for New Brunswick, are principles. We need to bring clarity in our province to our use of principles, and values, so that we can deal with the issues that cause divisiveness and slow the progress of solutions—and any chance of consensus.

One does not have to be a lawyer or constitutional expert to consider that principles, particularly when embedded in our Constitution, upheld by the Supreme Court, must be respected. If treated as an expedient, then citizens and their leaders must stand firm to their intent and application. These principles arose and evolved from beliefs core to our society.

We must respect our values and the values of others and other cultures, but universally we must protect principles. The co-mingling of these, intentionally or in ignorance, is a barrier to solving misunderstanding and conflict, and a barrier to collaboration and cooperation on issues of significance to the world, our nation, and here in New Brunswick.

"Boldness, leadership and stealth are all more difficult. (Henry) Kissinger describes four models of "world order" extant: Europe's Westphalian model of nation-states with equal status; the U.S. model; China's notion of itself as a great regional power; and an Islamic system of believers and infidels. These parallel universes can find common ground only if a "globalistic second culture and concept of order" is created. From *World Order*, 2014

The globalistic second culture, with regard to this brief discourse on principles, is one of understood and sacrosanct principles. Ongoing squabbles, disagreements, misalignments, and even political correctness, are underpinned by melding with references to values. **We only can overcome, and hopefully even transcend, misunderstanding and dissonance when we are speaking of and acting on principles.**

Principles are universal truths and therefore beyond reproach or indifference, and necessarily upheld and protected. Rights guaranteed by our Constitution, upheld by court decisions, are beyond argument or reproach.

"Expedients are for the hour,
but principles are for the ages."

Henry Ward Beecher

Our Values
as a Province

When one asks people what is important to us about living in New Brunswick, a variety of things are expressed in different ways, usually within the Canadian context and New Brunswick centric at the same time. So, we hear that in New Brunswick what is important to us is our way of life, our safe communities, our dignity as a person, and a government with our best interests including universal access to healthcare, education, justice and so on. Recall that **Values are those things that are most important to us.**

Values, while often titled or referred to as the same as principles by some, are defined by different people, families, groups, communities, and nations. Nations, created by circumstance of commonalities, as opposed to geopolitical border drawings by conquerors, would tend to be more prone to similar value definitions across its groupings and subgroupings.

In a nation such as Canada, we have more in common than not, a core of principles and way to live, across our provinces and peoples, sea to sea to sea. Thus, when it comes to our values, we have a general sense of agreement, consciously or subconsciously and articulated or just felt, within a range of defining criteria. At the same time, we have shades of differences from region to region, province to province in some instances, and other groupings and groups.

Within New Brunswick, we have a struggle of urban growth and rural depopulation, of demographic challenges, of linguistic rights and desires, of service expectations and fiscal realities. We need to sort out the elements of principles and values, so that a more productive, respectful dialogue and resultant decisions may occur.

If a people cannot express their values, if their leaders cannot articulate those values, then the very foundation is weak. This is true in a province (or a nation) or a profit or not-for-profit organization. In the absence of a strong sense of values, incremental change will be resisted and transformational change is a non-starter.

In the 19th century this may have been as basic as remain with the King and free of the USA, keep our borders secure, have the police and military available when we need them, keep taxes low, and leave us be.

As the 20th century progressed, with its evolving emancipation of voters, workers and rights, along with social support systems, expectations increased. Institutions formed, as noted previously best recognized by buildings—public schools, post offices, hospitals, liquor stores were added to the churches and banks. Over several decades these buildings became related to programs such as universal education, mail and parcel delivery in every corner of the country, hospitals in every community, and the right to liquor and beer accessibility.

As described earlier, buildings were increasingly identified with universal services, paid by taxes and delivered by government, the metaphor of the physical transformed to the programs themselves and unwitting politicians called these "Canadian values". Then all of these institutions and programs, one by one each in its own way, began to show cracks of failure, crumbling before us in levels of service, unable to meet rising expectations.

Predictably, proponents of the programs questioned opponents' contradictions with Canadian values. Politicians and third party organizations as well as those with a stake in the status quo, real or imagined began their "not like in the USA" or not "American values", all the while speaking of programs not values. And, so this went on, and continued in all of a lunacy that belongs to a Pogo or Bizarro comics box or perhaps more closely the pointedness of a Dilbert comics strip, so that nothing has changed, nothing has improved. The gap of expectations and actual outcomes is growing wider.

In times of change, particularly when transformational change is either thrust upon us by global threats, or when leaders need to be leading the transformation, a firm understanding of one's values and of their society's values is the basis of moving forward with confidence and competence, aligned with their people.

Sometimes, looking at the extreme end of the range of examples can be insightful. The media and its opponents, all with a sense of their self-acknowledged superior intellect, refer disparagingly to the Presidential Republican Party potential candidate Donald Trump. Yet he is the one in an age of cynicism willing to share how he feels, in the vacuum of leadership display 'who-he-is' self-confidence, with a populace rife with mistrust of politicians, and speak his mind on issues of which they are disenchanted and disheartened. This is why candidates like this strike a chord with so many, and not just in the USA. Agree or disagree, this trait of non-couched and non-politically sanitized communication and confidence is a missing one for most of the rest. The message is candid, unencumbered, and goes to the core of many issues. Perhaps not the way others would, but of interest to a level of significant numbers of people tuning in.

In the lapse of a true 'esprit de corps' in any group, as things get worse, something surfaces to bind people together. One candidate's straight forward, honest statements leading to polling domination is not dissimilar to another candidate's timely 'hope' speeches. As expected, partisans on both sides argue as to the lack of substance and credibility.

New Brunswick needs a leader with the trait of self-awareness and understanding of their personal values, linked inextricably to the values of our province, and the capability to extend this to executable actions. We need the traits of a leader to include clarity of purpose and vision, confidence with competence, and the capacity to transform this province with the people.

Values, while commonly named amongst a group, may be subject to differing definitions and expectations. While important to us, **the way we define and measure values may tend to change with time**, be redefined and expressed according to our evolving times and the context of current realities.

Each of us, as individuals, may draw from a common pool of values, but we have personal defined, and refined, view of each of those values. For example, values typically include Family, Work, Spiritual, Physical, Financial, Social groupings. Our view of those values affects our feelings, behaviors and actions. Sometimes we may keep these private, but always others will reach conclusions regarding those values by what they observe and interpret from our behaviors and actions, whether that is our intent or not.

For many, 'Family' may be defined similarly even if not as 'narrow' as it may have been in generations past. Even in the past "blood is thicker than water" was an indicator that the bonding of familial relationships is stronger than marital relationships and would trump loyalties. To others, the marital bond was/is a superior bond, and should one be forced to take sides (in war, heritage, community, etc.) the family of marriage is stronger than the family of blood relations.

No one wishes to be placed in a situation of choosing their family ties of parents, siblings and relations over that of their marital family of spouse/partner and children. But, families have been thrown into angst or torn apart from such situations. Many conflicts have and do occur from these definitions and parameters of the value 'Family'. Now, add in the accepted 21st century 'make-up' of a family – mother/father/children, mother/father/no-children, mother/mother/children, father/father/children, mother/father/children-from-different-marriages, single parent/children – and, the value 'Family' can mean different things to different people. In all cases, 'Family' is a value, and as a value it is cherished by our society and culture, and is a value deemed worthy of safety and security.

> "What lies behind us
> and what lies before us
> are tiny matters compared to
> what lies within us."
>
> Ralph Waldo Emerson

Even those with clarity as to their personal values can still struggle with 'balancing' their values. For example, the struggle with quality of 'Family' in time and relationships, while managing the aspirations of a 'Work' career or professional path, while maintaining good 'Physical' condition and diet, while growing one's 'Financial goals', while contributing to personal obligations of 'Social' objectives of volunteerism or ongoing friendships.

The challenge of understanding personal values and living those values should serve to highlight the challenges that an organization has with its values of say, Customer Service and Team Work and Resource Management and Performance, and so on. Profit or not-for-profit or charitable, every organization depends on its leadership to fulfil expectations based on their values.

Political entities and groupings and jurisdictions, too, have values. And the peoples within these entities have presumptions of their leaders and governments to live up to these values and fulfill expectations.

Consider what is important to us in our Province. As introduced above, what is important to us is our way of life, our safe communities, our dignity, accessibility to health and education, and a government of our best interests. To some these are simply aspirations, with different definitions by different people, different political parties, different special interest groups, even different communities.

Across the province, however expressed, from my experience as a citizen and a strategy professional, these are the bedrocks of our values. While these are shared in one way or another with other provinces, with many common points, we have our own unique beliefs and expectations.

While referring to the essence of the 'what' is important to us, and by putting aside all the programs and policies, the values of the Province of New Brunswick, could be expressed as:

Dignity and Well-Being

As a person, a group, a community, a people
Be who you are, with respect and respectful
Quality of life in health, education, work, recreation
Accessibility and inclusion of all persons

A Safe Place to Live

In our Communities
On our roads and highways and byways and trails and waterways
For family, as any of us may describe
Through expression, of who we are individually and collectively
Well-being protected and defended

Governance and Civility

Competent, capable government, accountable and fiscally responsible
Transparency and trust in policy, action and outcomes
Talents and skills of our people respected and leveraged
Resources optimization, environmentally, economically, socially
Services of value and value for taxation

Our Way of Life

Livable places for home, work and recreation

Neighborly concern, support, respect, courtesy
Opportunity for prosperity as each of us defines and lives
Contributing to others in our province, country, world

While in no way an exhaustive list, most of what we may use to describe our values can be captured in these few expressions. This, at least, is a start for us to reach our conclusions and beliefs of what is important to us. We can use it as a barometer of which political incumbents and candidates may be measured, and compared. Along with our entrenched principles, we can get to the core of our aspirations and the root of our many challenges.

Our best days of leadership were of Premiers with an innate understanding of our values, and a sense of vision communicated with their goals while at the helm. While fortunate in having these true leaders, the 'hit-and-miss' of having an incumbent of this talent is risky and the potential of casting about until another happens along is damaging for us.

The observations of others can be helpful to reinforce our own self-reflection. For example, The 'Living In Canada' website touting itself as "Your independent guide to getting the most out of Canada" states: "Most people who move to New Brunswick find they are welcomed into very friendly communities. In New Brunswick you get the chance to own an acreage of land that only the wealthy could afford in some places and the opportunity to live in communities where people still genuinely help one another."

A common set of principles and values shared by all and manifested in a common purpose pulling all together is what moves a people united. That is esprit de corps. Fortunately, we mostly agree on what is important. But then we allow our politicians to pull us into partisan talk of how to do things or what not to do so that we somehow transgress to disagreeing on those things we already know and agree are important. And, then, any hope of change, of collaborative movement forward, halts.

Without a solid foundation, understanding and behavioral alignment with values, a vision accepting to change, real change, is not likely. For more than twenty five years we have known the keys to successful change. Harvard Business Review highlighted "The most effective way to change behavior…is to put people in a new organizational context, which imposes new roles, responsibilities, and relationships on them." And, that three interrelated factors included *coordination*, high levels of *commitment* and new *competencies*.[≈]

The respected professor and author, Rosabeth Moss Kanter, wrote of the "environment that makes it possible for people to master change is characterized" by knowing what to *focus* on, the ability to move *fast*, and *flexibility* to keep redirecting.[3] That was in 1993.

Reference to this timeless material is simply to point out that the knowledge and skill sets required are known. The capability and capacity required of leaders are known, as is the aptitude and attitude. The leaders needed in time of uncertainty, those who succeed, have these attributes. Longevity in elected office is not always indicative of this, as often it is due to a number of factors of keen political sense, and occasionally an ability of pragmatism to continue the visionary trail of a predecessor even if the succeeding Premier is of a different party.

There are issues in New Brunswick that simmer, cause hurt and on occasion divide us. At some risk, it is necessary to examine the earlier reference regarding a topic of which those at the extremes either manipulate or react for their own agenda. These issues would not continue in our public discourse if they were not important.

The principle of bilingualism, as entrenched and guaranteed in our Constitution, is in a complex symmetry with the ideology of access and the applications of service levels that are indicators of success and form parts of our values. The co-mingling of these without open acknowledgement or clarity is the fuel that keeps our conflicts afire. It is here where politicians and linguistic rights groups must be more responsible in their leadership.

Ill-conceived actions taken or uninformed decisions made or biased statements shared regarding bilingualism have created conflicts with the value of Dignity and Well-Being. If 'accessibility and inclusion of all persons' is a defining indicator of this value, then all persons should be respected, whether from a minority or a majority. The minority rightfully achieved parity of services this past half century. Yet, we have an ongoing divide where many of the majority are feeling nearly as disenfranchised when it comes to access to public sector jobs as the minority were decades ago.

These actions can even creep into our other values of Our Way of Life, Governance and Civility, and A Safe Place to Live. Situations relative to everyday living and interaction with others are within our values because they are important to us.

Understandably, there are people who are upset that with the tiny pool of people we have seemingly two-thirds of our population who are not 'eligible' for many jobs. We need to resolve the conflicts. Likewise, when we are looking for the best talent and competency for a Premier the electorate need to be able to make their choice from the best of the whole pool of people. Many criteria and competencies are necessary. Drawing only from a third of our population limits choices and opportunities to elect the right person.

Outstanding leaders, of substantive accomplishment, are those who are moved and motivated by deep seated values supported by conviction and also with a correlated competence. The previously cited New Brunswick trio of premiers, arguably the most outstanding in our Province's history, were of this kind of leader.

At this time in our history, the dearth lies in the leaders made available from which to choose, from those elected as well as those hired or appointed. The conundrum is we cannot afford to wait another twenty or thirty years for a Fisher/Tilley or Robichaud or McKenna to be found, willing to accept the role, and elected.

What We Ultimately Seek
as a Province

New Brunswickers seem to have a mostly unspoken sense of what it is we seek for our Province—for us. We have much already as citizens, even with our very serious fiscal challenges. It is worthy to review some of this before addressing what else it is that we seek.

We are admiring of our former generations who arrived here, who in turn welcomed so many over the early decades, from United Loyalists migrating north to avoid the revolution in the United States, to Europeans escaping tyranny of lords and famines. Then, from the immigrants of the late 19th century and early 20th century, to post World War II, and the recent decades of global migration, and newly arrived refugees.

Rightfully, we are almost boastful of where we live, our 'Picture Province' and natural beauty of streams and forests, valleys and ocean-fed bays. National and provincial parks, the warmest waters north of the Carolinas at Parlee Beach, the UNESCO protected Stonehammer (Bay of Fundy Coastline) Geopark, the New Wonders global finalist Bay of Fundy with its highest tides in the world, and two of the world's most famous rivers of salmon. These form much of why we enjoy our 'way of life', and, much of what some are afraid we could lose.

For the most part, we feel blessed to have our low crime communities, safe streets and highways, and our abundance of access to water, forests, and natural playgrounds. Roadway ramps and main streets motorists allow other motorists to enter; Reader's Digest award to one of our own for "most honest city'; inclusiveness in our schools; and volunteerism remains intact.

We are concerned, worried, and frustrated, with our provincial fiscal situation, with many of us embarrassed with our dependency on federal government transfer payments. There is nothing inherently wrong with 'transfers' across the country to share in the wealth of different regions at different times. It is only a few decades ago that Central Canada 'subsidized' the Western Provinces, and before that when it was the Maritimes trading east-west in place of south-north for the benefit of Upper and Lower Canada so that our young nation would survive.

Those who know our history can speak of the economic strength of New Brunswick's export and trade economy with the USA pre-confederation. Then the change to east-west trade, from north-south, and the demise of ship building and related exports—the era of wood wind and water (sail)—began a downward trend in our self-sustainability, interdependent equal amongst the provinces, and population stagnation.

While many of us aspire for a better, more fiscally secure future in our province, realistically without the largess of the federal transfers pre-Chretien/Martin/Harper era, some continue to yearn for those days past. **Insufficient ground work to change how we manage this province, become a 21st century jurisdiction, and increase our productivity as a people, has us languishing to a point of considerable concern.**

Citizens have grown tired, and even cynical, of political leaders who speak of 'vision'. So much that the 'vision thing' is a turn-off for many, leading some newspaper editors to suggest that a Premier ought to forego the 'vision thing' and just get on with what needs to be done. We now have one.

The problem with vision is not that it is a waste of time, it is the waste of not putting in context what it is, why it is relevant and how it will be fulfilled. Moreover, leaders even when expressing some modicum of vision have avoided what they will do in their term, at least in any measurable or accountable way. And too frequently we have leaders citing goals that overlap and extend to mandates into the future. Is it that they are avoiding accomplishing something due to lack of knowing what that is, or how to achieve it, and therefore avoid metrics and accountability?

Likely, the challenge of vision is more due to a cognitive dissonance in our provincial society and amongst our elected leaders, their supporting cast of civil servants, and the population as a whole. Paradoxically, it is a lack of clear values and vision and mission that is primarily responsible for the dissonance. **Actions and behaviors will conflict with individual identity, and collective identity, when not based on common definitions of values**.

Unfortunately, the electorate's discomfort can turn to 'throw the bums out' or attention to a positive and hopeful message even when it may lack substantive action. Leaders, at the point of being uncomfortable with the status quo make changes but these are negligible to real improvement and too little for transformation. All of us are less than satisfied with the outcomes, as leaders and as citizens.

So, let us turn to that we can begin to form what it is that we ultimately seek and in way that all of us can align, have 'buy-in', support and act upon. We have foundational elements and pointers to go with our intuition, feelings and opinions.

We have symbols emblematic of who we are and our vision, from the national flag adopted fifty years ago, to the official provincial logo, updated in recent years and now graphically signifies movement forward.

Our provincial flag is meant to be representative of who and what we are. For New Brunswick, the flag was modelled after our coat of arms, and is a graphic of who and what we were about in the 19th century.

Today, it still can be a metaphor of our current direction:

Steering our own ship, oars in the water, optimizing the winds.

As the official website of the Province of New Brunswick describes: "Our provincial flag, based on the coat of arms, was adopted by proclamation on Feb. 24, 1965. The symbols depicted on the flag are taken from the Coat of Arms assigned by Royal Warrant of Queen Victoria on May 26, 1868. They are a gold lion on a red field across the top and an ancient galley with its oars in action across the base.

"The province takes its name from the Duchy of Brunswick in Germany, which in 1784, the year the province was established, was in the possession of King George III. The arms of Brunswick consist of two gold lions on a red field, and the arms of the King contained the three gold lions of England. The gold lion in the flag therefore reflects New Brunswick's relationship both to the Duchy of Brunswick and England.

"The galley is the conventional heraldic representation of a ship and reflects the two principal economic activities, shipping and shipbuilding, carried on in New Brunswick when the coat of arms was assigned."

That was New Brunswick in the 19th century. To our detriment, we are now clinging too hard and for too long in the 20th century when we now have the opportunities of the 21st century.

In recent years the ship was transformed to a modern, official logo of the Province of New Brunswick showing a ship full in the wind, moving forward in the waters. It is a pleasant, positive and proud image, modern in its graphic and complementary to the flag.

The stylized ship from the official logo is modern, bold and forward moving. **The full sail ship remains representative of a people with a hard-working heritage, self-setting direction and buoyancy through trials.** Principles and values are intertwined.

Inherent with the modern version, we have a graphic also of what it is we ultimately seek—our vision. Notice that the direction has changed as if to signify that we are moving forward once again. The sail is full, as one would be 'puffing' one's chest out, with pride but without arrogance. And the ship rides high on moving waves.

No oars showing reflects our modern economy. It also indicates how our government should operate.

This stylized ship is the graphic representation of our vision, by my observations, that we seem to collectively have for our Province. We are proudly sailing forward, using our sails appropriately to catch the winds which we choose, riding the waves of global shifts and opportunities, and safely housing everyone within the strength of its hull.

For a vision statement we could consider the words from our motto, or coat of arms, should either still be relevant. If the latter are no longer applicable, then it is time to remove them to the history books and museums to remember and celebrate our past, and replace with a modern New Brunswick phrase. However, the phrase does remain relevant, particularly when complemented with a contemporary purpose.

New Brunswick's motto is:

Spem Reduxit – Hope Was Restored or (It) Has Restored Hope.

Our traditional ties were to the sea (we were, after all, commonly referred to as 'Herring Chokers' much as Nova Scotians have been called 'Bluenosers'), as well as to the forests and rivers. In recent decades, these ties have expanded to highways of vehicles and information technology.

A parallel to our past is noted in the excerpt at www.lib.unb.ca/winslow/reduxit.html. From Ann Gorman Condon, *The Envy of the American States: The Loyalist Dream for New Brunswick* (Fredericton: New Ireland Press, 1984), pp. 131-151., we read:

"Stripped to its essence, the political philosophy of the Loyalists who were appointed to organize and govern the new British province of New

Brunswick centered around a profound belief in the positive aspects of power. Like virtually all the Loyalist participants in the American Revolution, these men were convinced that Great Britain had lost her thirteen colonies through a failure to govern.

Even the dour [Ward] Chipman [Colonial Administrator, N.B. 1823-24] permitted himself to hope that "we shall have as good a society and live as happily and chearfully [sic] in the province of New Brunswick as in any part of the King's Dominions."

Describing what it is that we ultimately seek is also defining what our vision is. **Full sail, no oars showing is relevant to this modern century. In today's world it is intellect, education, advanced skills and uniqueness that will move us forward. It is aligned principles and values with clarity of vision that forms an esprit de corps for a people to be in unison of purpose.**

So, where is the Vision? Have we lost it? How to reach toward that appears to be either unknown, inappropriately articulated, not agreed, or perhaps not important.

The vision is a beacon toward which we move. As we get closer, we see even further beyond, such that a vision is never really reached. As we discover more, learn more, savor more, and reach more, a new destiny is seen and the vision is stretched further out.

In this light, and given our heritage, our vision can remain the first half with our motto, with a second half, an additional beacon that beckons us.

We have restored hope, in harmony, community and opportunity

As we consider this vision, we can assess our Premier candidates as to their intended contribution to our future. With a destiny agreed, it would be up to the political party nominees to add context to this vision relative to the times. Then, the electorate can decide if it agreed with their belief of this vision and what their next four years will contribute toward that objective given the current circumstances with which we find ourselves at that time.

Premiers Fisher and Tilley likely were seeing, given their times and the threat of American continentalism, a vision of: We have restored hope, in harmony, community and opportunity—it is with security, we remain subjects to our Crown.

Premier Robichaud likely was seeing, at that juncture of our Province, a vision of: We have restored hope, in harmony, community and opportunity—we have equality of our linguistic peoples, and, our rural and urban citizens.

Premier McKenna likely was seeing, given the decline of traditional business and loss of jobs, a vision of: We have restored hope, in harmony, community and opportunity—we are in sight of self-sufficiency with job opportunities from our technological innovation and our bilingual capability.

A Premier in the current term could be seeing, given our fiscal dilemma and emerging threat to our health, education and social systems, a vision of: We have restored hope, in harmony, community and opportunity—we are taking control so that we can be directing our future

The Premier, and team (party) who lives up to this vision 'granted' by their election would more than likely win a re-election. The people will decide at the polls, but with a more explicit reference, as will be addressed further. In a modern, respectful democracy this may also bring more clarity for voters to make their choice at the ballot box.

During those years when we had a premier who understood, to his core, our direction and his leadership role, we have leapt ahead in transformational ways. Our future was assured by vision and actions of significance of that time. Premiers Fisher and Tilley, Robichaud, and McKenna, had clarity of vision from personal perspective, an alignment of passion, and fortunately for New Brunswick each had the core competencies to execute and succeed.

During those times, and the terms of these premiers as previously written, we also were fortunate for at least one or two terms, irrespective of the party affiliation of the succeeding premier, to have some continuity thus ensuring all was not undone. Party leaders were elected by their members, with at least one of them a reasonable enough choice for the electorate to award office.

Now it seems that as a people we have an inability to elect appropriate leaders, with the 'next steps' requisite competencies and direction. The port seems unknown, or unreachable, and as the tide ebbs and flows, our good ship New Brunswick bobs about taking on water, sails inadequate for the winds, keel too weak to steer, and on the edge of a wave that can succumb.

"No wind favors him who has no destined port."

Michel Eyquem de Montaigne

It is almost as if any two strokes forward are followed by one stroke steady, to be superseded by three strokes back. And, we watch frustratingly and incredulously at the worrisome situation of it all, as we go about our daily lives and try not to fret for our future.

There are visions of platitudes and vague notions of balanced budgets and return to programs for the people, and social license, that deservedly are subject to criticism. One of the biggest critics of weak vision was iconic CEO Lou Gerstner of IBM fame, who was known to warn of vision and forecast vagaries while urging well-grounded strategies that are well executed. He was a visionary.

Of course the 'vision thing' is relevant to New Brunswick and New Brunswickers now, as it has been in our past. Vision can have a pragmatic perspective by providing a context of where positions taken and decisions made are taking us and, equally as important, if these are moving us toward where we want to be.

It is a mistake to overlook the importance of a vision with meaning and comprehensibility. Our leaders should not be allowed to bypass it, or to provide a wishy-washy piece of jargon filled phrase. Disappointed voters cannot recognize what they had expected to occur, and so feel they have little choice than to vote for the 'others'. 'Where there is no vision the people perish', states Proverbs. To which may be added, or follow any ostensible vision presented.

New Brunswick needs a Premier, at this time, who should at least be seeing, given our fiscal crisis and threat to services: We have restored hope, we are directing our future.

A clear and relevant vision has to be accompanied by a measurable and accountable path for the Premier's term. It has to be clarified by a proposed mandate, working toward our vision, while consistent with our principles and values, clearly articulated by the Premier. Or by the people to our Premier.

Our Reason for Being
as a Province

When we consider what our reason for being as a province is, some of the descriptions used in regarding our values frequently come into the discussion. While there is congruity amongst values and vision and mission, each provides a different element to our identity, to who and what we are.

Knowing and believing our mission is akin to the keel of a ship—it establishes a basic foundation and its strength ensures direction in the water. A sound keel enables forward thrust of a ship with the subsequent lift to counteract the leeward force of winds. No surprise then that to lay the keel is a significant event in building a ship. So, too, is it critical to any organization, including a province.

A leader needs to outline clearly how they will 'lay the keel' for their term in office. Rarely do we have it communicated to us during the election campaign, and so rarely does it occur once the outcome of the election is determined. What follows is a brief commentary and suggestion as to a relevant statement as to why we are a people in this Province of New Brunswick. From this should, in essence by the electorate, be delegated a 'commission' to each Premier and government.

Any reference to our Province's reason for being, or mission, ought to be within the context of a province in the confederation that is Canada. Looking 'out' at the 'bigger picture', some would highlight the key words from our Constitution and suggest that in Canada our mission statement is:

…a nation of peoples living in peace, order and good government from sea to sea to sea…

For our closest neighbor and ally, the American declaration expounds a country of life, liberty and the pursuit of happiness. The 'American Dream' is ubiquitous, internally and externally, to the USA. Perhaps a lawyer would argue that we would need to dig deeper to understand both the intentions and the constitutional guarantees implicit and explicit in the American, or Canadian, words. However, a mission statement is not a legal statement as much as it is a defining statement as to why we are.

This was the passion and motivation of Sir John A MacDonald, our first and greatest Prime Minister, and all of the Fathers of Confederation. **For Canada**, this is our reason for being as a nation.

A nation of peoples living in peace, order and good government From sea to sea to sea

Above any other expectation we may have of our federal leadership, we expect our Prime Minister and government to uphold, protect, respect and govern to ensure this is so.

"The Government are merely trustees for the public"

Sir John A Macdonald

We hear and read a lot of statements, and introductory phrases to a point being made preceded with "from sea to sea to sea" or in contemporary times "coast to coast to coast". When we say 'from sea to sea to sea' it should be implicit that the rest follows, "a nation of people living in peace, order and good government." Implicit or explicit, it should be referenced with sincerity and with respect to Canadians.

A Province of New Brunswick mission statement would be within a similar context. Likewise, most municipalities within New Brunswick would be a variation of this theme as it pertains to that community. Thus, the reason for being of our province, the mission of the Province of New Brunswick could be expressed as:

A province of peoples living in peace, order and good government

In New Brunswick, there is a crack in our peace, Anglophone/Francophone/Bilingualism, rural/urban and south/north. Our order is out of sorts fiscally, as well health, education and social services. This province's government is dated in its governance, lacking in capacity and capability, and reliant on the largesse of the federal government transferring the surplus of wealthy provinces.

As with vision, we must have clarity as to our mission. There is not a politician in our Province who would disagree with this phrase, nor not wish to fulfill it in their mandate. It may be a surprise if any in the Legislature could cite this or provide a context of it to our current times.

Once we address with clarity the mission of our Province, we then turn to: What is the reason for being for our government? Each political party, as it seeks to be the new government should seek a mandate that is clear to the population. Not a mandate based on 'anti-whatever' or for 'what-it-might-be' but a mandate of clear mission for the four years of government it is seeking support from the electorate.

In times of clarity of purpose and expectation by the electorate, the mission would be clear from the people, or at least clear to the people. Then, the party leaders would agree on the way to best describe that mission, or as a minimum their variation on that theme.

Subsequently, each of the political party leaders would explain, in detail with clear objectives, timelines and costing, as to how they propose to achieve their commitment if elected.

In the absence of such clarity of direction, each political party platform should be within the umbrella of a stated mission for the province. A party leader ought to be able to, at minimum, complete with a reasonable level of clarity this statement:

"In the next four years the reason for being for our government, if elected will be to…"
Followed by, "And we will…commitments to the citizens."

As an illustration, consider:

A province of peoples living in peace, order and good government—and by Righting Our Ship we will in 2018 be in a zero deficit financial situation and be moving to better health, education and social systems.

We should have a higher expectation of a party leader, and their party, as to their mission to govern, their values, their collective competencies, and their intentions. A premier-nominee, irrespective of their party, ought to have a very detailed resume published, not the promotional, communication controlled back of a brochure biography with which the party, and the reporting media, seem content.

Could you tell me, please,
which way I ought to go from here?"
"That depends a good deal on
where you want to get to," said the Cat.
"I don't much care where–" said Alice.
"Then it doesn't matter which way you go," said the Cat.
"–so long as I get SOMEWHERE,"
Alice added as an explanation.
"Oh, you're sure to do that," said the Cat,
"if you only walk long enough."

From Alice's Adventures in Wonderland

By 'commissioning' a newly elected government to a commitment the elected Premier candidate provided, and to which the electorate awards with power, the people are essentially agreeing to an interim (four years) mission to the Premier and caucus. This 'sub-mission statement' is good governance.

During my years providing consulting, coaching and facilitating of strategies, plans and initiatives with profit, not-for-profit, as well as provincial and federal government groups, there has been great success when the Board or Executive has adopted the sub mission approach for hiring and holding accountable their most senior management executive. With the mission statement as the 'keel' for the long voyage, the sub mission statement provides clarity as to the direction over the 3-4-5 year contract. In provincial politics, the contract period is now an accepted fixed four year term of government.

Without a doubt, there is a trust element, but then every election has a trust element. Trust can be a trust in capability (as in, we trust that they have what it takes to get the job done). Or, it can be a trust in integrity (as in, we can trust that they are being honest with us as to what they promise to do). We need to be in the position where, as voters, we can place our trust in both aspects with our Premier and Ministers.

This is far different than making altruistic commitments, avoiding the tough realities, or the familiar grasping of straws, sometimes because they have a self-belief, or altruistic obligation, or because they really don't know what should be done, or voters are so cynical that many have little trust in their political system.

How would this look? Let us look at an example relevant to our current situation. With the overarching mission of New Brunswick being "A province of peoples living in peace, order and good government", a (sub) mission for the current government mandate could have been proposed to the people of New Brunswick:

Get our fiscal ship in order and ensure our essential services are put back on track to be sustainable

For the immediate year at hand, in the absence of capacity and experience, as a starting point this could have been followed by a commitment for the NB Provincial budget 2015-16 to have three key outcomes:

1. Immediate shoring up of revenues: HST up 1% 1April, 1% 1November, with an expiry of 2017-03-31.
2. Get government structure back in control: Freeze all civil servants positions; except doctors/nurses to be replaced at attrition, and teachers at current ratios, to 2016January.
3. Work with experts within and without the civil service to adjust government, beginning with a full review to extend through the entire government of NB for a 2016-17 zero deficit budget.

Even at best, these three actions would have been only temporary, interim measures, and observations indicate some variations were favored by some. These would have provided some breathing room to get the requisite debriefings of the best of the predecessor government, the input as offered by former Ministers, and other external advice. Then, a readiness with an informed opinion would provide a better guide in the strategic and tactical decisions for the province.

For those of us whose tendency is toward lowering taxes collected so as to leave more with the people and less with governments who like to spend, the increase in HST is not a favorable option. However, as a stop-gap, as long as the legislation includes a temporary period, say one year, at the end of which time the renewal needs to come back before the Legislative Assembly, the province has at least an increase in revenues for this period of time.

For a person's eye, an area of diminished or absent vision is referred to as a scotoma, or blind spot. While not alone amongst the provinces, we do seem to have a strategic scotoma, with the blind spot more with mission than vision. This may be from a lack of creativity, or fear of significant change, or capability.

Many leaders in this province could describe a vision of sorts. And, most of these visions would be of a better New Brunswick, likely of a self-sufficient province, with full employment, families living together in their communities, harmony of our linguistic peoples, etc. Note the mix of vision and values and mission here. We do not entirely lack a vision, of sorts. It can be implicit, but most people will 'know it' when they hear it.

We lack a mission, and most particularly a mission that is explicit in its clarity of direction and intent. Consequently, we lack a sub-mission, with its necessary mandate to commission our government for its objectives during its four year term.

Some will argue that there are 'visions' from Premiers other than the esteemed group indicated herein. That sort of vision, tends to be less of a macro or destiny sort and more of a strategic objective. Furthermore, many of these strategic type objectives are beyond the term of the government, with little in the way of metrics or accountability for the government's term in office. We need an accountability framework for the current term.

> "It is a mistake to look too far ahead.
> Only one link in the chain of destiny
> can be handled at a time."
>
> Winston Churchill

For obvious reasons, the senior civil service, led by Deputy Ministers, manages the initiatives, strategic and operational, of the government. Some department heads are competent, or competent enough, for their position, whether they are maintained as political parties take power or appointed due to political alignment. Some are very competent, leaders in their fields.

Naturally, it would be expected that the civil service may have its own perspectives, as it is intended to be non-partisan and non-party aligned in its work, seeking to influence their minister directly or in response to direction. When successive governments seek input from their bureaucracy, it is to lean on a knowledge and expertise. To the keen observers, many of these ideas, suggestions and recommendations, appear to be recycled. Look in the drawers and archives, dust it off, update with an amended addition or two, and present in the hope that their politician will be accepting. This is not always entirely to the fault of the senior administrators.

Fortunately, in Canada we have decades of internationally recognized competence in our civil service, and low corruption in our government and politics. Yet, we are dissatisfied, as we should. Even in recent memory we witnessed building and construction at the direction of a cabinet minister (real or perceived), sometimes even the location when best located elsewhere; MLAs being given authority over dispensing summer job grant monies; lack of transparency.

Many of the deputy ministers and directors may be lacking in the competencies if a government is transformed to one of oversight rather than doing. But, in the absence of clarity of mission, how can one assess, or even criticize, our professional civil servants for their current ways and means let alone what might be?

Nearly fifty years ago, Dr. Peter F. Drucker, in his 1968 book "The Age of Discontinuity: Guidelines to Our Changing Society" dealt head on with the failure of bureaucratic government as well as the challenges of all very large organizations. He further elaborated that government had proven by that time it was very effective in two things, waging war and inflating currency; and in most other things it can promise with rare accomplishment. The latter failures include running industrial enterprises and the inability to stop doing anything. His conclusion alludes to: governments have to stop doing.

Government is not the only bureaucracy that he put on watch, as over the next number of years the international conglomerate model was reaching its pinnacle, before imploding. Most noticeable to observers would be the significant downsizing of corporations that occurred in the late 1980s, culminating in the great recession of the early 1990s. Some global wealth advisers are signaling the most recent years of mergers and acquisition return to mega and far reaching diverse corporations is once again reaching a peak.

Corporations sometimes forget why they exist. So do **governments sometimes overlook their reason for being**. This is why mission is critical, and far more than an exercise to fill in the blanks so the check mark can be placed by mission statement on the strategic plan.

In the David Osborne and Ted Gaebler [4] seminal book on 'Reinventing Government' an entire chapter is written about and reporting on "Mission-Driven Government Transforming Rule-Driven Organizations."

Rather than "rule-driven government" the "obvious advantages" of Mission-Driven Government are, according to the authors:

Mission-driven organizations are more efficient than rule-driven organizations.

Mission-driven organizations are also more effective than rule-driven organizations: they produce better results.

Mission-driven organizations are more innovative than rule-driven organizations.

Mission-driven organizations are more flexible than rule-driven organizations.

Mission-driven organizations have higher morale than rule-drive organizations.

Osborne and Gaebler go on to report on family services, state departments, municipalities, and other government organizations.

New Brunswick has a mission, as does it have historical reference to a vision, to values, and to principles. The failure has been to ensure that each government knows and believes and governs by the mission and more particularly to a commission or sub-mission the electorate confirms when it is made our government.

The public has a right to expect its government to know why it exists, and what it exists for and to do, within the larger parameters as to why our province exists, and to govern to that mission approved for them by the electorate.

Chapter 3

Expectations Fulfilled

of a 21ˢᵗ Century People

Much more is expected by people of the life they wish to live, the role of government, and the assumptions of politicians and their civil servants decorum, than many experience. For some it is a matter of opportunity and high achiever success orientation, while for others it may be a matter of entitlement, with yet others who likely form the majority it is a simple matter of living their own lives as they choose with their families, friends and pursuits.

In some ways, not much changes over the decades of this modern world in which we live. Except when it comes to politics. We are in a nation of consumer savvy, technology connected, higher educated masses of people, accustomed to growing economies and growing government spending on health and education and other services.

We expect our governments not only to maintain that to which we have become accustomed and taken for granted, and pay for with our hard earned money, but to ever improve and enhance along the way.

The writer and philosopher, John Ralston Saul, Tweeted:
Citizens now believe that they are client/consumers of democracy instead of its agents #canpoli @stratfest #stForum   (2015-06-25 @JohnRalstonSaul)

Now, one can never be sure as to why JR Saul writes or speaks, although one can usually be assured it is to propagate his view of politics and culture. This particular statement does strike on an important point. That is, as voters and taxpayers, as we receive increasing depth and breadth of products and services from our government, we have also become client/consumers.

We can wear two hats, as voters and as client/consumers, and we do wear two hats. The government and its civil service need to realize this is our prerogative, and we have expectations with this dual-dimension. Likewise, we cannot abdicate our responsibility to vote for responsible government, if we are not ourselves responsible people – the agents to which the Saul Tweet refers.

Now we are fully aware of the cynicism, skepticism and anger of the 21ˢᵗ century democracy's electorate. And, it is not just here in New Brunswick, or in Canada, but across the western democratic world. As we have increased our education, gained more access to the world's knowledge via the Web, gained confidence, and the gap has closed with the former elite of our society.

Our expectation of what many consider a more democratic democracy will only be fulfilled when our elected officials, at all levels of government, demonstrate Clarity and Truth in their capability and capacity, as well as intentions; Accountability and Trust in policy, action and outcomes and fiscal responsibility; Transparency and Openness in their goals, execution, and reporting; Representation and Consultation with the people for services of value and value for taxation.

Clarity and Truth

The expectation of Clarity and Truth from the politicians whom one elects should be without need of comment. Regrettably, a broad segment of our society believes that while most people go into politics mostly for the right reasons, once there for a period of time become less than truthful, less than honest. These men and women who are elected, many of whom I know, are there and stay there for the right reasons. It is just that politics and party politics seems to get things off track a tad.

Frustrations are mounting practically everywhere in modern, western democracies by an electorate that is educated and mindful of some politicians disrespectful to the straightforward, real answer, and sometimes of saying one thing but doing another. Provinces and States, with a recent example in Alberta, have shown just how this frustration can be released at election time. More than one high profile US 2016 Presidential candidate is attracting significant support due to their frank, non-politically-correct statements—because they speak from their truth and belief systems.

One of the small curios that has been in my family for decades is a bronze trio of wise monkeys in the See no evil—Hear no evil—Speak no evil pose. Ironically, we see public figures using these actions in a way to move hidden agendas forward, or to avoid taking positions, or to 'tow the party line'.

We seem to have had our share of party leaders, premier candidates, and premiers, who take turns which of the three blind monkeys they are, perceptions being people's reality.

In nomination mode by their party, a leader can be blind, covering his eyes to realities so as to hear nothing contrary to electoral victory, and speaking a good talk, placing a positive spin on most topics to attract favorable polls from the majority. In full accord to the charade, cognizant or not, the party members present at the nomination meeting are likewise with their favorite.

Upon good electoral fortune elevating a party leader to Premier, on go the ear plugs deaf to creative solutions, even when there are only a few, from those in opposition, as it may portray the government as not innovative on its own or an idea better than one it had originally. Good legislation is left less than it could be without the eclectic collaboration of input from others, and augmenting from the experienced of governments past.

Then, as if to be aligned less with values and more with political wins, now is the leader covering his mouth lest transparency be an evil, and collaboration becomes in reality consultation. Within days of electoral victory, suddenly the cupboard is bare, the realization of the "real" fiscal situation of the province now that we "see the books". An epiphany that an informed electorate can only wonder as to how it elected what must have been a less than stellar opposition to an even less than stellar government.

In the role as leader of the opposition, this same person would be the blind monkey covering one's eyes, blind to what is best and proper for the citizens even to the point of criticizing the government in power for policies, actions, and civil service activities that would be approximate to its own actions as a government. Not hearing, nor fully listening, to the governing party propositions or the electorate feedback, choosing words of discontent in the name of 'opposition'. None of these, government or opposition, are dishonest people, so one wonders why the roles are assumed so quickly.

Now, this allegory of three monkeys is not directed to any party or leader. This is an illustration as to what people perceive, and as we all know perception is reality, as well as what actually occurs.

> "There were, unfortunately, no great principles
> on which parties were divided—
> politics became a mere struggle for office."
>
> Sir John A MacDonald, Canada's first Prime Minister

Too often, the truth, at least the full truth, is beyond what one hears from public personalities either due to intent or lacking of them or us. Without us questioning these people further, perhaps beyond the surface of what we want to believe, the public as a whole and the media/reporters who have an obligation to be our 'fourth estate', allow the truth to be withheld. The proverb of See no evil—Hear no evil—Speak no evil, is meant to be a way of living, not a convenient technique of deception.

Trying to get the real facts at the root of issues such as the size of our civil service and what those numbers really mean can be an experience in frustration. Not all citizens are researchers or investigative reporters, and should they need to be so they can locate information of interest. Simply stating the number of 45000 with regard to civil servants does not provide a foundation for an appropriate or accurate assessment of comparative ratios or otherwise.

On occasion, thanks to a diligent reporter digging through various sources, we read reports with some details. From this, we know that as at the end of 2014, of the 45465 civil servants on the New Brunswick payroll, there were 19464 in health, 16797 in Education, and 9204 in the civil service general. But, any one citizen should not have to wait for these infrequent insights.

Today, citizens need, and have a right to, easy and unfettered access to most data in government. On the topic of employees, details should be readily available with regard to the groupings of schools and school districts (teaching and non-teaching), hospitals and provincial health centers (medical and administrative), and NB Power and NB Liquor (when either or both are lumped into the larger number), and the separate number of civil servants employed by departments (administrative and labor workers). With this more appropriate data, intelligent assessments and decisions can be made by voters.

Finally, should one wish to make comparative judgments, such as to other provinces, it is not shown. For example, one needs to consider how 80% of our country's school districts have contracted school bus services, but not us.

Unquestionably, we need to do things differently in New Brunswick. We are an intelligent people who need to make intelligent decisions and communicate to each other intelligently, including the media and our politicians. Mixing facts, stressing perspectives, stretching points, do little in providing clarity and often border on the truth. It may be 'good politics' but it is not genuine.

Every field has its own vocabulary and way of communicating within, a nomenclature, and accompanying acronyms and jargon. When this is used outside of the insiders, it is unintentionally a failure in communicating well, or intentionally showing off, acting superior, or misleading. Political circles are not any different.

In lieu of clarity, nebulous, fuzzy or hazy statements designed to obscure or avoid are frustrating and insulting to a modern citizen. On the other hand, if such talk is due to lack of insight or capability, then the electorate needs to have reference points to flush out the situation, reveal the truth.

Voters, cynicism aside, expect an honest vocabulary whereby a politician would use terms, answers and explanations that are straightforward, understandable and not misleading. By way of a recent illustration, when it comes to cutting taxes, a concept to which voters are typically receptive, the objective becomes muddied and they might agree to not wanting to see revenues reduced when linked to service reductions. While taxes and fees form part of a government's revenues, reducing revenues' is a ridiculous piece of terminology.

Generally speaking, politicians need to come clean on discussions regarding taxes and services, and revenues and expenses. When a politician criticizes another politician of reducing revenues or cutting revenues instead of investing in infrastructure and programs, it is a deliberate use of words for euphemistic numbing of the voter.

Also related to finance, voters would be better served, and communication more effective, if there was a consistency of accounting, and reporting, from one governing party to the next. Changing accounting methods for more attractive reports is a lack of clarity and of truth.

Quarterly and annual reports indicate our provincial GDP (Gross Domestic Product) which is an aggregated figure to indicate the size of an economy, with period to period comparison reflecting the productivity of the jurisdiction. It also serves to indicate the success or failure of a government's economic policy.

From the Department of Finance website we can see anemic 'real' GDP growth in our province:

2015 at 1.5% (Reduced to 1% by some economists)
2014 at .0%   ~ 2013 at -.5%
2012 at -1.1%   ~ 2011 at .03%

The honest answer, at the basics, is that as a province we are not exceptionally productive or competitive, or amply innovative, or else we would have a robust growth economy. This is as relevant to most of our businesses and workers, as to our government. People do not like to be told they are not productive enough as for many that translates into not working hard enough, which is not true necessarily.

"The liberties of a people never were,
nor ever will be, secure,
when the transactions of their rulers
may be concealed from them."

Patrick Henry, American colonial revolutionary

Compounding our circumstances is the growing demographic shift to significant numbers of seniors coinciding with the slower growth in the population of our young people. This is creating further strain on health services and on budgets, and requires a strategy far sooner than later.

What is true is that as a province we have two major challenges, if we have a real concern for our future collective self-determination and prosperity. **In tandem, we need our provincial government to transform the way it governs, and we need our businesses and workers to increase productivity.**

This means the government needs to be straightforward with the numbers making the time that it will take to help citizens understand the numbers and gain confidence in the truth of the figures. And, it means that businesses need to invest, and workers willing to adjust, in higher productivity methods, equipment and outcomes.

From the economic benefits of developing our resources, to environmental protection, to cost containment of education and health expenses while maintaining the services we expect, and continuing on with why certain decisions are made, **citizens just do not know what to believe, or in what to have trust**. An unending spiel of speech, whether with scary scenarios or positive commentary, will not mend our sails let alone re-set the keel.

However, **politically led dialogue with a level of intellect paired with capability, will eliminate the cynicism**, if it is straightforward, understandable, commonsensical and honest. If we cannot have a leader of the stature of the aforementioned trio, let us at least have the truth and the level of clarity to which our leaders should be capable.

Transparency and Openness

In the 21st century, we expect our governments to be open in their ways and means, and transparent in the fullest sense while respecting privacy. Yet, full disclosure, even in hard numbers of financial reporting, may be suspect, and right to information, mandated by our courts, delayed or scuffled.

The lack of openness only perpetuates the suspicion and distrust, further fueling the skepticism of citizens. Similarly, citizens no longer are accepting of the excuses of what continues as a para colonial parliamentary management style. Democratic reform can be immediate through government reform, from attitude and capability, not procrastination to legislative or constitutional changes.

When one of my forefathers, William Henry Steeves, a government reformer, represented our pre-Confederation colony at the 1864 Charlottetown and Quebec Conferences, his was an era of political appointees to post master positions, contracts to favored road makers. It was an era of opaqueness, not transparency. It was an accepted practice, even when it was known. But that was a different time, with a people of different expectations.

True, as a Father of Confederation along with Leonard Tilley, Charles Fisher and five other New Brunswickers, WH Steeves would eventually be accountable to the voters of this province. But as the first Chairman of the Public Works Department, the budgets may have had to be approved in the legislature, but procurement and construction was not subject to the policy, process or scrutiny now expected. As it was said, that's just the way it is. Not anymore.

Lack of transparency has, in the past, been the kindred spirit of politicians and their appointed senior civil servants. These two groups got along well, for the most part, as they planned and executed projects. With little transparency, less time had to be spent on explaining, or influencing, or persuading the public to get on board.

Opaqueness went hand in hand with elitism, while *transparency* is coupled with *accountability*. At the same time, *clarity* is lacking when less revealing of details is provided. Likewise, the quality and occurrence of legitimate *representation and consultation* is lessened. This creates an environment where the four keystones of our expectations as a modern electorate are all weak.

Across all sectors of our society professionals are being challenged, with the 'old school' (not necessarily age related) resisting and sometimes angry with, and the progressive amongst them embracing the engagement and input of their clients and patients. The latter also respects the right of people to manage their bodies, and have oversight of their children's education, their legal decisions and financial assets, etc.

Modern professionals, including politicians, recognize that more informed people make more informed decisions, take ownership, and might even provide an insight or teaching moment to the professional. A 'progressive', although arrogated as a term by the 'left', is any person of any political or professional propensity who contributes to society's progress.

A tenet of transparency is our right to information as well as a window to accountability, clarity, and representation. In today's world, every government at every level portrays in its transparency, or lack thereof, that by its behaviors and actions if it is aligned with the values of its people, and not compromising the principles of its society.

Telegraph-Journal 2015-10-24

The Telegraph-Journal, provides a succinct message on the right to information in its October 24, 2015 Editorial, with this excerpt capturing the key points:

"Why is the right to information so important? It goes to the heart of government transparency and accountability. The Supreme Court has said access to information legislation is crucial to democracy. Government must understand it is merely the keeper of public information and the public has every right -- barring a demonstrable need for secrecy -- to see it. In New Brunswick, public bodies such as government departments and municipalities are required by law to respond within 30 days to an information request unless an extension is granted for a large or complex request. The average response rate in the audit by the province was 42 days; in Fredericton, 59 days.

The province received a failing grade in the length of time to respond; it managed only a 'C' grade in the completeness of disclosure. Of the 15 requests made in the audit, the province fulfilled only nine. Two cities went even further to deny releasing the information, appealing to provincial access to the Information Commissioner for permission to ignore the requests. The Commissioner ordered them to comply with the law."

The editorial concludes: "What information is released, and when, cannot be left to a political decision -- or even the whim of a bureaucrat. New Brunswick has laws governing access to information -- the public's information -- and the province and cities must be held bound by them. All information held in trust by governments must be made public by default, and the onus must be on government to prove in any case why it should not be released. It should not be the public's job to fight for access to what is rightfully their property."

Now, it must be clarified that this raised bar for transparency does not mean or even infer, corruption or corrupt government. While there exists the occasional scandal at the provincial and federal levels, some justly labelled with others as a result of incompetence, we are not a corrupt society by most standards.

As a country, we are one of the "cleanest" less corrupt countries in the world—in fact, in the top ten, according to a 2014 Corruption Perceptions Index (CPI). The number-one or cleanest country in the world is Denmark with a score of 92, followed closely by New Zealand at 91, and then rounding out the top 10 in order—Finland, Sweden, Norway, Switzerland, Singapore, Netherlands, Luxembourg, and us, Canada. We are ranked number 10 with a score of 81, which means we slipped a notch. In the 2013 CPI, Transparency International© had Canada tied for 9th place with Australia, and in the 2012 Index, we were also tied for 9th, but this time with the Netherlands.

The Reputation Institute in its Country RepTrak® 2015 report ranks Canada as the Most Reputable Country in the World. Its highlights that most reputable countries in the world are the ones with less corruption, the ones that are peaceful, and are the happiest. Our gap between external and internal reputation is amongst the smallest at 6.2% (compared to the UK at 6.6% and the USA at 19.8%). The key factors are Effective Government (#4), Appealing Environment (#1) and Advanced Economy (#5), accompanied by emotional factors of esteem, admire, trust and feeling.

As with so many other changes, managers in both the private and public sectors are struggling to lead an enlightened and empowered workplace. **Politicians, along with their senior civil servants, likewise have not kept pace with the educated, empowered, less intimated, more emancipated, and somewhat more aware people who elect them. Neither their skillsets nor their attitudes have kept pace with society's expectations.**

In the case of transparency, attitude is the precept to aptitude. For the most part, we already have the capability and the technology. To begin with, we can expand the government's website and create links 'to all things Government' as well as augment the site for easier macro and micro access to information. Then, we post it with minimum of delay, as established by timeline protocols relative to the privacy of person, security and other confidential criteria.

Transparency begins with ease of access to find, read and understand information and statistics in our province. The list of access to information is encompassing of much of government at provincial and municipal levels as well as crown corporations, commissions and boards.

This list includes transparency as to quality of services provided by provincially funded programs as well as key industry sectors affecting children, food, and vehicle safety.

~Restaurant health inspection ratings

~Day Care operations inspection ratings (and eventually client assessment ratings)

~Hospital ER wait times, bed occupancy rates, surgical availability (Eventually, surgical success metrics, illness levels of inpatients, complains/resolutions)

~Automotive/Vehicle Repair and Ownership satisfaction ratings with links to recalls, etc.

~School ratings K-3 4-8 9-12

Technology is in place now, at least at a sufficient and working level, for our province to implement an Open Data Transparency Policy. With an open attitude, this can begin almost immediately without legislation. An all legislative committee can draft the applicable legislation in the mid-term.

The Telegraph-Journal commented in its March 3, 2015 edition:

"The City of Saint John has developed its first open data policy, an attempt to put more city information in the hands of citizens. The policy is an important step by Common Council to provide more accountability and transparency around city spending.

"Larger Canadian cities have shared data sets for years but the new Saint John policy positions the city in the forefront of open data in the Atlantic region. The Saint John Police force already provides crime data on a website, but the new policy will see all city departments, as well as agencies, boards and commissions, share more about where money is spent and what services are offered.

"The possibilities for open data are endless, from mapping transit routes to property tax information, building permit trends, land use and rezoning reviews, to traffic patterns. If the data is presented clearly, it can be used by the public both to better understand how their city operates and to offer suggestions on better use of public money.

"Open data is a shift away from providing information only when it is requested by the public to providing it by default. Putting more information in the hands of voters may eventually result in more suggestions that will help council decide on priorities and make important decisions. It can also arm potential investors with the information they need to better plan business ventures in the city.

"Information is power, especially in today's digital world. Opening up the information collected by city hall is a positive step in Saint John's evolution to a connected and engaged city. Council has nothing to fear by opening up the flow of information. A better-informed electorate is a sign of a healthy city."

To which can be added, and a healthy province, and a healthy democracy.

> "A lack of transparency results in distrust and a deep sense of insecurity."
>
> Dalai Lama

Transparency, of course, is expected at the Legislature level of our government, by the MLAs generally, and always by those in the Opposition ranks as part of their holding the governing party accountable. We elect our MLAs to represent us, and have input into lawmaking even if they are not a Cabinet Minister or member of the governing caucus.

In a unicameral legislative framework, as is the norm in Canadian provinces, committee work provides more than a venue of opining from other than the government members, it provides the debating and vetting of legislation prior to it reaching the Legislative Assembly. This enables a sitting legislative assembly to be more meaningful in its work, and more refined and discriminating in its deliberations.

While not as apparent as some may say that it is at the federal level, our province has seen some erosion of the importance and the legitimate use of committees and their work. David Coon, the only member of the Green Party elected in this province has been quoted as saying that over the past decade or two "power has been stripped away from the legislature to the executive branch, which is undermining the ability of the legislative assembly to do its proper work."

Most of the observing adult population would assume that the committee work exists, either because one hears or reads of this or that going to committee, or views across the border television shows and movies with the USA committee system in full camera. Ours is not as open a democracy in this regard. Rather, we have regressed to a more colonial atmosphere, it seems, with the television camera.

While once perhaps not questioned, at least in public to people in power, today much more is expected. Nonetheless, for all the best efforts of diligent reporters, queries by others on occasion, and even requests through access to information, privatized highway operations are without tolerable disclosure as to terms. Nor is much known about the details regarding the 'non-retail' services of Service NB other than the descriptions of laundry and IT and other 'government' services in brief, broad overviews, and without detail or financial disclosure.

These are not signs of transparency in government. True enough to our principles and values, Integrity would dictate that proprietary methods and processes have to be kept in confidence, before and during as well as after a contract. Likewise, contractual details that may compromise current and future bidding must not be compromised. However, the governments gross expenses, project by project, and contingent liabilities, and performance penalties, do not need to be kept secret from the paying public. That simply is not proper.

Somewhat gradual in getting to where we are now, power and decision making is more centralized around the power of the Premier's office but without the checks and balances of the less cohesive 19th century looser party system. This may come under renewed scrutiny by media and others with our post 2015 federal election, if comments made are any indication.

Ironically, this regression in balance of power has occurred parallel to rising expectations and scrutiny by our more educated and now empowered populace. MLAs are part of this populace, and more frequently appear to becoming restless in their inactivity, disenchanted by their warming of the back benches. Their input would provide a broader perspective to legislation policies and bills, with better chance of it reflecting their riding's constituents.

While the respective legislation serves to protect the privacy of individuals with regard to health, education and other records, the various Protection of Privacy acts also serve the purpose of those who use it to hide access, whatever their reasons. In recent years, there have been some minor breakthroughs in transparency. Release of health department reviews and ratings of food and restaurant facilities; daycare operational reviews and ratings (although this battle is not quite over).

The Open Government Partnership (OGP at its website _www.opengovpartnership.org_ we explains that OGP "was launched in 2011 to provide an international platform for domestic reformers committed to making their governments more open, accountable, and responsive to citizens. The following excerpts from OGP reflects the points made above.

"Accountability – There are rules, regulations and mechanisms in place that call upon government actors to justify their actions, act upon criticisms or requirements made of them, and accept responsibility for failure to perform with respect to laws or commitments."

"Technology & Innovation – Governments embrace the importance of providing citizens with open access to technology, the role of new technologies in driving innovation, and the importance of increasing the capacity of citizens to use technology."

"Citizenship Participation –Governments seek to mobilize citizens to engage in public debate, provide input, and make contributions that lead to more responsive, innovative and effective governance."

"Transparency—Information on government activities and decisions is open, comprehensive, timely freely available to the public and meets basic open data standards (e.g. raw data, machine readability)."

So, as we see, all democracies, mature and less so, are receiving attention with regard to transparency and openness. One would assume that the more open, more respected democracies, have a higher sort of expectation place upon them based on an existing state of democratic principles, relatively low corruption, and uninterrupted and uncorrupt electoral administration.

The review of the current government with regard to Legislative Officers while prudent should also be strategic. These officers include, Auditor General, Chief Electoral Officer, Access to Information and Privacy Commissioner, Child and Youth Advocate, Commissioner of Official Languages, Conflict of Interest Commissioner, Ombudsman, Consumer Advocate for Insurance.

There is overlap amongst many of these roles, something that easily occurs as additional specialties are added. Should each of these oversight and/or liaison roles fulfill a legitimate gap in our society that will not sufficiently be addressed upon consolidation of roles, then there should be concern.

Some of these roles, or at least portions of the roles, could be acceptably fulfilled by the posting of 'all things Government' as much of our issues as citizens is the 'secrecy' in the lack of full transparency and openness. Streamlining would have three Legislative Officers, which is much more appropriate to the budgets and the roles needed for this province:

~Auditor General
~Chief Electoral Officer
~Chief Advocacy Officer for People & Ombudsman Office

The Chief Advocacy Officer could have direct reporting Assistant Officers in official languages, youth, women, disabled persons, conflict of interest, and consumer advocate. **With all of the five previous Legislative**

Officers and their offices brought under one Chief, cross files and energies would be more efficient and effective. While significantly less positions are required with five less officers, the big savings to taxpayers would come from a reduction of six very high paying executive positions and their executive assistants, offices, IT support, telephones, and other expenses.

With a new age of transparency and openness, the need for an Access to Information Officer is redundant. Any future difficulties would be addressed to the Chief Advocacy Officer. Faster access, more efficient and effective workflow, as well as a lower budget requirement, is a strategic solution to a number of issues.

Transparency is a philosophy and a way of operations that a government embraces, a modus operandi as mentioned above. **Yesteryear (and to some still, yesterday), opaqueness was the best friend of a politician and their partnering senior civil servant**. It provided more latitude and discretion while saving time from explaining, justifying, and procuring.

Today transparency is the enlightened politician's best friend. And for the senior civil servant the modus operandi that can transcend politics, conducive to evidence based decisions and an open governance workplace.

> "Government ought to be all outside
> and no inside...."
>
> Woodrow Wilson, US President

Representation and Consultation

Representation has come to mean many things to the New Brunswick electorate. At the riding level, representation is the Member of the Legislative Assembly (MLA), elected by the voters of that riding. There are not any members 'at large' in our province as there may be councilors in some municipalities. (Nor should there be as ridings are representative of peoples.)

At the provincial level there is the representation and leadership of the Premier with regard to the best interest of our Province and citizens. And, there is the broader expectation that the Legislative Assembly as a whole will be 'representative' of our interests and concerns.

Representation at the local riding level begins with the election of a candidate amongst other candidates as a Member of the Legislative Assembly. The MLA represents a riding that has been as of the current election outlined by boundaries subject to a process established in the *Electoral Boundaries and Representation Act.*

The most recent 2014 distribution saw a reduction to 49 seats in the Legislature which resulted from the Commission, established by statutory requirement for redistribution following every second general election in the province. The boundaries are to be within the range of 95% to 105% of the 1/49th of the number of registered voters in the province; "extraordinary circumstances" allow an exception.

Communication is critical to one's constituents, on the broader pan provincial level by the Premier and Cabinet Ministers, and at the riding level by the MLA. Sometimes this is done by way of presentations, speeches, newspaper commentaries, social media, and news reports.

Communications, on other occasions, maybe town hall meetings, or special interest group, or elected officials associations. Consultation is required for better understanding, input and dialogue on issues. This adds, by additional information and goodwill perception, good communication when it is used sincerely and effectively.

"What we've got here is failure to communicate"

Actor Strother Martin as the prison camp warden
in the 1967 Paul Newman movie, Cool Hand Luke

Consultation is not collaboration. It is important that, intentionally or unintentionally, politicians be judicious in their use of the word collaborate or when inferring collaboration. When one collaborates, the process and the outcome is geared toward a joint decision. Since nearly all consultation is seeking input prior to making a decision, the politician as well as the attending bureaucrats need to be honest in being clear as to their method and intent.

It is unfortunate that too often people think that the politician wants to collaborate, and the politician knowingly or unknowingly overlooks this nuance as it keeps the proceedings calmer and less confrontational. However, when eventually the decision is introduced in legislation or otherwise announced, people are dissatisfied, frustrated, and often angry.

The earlier reference to the David Alward term of Ministerial expected consultation when it was used it was productive. Those ministers most successful during the term of his government—with difficult and demanding portfolios—were also those who consulted more than their colleagues, and most of their predecessors. The remaining ministers, with minimal to nil or too-little-too-late consultation, created the problems for which some would say his government failed to win its second term, leaving it vulnerable to not effectively communicating and appearing to have a one topic strategy.

Extending the comment on the creation of Regional Service Commissions, the beginnings of major modernization of government, internal justice productivity, and the financial budgetary process and decisions–all were done with less conflict, and more results, than the projects of ministers who failed to consult as their Premier had requested and directed. The subsequent government also sought wide range input as it planned its range of cuts.

The initial regionalization concept was created by the Liberal party, and shelved in fear of forced amalgamation as proposed by the government's chosen author, Jean-Guy Finn. The reason given by Premier Shawn Graham was the expense of implementation. Most who are politically astute know that it had more do with the issue of amalgamation, and how unpopular that can be to a political party seeking a mandate from the rural populations.

Communities, including my own community of Pointe-du-Chêne which is an unIncorporated area formally referred to as a Local Service District, were asked by the Liberal Minister to put reports regarding Rural Community status on hold pendng the Finn Report. The 'rules' on minimum population and minimum tax base to qualify for the quasi-municipal designation were increased. Once the latter was shelved, all reports also essentially were shelved.

Minister Bruce Fitch leveraged a knowledgeable and competent senior civil service team to consult widely, perhaps as well as any other time in our history. Open public sessions; gatherings of mayors and Local Service District chairs; frequently expanding the net to include fire chiefs, police chiefs, planning commission directors, and other senior officials.

Wisely, once the decisions were made, the Minister travelled the province, once again, explaining the approach his recommendation to Cabinet would take. He listened, and his team took notes. He answered questions, and clarified details, and took suggestions under consideration.

Then, following a transition period of several months, the RSC Boards met monthly in a sort of developmental mode leading up to the legislated date. The kinks were worked out, relationships began to build, and decisions as to direction and budgets were discussed.

When 01 January 2012 rolled into being, the RSCs around the province were prepared to begin a new era. Some boards and regions began to work together immediately, while others experienced resistance internal to their Board which thwarted progress. All Boards now had regional decision making, and commissions such as planning (buildings and houses) and solid waste reporting directly to the peoples elected mayors and president/chairs.

Consultative meetings are by their nature input generating and information gathering, but what made the RSC development successful, was the well-designed meeting method with a broad range of contributions from mayors, councilors. Local Service District leaders, fire chiefs including volunteer departments, police chiefs, municipal officers; and the general public meetings.

At various times, there was a co-mingling of the various participants, or tables of like roles. In all cases notes were taken, reported to the group assembly, discussed openly with the minister and his key assistant deputy minister, and clarification made and sought. Reports were used to summarize the province wide rounds at each phase.

Did all of this take longer than a minister and department staff making the decisions unilaterally? Likely, much longer, but this situation required consultation with some collaboration, and while exhaustive for this minister and his team, it was a forward-moving way to accomplish change. Not everyone was entirely satisfied, but it is a credit to our two main political parties that the blueprint for the change after a short shelving was picked up and implemented.

> In the 21st century, we expect our governments to
> consult to a level required for the issue at hand,
> then govern according to their mandate
> and our values.
>
> *cfs*

Naturally, not all consultations need to be of this large a scale (although, the finance ministers of two governments also consulted widely). Nevertheless, we are challenged with a perennial problem that has become chronic, and the people need to be consulted, listened to and kept informed.

Can consultation be used as a cop out for a sitting government and its elected officials to avoid decisions? It should not be. There is still a responsibility of the government to make the final decisions and take the positions most appropriate for policy and for law. Representation means that you are representative of the people who elected you, members of the legislative body. Appropriate consultation serves to enrich that role.

There always will be some tension amongst groups, of a list of priorities that is too long, of demographic requirements, and of rural and urban interests. At times in our fair province the tensions are very high. It is unfortunate when certain groups and sometimes certain politicians stoke the flames for personal gain. It is fortunate that, even in the absence of explicit values this is rare, and particularly of the most important 'people' issues.

Lamentably, amongst some individuals and **groups there is discontent that is disruptive and gets in the way of change that overall is beneficial.** Still, these groups are rightful of representation as well, and deserving of a listening and compassionate government. My observations are that the most divisive issues that rear up on occasion, or simmer below the provincial discourse, can more suitably be resolved with dialogue, particularly if facilitated in reference to our principles, values and how we go about governing.

The previously noted lack of transparency within the Legislative Assembly committee arrangement also is indicative of the fog encompassing consultation at the MLA level. If our committee framework and usage of that time and talent were enhanced, then consultation at the legislature level also would be enhanced. The representatives of the people would be more enabled to actually represent the people of their riding and all of New Brunswick.

The Legislative Assembly committee work ought to be in a climate of consultation and substantive debate, with a mix of collaboration, of the elected representatives of this province. Majority can rule in short order at a committee, but it need not be, and while expedient it is at a loss of better quality decisions and recommendations. Both government and opposition need to move, while maintaining their valuable roles in our democracy, to a more constructive to and fro—it will be more enriching and contributive.

The ridings, 49 as currently we have, in our province distinguishes a core element to our representation. In our representative democracy, most often termed 'First-Past-The-Post', we do not elect MLAs at large, we elect amongst candidates to represent a particular riding. The ridings are to be reflective of a group of citizens within the defined geographic boundaries, and with commonalties of interest, language, community, and so forth.

Some may object to an MLA elected with less than 50%+1 of the population, but that does not equate to a 'better' system with all the 'leftover votes' tabulated for additional seats to 'represent' the political suasions of those whose candidates lost. If this was enacted, as some suggest, this would lead to a less pure right to representation. The only fully democratic replacement for 'first-past-the-post' is the 'run-off' between the two top vote receivers. The Thursday, or the Sunday (as in Europe) following the election, in the case of any election with a less than 50% +1 resulting winner, would have the two top ballot nominees in a 'run-off'.

The ranked-ballot is a lazy and cheap way to compromisingly resolve the first-past-the-post lack of majority election. Second and third and fourth choices cumulative totals are simply implausible. If one had no choice other than their preferred candidate, then not selecting alternative options on their ballot would make their vote weaker than other votes. Finally, we have had since the 1960s legitimate universal suffrage for all persons in Canada so to regress to another sort of inequity would weaken the foundation of our democratic rights.

The electoral riding is to be representative of the people, and the run-off is the only alternative to First-Past-The-Post for an appropriate representation of people. Wide-spread, yes exhaustive, consultation, coincided with well-formed deliberation, then a one year 'cooling period' prior to referendum, or the next election, would be the minimum to consider representation change.

Accountability and Trust

The government, politicians and civil servants, is accountable to its citizens and taxpayers. This accountability occurs in a full and tangible way only once every four years at election time. In some provinces it may occur during referendum on particular topics, but to this point in time not in this province.

We expect our governments, at all levels, to be accountable in a meaningful, policy and process supported, and measurable way. Yet, the cynicism and skepticism present today would signify that the electorate is not lulled into a sense of trust that it may have had in the post-1945 era.

The checks and balances and scrutiny by appointed officials such as the Auditor-General to ensure accountabilities of publicly elected officials should not be overlooked or considered to be nothing more than another layer of bureaucracy. This is an oversight that is one of the hinges of our modern democracy between elections. However, it depends on those being held accountable also to be accountable within as the hinge can enable a closing as well as an opening. (Consider when privacy act or confidentiality reasons are invoked to prevent scrutiny.)

There is a plethora of accountability and/or governance acts, so it is not the lack of legislation that is the problem. There are federal and provincial acts by various names. Likewise in other countries.

The Federal Accountability Act, or An Act providing for conflict of interest rules, restrictions on election financing and measures respecting administrative transparency, oversight and accountability, enacted by the Parliament of Canada was assented to on December 12, 2006.

In New Brunswick, the Bill 87 Fiscal and Transparency Act was enacted in 2014 May, and deals with Fiscal Accountability for Balance Budget, Fiscal Reporting; Transparency in Elections, for Costing of Election Commitments, Legislative Library Research Support; Miscellaneous Provisions, such as reviews, regulations; Consequential Amendments, Repeal and Commencement. It did not last long as it was amongst many Acts repealed by Bill 14, an Act Respecting Responsible Governance, enacted 2015-02-20.

In either of the federal or provincial acts, one would be hard pressed to identify much real impact on activity or approach that was different afterward than before. In the House of Commons or the Provincial Legislative Assembly, one would easily on almost any given day of a sitting, hear answers of clarity lacking, diversion or avoidance. The disrespect this accords exceeds even that of the vitriol in the voices.

The work of certain former Ministers of Finance and Auditors General, taking on their role with fresh eyes as a seasoned and successful professional, introduced New Brunswick to a more open financial process and reporting format. Surely a professional accounting expert in government policy could facilitate the A-G and Finance Minister to an agreed format.

Accountability is evident to the electorate by the actions and behaviors, attitudes and openness, of the MLAs, and more particularly the Cabinet Ministers and the Premier. Far less frequent than it should be apparent, accountability is lacking, as are the mechanisms when this is occurs. The politicians know this. The electorate knows this. And, when governing parties change, nothing much else seems to change despite the commitments likely made in all sincerity.

An accountability framework, structured to meet the levels of scrutiny of the bills enacted, must have explicit benchmarks, metrics that are trackable, and the appropriate 'watchdogs' supported not just appointed. Trackable means also detectable, providing another linkage between accountability and transparency. This will equate to easier and user-friendly accessibility on the government website, with summaries as well as detailed statements and reports. And will build a trust amongst civil service and politician and voter.

Trust in leaders is both a trust in integrity and trust in confidence, as was covered in the section on Our Reason for Being. Since not everything is, or can be, explicit trust is hand in glove with accountability.

The financial reporting and fiscal updates ought to be the easiest to apply accountability. Operations and certain programs and policies, while in some situations more difficult to measure and report, can be applied. It begins with defining, measuring and reporting outcomes.

In her Massey Lectures series, Professor Janice Gross Stein states, "Accountability is about evaluating performance, meeting legitimate standards, fulfilling legitimate commitments, and holding responsible those who fail to meet the standards. The right to judge government performance flows naturally from the role of citizen, as does the right to sanction those who fail to meet the standards."

The professor, in her postulation on efficiency, precedes this with "Efficiency in the provision of public goods needs to be joined by a conversation about accountability. States are facing newly intensified demands for accountability from their citizens. And it seems likely that these demands will grow as states turn to markets to provide public goods."

Righting Our Ship will occur partly in response to a citizenry calling for increased accountability in the running and of the outcomes provided by our governments, whether delivered by the public sector or the private sector. Where private sector delivery shortcomings have occurred, it has been in part as a result of lack of transparency in the request of proposals and contracting, and lack in quality of oversight by the civil servants.

Compatible with a later point to Righting Our Ship, Janice Gross Stein subsequently comments, "These new responsibilities of the state are likely to cause deep unease inside and outside governments. Accountability requires transparency, standards, open evaluation, a capacity to learn quickly and to correct deficiencies when they become apparent. Transparency is not typical, however, of hierarchical organizations that habitually respond to direction from the top, are acculturated to secrecy rather than openness, and in their capacities as custodians of the public interest, are deliberate and conservative rather than nimble in their ability to adapt." [5]

Genuine accountability requires a Premier and Ministers willing to accept full responsibility for their actions, the first step in accountability. Transparency and openness is requisite to appropriate reporting to the public to ensure accountability. **A strong sense of purpose and values instills a confidence and self-esteem in a leader to be accountable**.

Perhaps, in addition to an election every four years, accountability to the people of New Brunswick can as it should, with modification and willingness, be through the Legislature Standing Committee on Public Accounts. This committee, comprised of MLAs from the political parties represented in the provincial Legislature, has reporting to it the Auditor General, and its responsibilities of most interest to the public would be holding the executive council accountable. It is unfortunate that the public is not allowed to view most of the meetings.

However, this accountability too often is masked by the party in majority shutting down discourse, making motions to speed up dialogue, and doing, what appears, the minimum necessary to move items of 'government priority to the Legislature, or stall other matters of which it disagrees.

Currently, as is policy, the chairperson of this committee is a current opposition member, with the vice-chair a sitting government member, and with the majority of members of the governing party. Legislature Standing Committee on Public Accounts also has appearing before it the senior officials from each department, providing a venue outside the Legislature for accountability of the departments, rather than the ministries (to which this will be addressed in a subsequent chapter).

Obviously, there is little inherently wrong with a majority rule, in any standing committee, by the party majority in the Legislature. Admittedly, having never been a member of the Committee, these comments are based on observations, conversations, perceptions, media reports, and other sources of information. Nonetheless, more openness, genuine concern to be representative and reflective, and with more accountability, these meetings could be managed with more time allowed for in-depth discussion, consideration of different views, and to and fro of healthy debate.

All of this may cause rougher waters for the governing party and perhaps take longer to navigate, but the proceedings would be more genial and constructive. Any standing committee, if in spirit rather than political affinity, can be more representative of the people if the representatives, the MLAs, represent and reflect the diversity of the citizens.

A premier working with the opposition leaders can take great strides, without legislation, in renewing, recreating a standing committee practice of intent and behavior. There is much in our Parliamentary inheritance of protocol, practicum, and process that is not legislated, instead occurring through convention and precedent. Likewise, the demeanor of the Legislature could be improved without harm to the vital role of the Opposition in our democracy if political parties could find ways to add more intellectual techniques and refined methods.

"A smooth sea never made a skilful sailor"

An Old Saying

Fulfillment *Through Transformation*

There comes a time in most organizations when evolving is no longer sufficient, incremental changes that once resulted cumulatively into eventual significant change is now no more than tactical and small movements, and much more is needed or else small failures lead to the big failure. Death by a thousand cuts provides many incremental savings points as it inflicts many incremental services reductions. Slow and painful, death still it is.

While we are not under water, yet, our province is sinking, abated only by federal transfers financed by the richer provinces. The enigma may be that should the significant budget propping of federal transfers diminish by dollar amount be coincided by percentage, we will sink.

Righting our ship will take nothing short of transformational change. The incremental changes we experience fall short. And, the latter are frequently, although well intentioned, minor corrections with negligible results. We seem to have found ourselves caught in a going nowhere fast mode, exchanging one ballast for another, one small turn here followed by another turn there.

Surely it cannot be overstated that our Premiers, of whichever party, are concerned with our state of affairs including the debt and deficits, the threat to health and education and social programs for our people, and the lowering opportunities for jobs and self-fulfillment. However, concern does not translate to progress or success without accomplishment.

For transformational change to occur, we need transformational leadership attributes of a Premier with a defined relevant mission to go with a compelling vision for our times, remedial actions pertinent and clear, so that people understand where they are being led and the 'whys' and 'whats' to get there.

The very real and very large challenges taken on by recent governments are overwhelming for them, and the decisions appear beyond grasp of the leaders to transcend fear of political retribution. Positions need to be coalesced for decisions, choices made, and actions determined for us to move out of the dangerous waves in which we find ourselves locked. And bold must be accompanied by acumen.

> "You seem to be a leader,
> but you can't seem to make up your mind."
>
> Purple Rain, Prince's 1984 rock musical drama

From mission to strategic decisions to tactical methods, and a lot of grit and determination, there is a significant shift that is required. For politicians, both in power and in opposition, the shift has to begin with them. A governing party needs to transcend above just tolerating other MLAs on Committees, and those in Opposition will need to be more creative and constructive in their role in our democracy. This may prove difficult for some.

Not even a *sense* of fulfilment will arise from a canvas left to paint once some ideas are gathered, a smorgasbord of nip and tucks applied, with little behavior and attitude change by the political class. Nor can the hope that a largess on behalf of Ottawa will make things better, as at best that will be temporary, and a momentary stop gap. The growth of population, even with a fairer share of immigrants locating in New Brunswick, will not bring back the somewhat good times of the past.

From the 'Over the Cliff?' [6], comes this warning, "For several decades, New Brunswick's economy has surfed on a rising tide of labour force growth, fueled by the baby boom generation and the steady, largely successful march of women towards equal participation in the workforce. The tide is now receding, dragging down the economy with it. A new Age of Diminished Expectations is upon us."

Richard Saillant pulls no punches, and provides well-researched data. His is a prescription of reduced programs and increased taxes. And that will certainly lead to his proclaimed 'diminished expectations". This does not fit well with the 'positivity' that wins elections.

Our governments and those who elected them are in this mess, primarily for the same reasons as our provincial counterparts, the spending and expectations fuelled as Professor Saillant describes. Unlike our counterparts, we and our Maritimes cousins are without the richness of natural resources or size of population that they may yet be able to muster to correct their displacement in their own sea of debt, deficit, and discord of services.

Consider: **What if our expectations are that our government transforms the way it governs, re-models our service delivery, create transparency with appropriate communication, metrics and outcomes?** Focuses on the outcomes that New Brunswickers need, want and must strive for? Does not allow old tendencies, preferred policies to protect power, or paradigms that were never real anyway?

It *is* possible to have realistic expectations of the short term, be guided by a plan that is driven by our values and mission, clear as to the outcomes and receiving quarterly updates that reference the metrics and report the facts (pleasant or otherwise)—for each year and for the term of a government.

Moreover, we need a beacon that is a well thought through target into the next two terms, based on the consensus of the Premier and the Opposition Leader and their respective MLAs. **Instead of the diminished expectations that are threatening to occur, we can have expectations launched from our self-determination and the resolve to take control of our province.**

For transformational change to go beyond just talk and hope, it must be led by a leader capable of transformational change. Frankly, most leaders, public or private or political, are incremental change or status quo leaders lacking the wherewithal, let alone the vision, to transform. They are competent at managing the incremental increases in sales, or quality improvement, or earnings for shareholders. And rarely does a person from this cast, lead the transformative advancements of Jack Walsh or Lee Iaccoca, or the entrepreneurial legacy of Frank Stronach.

Expectations fulfilled of a 21st century people will not occur unless we have Members of the Legislative Assembly, led by a Premier, collectively in their important roles, who are truly representative and consultative, epitomizing clarity and truth, demonstrating accountability, and acting in openness and truth. Anything short is not transformative, nor respectful of the people on whose behalf they govern.

We don't expect every national leader to be a Sir John A MacDonald, Abraham Lincoln, Sir Winston Churchill, Franklin D. Roosevelt—superior in oratorical delivery, poignant in their words, inspirational in their innate feel of the values of society and the movements of the world around them. We don't expect every Premier of this province to be a Samuel Leonard Tilley, Charles Fisher, or Louis J Robichaud or Frank McKenna. We do need one now.

Transformation, even when the goal is communicated and consensus gained, can be messy, confusing, and at times scary and sufficiently ambiguous for a want to return to the status quo. Many succumb to the ambiguity, hastening back to the status quo where they are comfortable even in their dissatisfaction. Transformational leaders inspire and invoke a contagious confidence to proceed toward the goal. We are in the midst of stormy waves and we know that the status quo is not an option.

You will never be who you were.
You *can* live up to who you are and wish to be.

cfs

As we read from the Provincial website, it is our coat of arms from which the earlier topic of our motto, and mission statement arose:

The supporters on either side of the shield are white-tailed deer with antlers, each with a small shield or escutcheon suspended from a friendship collar of Maliseet wampum, the original of which is in the New Brunswick Museum. One shield bears the Union Badge representing the British connection in New Brunswick's history and the early English, Scots and Irish settlers; the other bears the Royal Arms of France, the symbol of public authority during the French regime, and refers to the French settlement in the province.

The motto, *Spem Reduxit*, taken from the first Great Seal of the Province, is at the base of the arms on a ribbon and can be translated as *hope restored*. This refers to the establishment of the province as a home for the refugee settlers, the United Empire Loyalists, whose arrival here prompted the creation of New Brunswick by the British government. [7]

Let us also consider, the hope restored for Acadians and other rural county residents during the Robichaud followed by the Hatfield era; the hope restored in the creation of jobs in a modern economy during the McKenna followed by the Lord era; and the fulfillment which can be reached if we once again, induce hope restored. **Hope restored, if we are willing to correct our financial situation and to rehabilitate our health, education and social systems, transforming to a New Brunswick of the 21st century.**

We can have the previously described 'sub-mission' or commission for our times, and seek fulfillment, if a Premier was capable to take on the responsibility for us being:

A province of peoples living in peace, order and good government –and by Righting Our Ship by 2018 be in a zero deficit financial situation and be moving to better health, education and social systems.

And, this Premier would be moving us to keep our eye to the future, with our vision for what we can ultimately be, and specifically in four years we can say:

We have restored hope, in harmony, community and opportunity—we are taking control so that we can be directing our future

If we were to look at how this might positioned and communicated as an election platform, aligned with an accepted and long standing vision and mission for our Province, we could in everyday language only use the 'updated' and 'current' elements, as:

We are Directing Our Future:

By Righting Our Ship we will in 2018 be in a zero deficit financial situation and be moving to better `health, education and social systems

And so it is, with a concise message and inspiring communication skills, a Premier would be painting a picture, and having us seeing that we are directing our future, with the Premier and their party's mission (if we choose to elect them).

Chapter 4

Governance

for a 21ˢᵗ Century People

As an area of policy, by public officials toward private sector corporations, or by the corporations themselves, governance has been debated, researched, experimented with via legislation, on practically everything from banking to oil to Non-Government Organizations (NGOs). Good governance is not a policy. As long as it considered a policy it is not a core value, and will be treated as a policy that can be changed by the executive and board.

Partially paraphrasing an earlier statement, while governments ought to be run with modern principles of governance, sound business practices and business-like processes, social license given to it at each election, and above all with respectful deference to the people and for the people, they cannot be run like a business. On the other hand, good governance in a modern democracy would be considered, by most, a precept of good government as it is with good business, profit or not for profit.

Somewhat naturally, and expectedly, governments in the democratic world have forgotten, consciously or subconsciously, with intent or without intent, to review the governance of government. Good Governance in government? Good grief! Of course it should be reviewed in a modern democracy.

Over the decades, we have seen a gradual *in*-sourcing of tasks and jobs, and equipment and people. In the earlier decades of the last century, this was because there may not have been sufficient capacity in private industry. As the century progressed, it was because those in government were convinced doing things not for profit could be done less expensively. As well, sometimes it was thought quality could be improved by making the workers part of the civil service reporting directly to their political masters, when in reality it was better oversight and more comprehensive contracts that were required.

And so we found our New Brunswick government doing more and more, growing in scope rapidly, reaching for our small province almost dizzying heights of numbers of employees. Then, runaway costs took over, and with the hull overburdened and bloated, we were overcome to the point of not only less able to row, but also steer our way forward.

Ours is not the only government to succumb to a bias and philosophy toward steering more to the point of too much. Big government has become pervasive, bogged down in bureaucracy to the detriment of outcomes.

Good government, effective and efficient in its duties, will row as little as it can so that it can focus on its capability and capacity to steer. Federal, provincial and municipal, it is not a matter of an ideology of smaller government—government with ever growing responsibilities and obligations for services is bigger in-our-lives government. This is not the same as the mistaken bigger government is better if it has more employees.

> The word 'government' is from a Greek word,
> which means 'to steer'.
> The job of government is to steer,
> not to row the boat.
> Delivering services is rowing,
> and government is not very good at rowing.
>
> E. S. Savas.
> Chairman of the Department of Management,
> City University of New York

Good Governance

Consider the following perspective. There are two elements or levels of governance in government. First is that of the politicians and the cabinet of ministers. Second is the appointed senior civil servants and their departments and/or teams.

In our parliamentary democracy, the Cabinet is essentially appointed by the Premier, or the Prime Minister, (we will leave aside the Governor General or Lieutenant Governor conventions for now) from the elected members of their caucus. Occasionally, the Speaker of the House or Assembly is appointed from another party so as to maintain majority status for the governing party. As well, occasionally, at the federal level a Senator is appointed to the Cabinet for either political reasons or a competency requirement by the Prime Minister.

As a matter of normal course, the Premier makes choices for Cabinet positions from those who were elected by the electorate in their home riding to the government caucus. These MLAs become Cabinet Ministers, heads of Ministries, but they succumb to the role of Minister as Department Head with a Deputy Minister as Vice Department Head, as will be addressed in the respective section below.

Sometimes, it is an elected government, reaching down into the operations of the civil service where it ought not to go. Or, appointing a person to a position below the Deputy Minister level, or directing the 'how' rather than the 'what'. **Ineffective delegation from political leaders follows weak strategic objectives (or strategy at the wrong levels) to operational and business planning to tactical execution.**

These misfires are not always at the fault of the senior civil servants, who when appointed suitably and with the requisite experience and skill sets, are professionals who work professionally. Where professional deputy ministers and directors are in place, their frustration can be very similar to the citizens of their province. On the other hand, strong deputy ministers, very capable in their duties and knowledgeable of their areas, have opinions and biases of which they skillfully maneuver, and frequently out-maneuver their Minister.

One example of governance being hindered by the civil service, is at the federal level in Canada. In October 2014, Prime Minister Stephen Harper shared "...bureaucratic initiatives... that we think are effectively trying to put the long gun registry back in through the back door. This is not something we're going to tolerate." [8]

Similar activities occurred during the budget cuts to federal departments where the Finance Minister insisted that services to Canadians by front line workers would not be affected. Within a day or two of the Budget presentation in the House of Commons, there were border security guard positions and veterans support offices closed by their respective departments. This, by any observer was a senior civil service, comfortable in their job security, giving the proverbial finger to their government. How would those who mistakenly accused the prime minister of such orders, the latter's expectation clearly was administrative positions in Ottawa and not field roles, think otherwise?

Irrespective of your stance on the long gun registry, this was a Prime Minister stating that the bureaucracy was not going to do anything but what Parliament says it will do. From those who are of a contrary opinion to the long gun registry cheers go up for democracy. Of those who are upset with the VAC office closings accusations of meanness and insensitivity are proliferated by the equally unknowing media. (Another government may request re-openings, to which a 'compliant' civil service will 'dutifully' oblige—because it is in their personal interests to grow their ranks.)

Occurring far more frequently than most citizens realize, it is no wonder that **voters are left wondering why politicians don't just make things happen**. Side-railing by senior bureaucrats works because theirs is a competence, confidence and experience that trumps their Ministerial bosses. Dismal as it seems, our government lacks good governance at the government level, the civil service level, and between the two groups.

Similarly, within N.B., department executives, deputy ministers and their directors, have a capability to manage what they believe is correct, and the Minister to whom they report, the person appointed by the Premier, is often influenced to do other than what is expected or mandated, and sometimes even stone-walled in execution. It happens because senior bureaucrats are more knowledgeable and skillful in their subject matter area and their management capability.

As another example, the 1980s saw the Greater Moncton International Airport (as it now is called) local political business community bid for regional control and privatization from Transport Canada stonewalled, delayed and otherwise curtailed. This was like the conducting of an orchestra by the Regional Director General of the day whose personal bias was toward a strong and centralized Halifax airport hub. Community committee after committee would go to the federal Transport Minister, in what seemed like regular eighteen month rotations to the latest person in that cabinet role, only to have a study initiated. The study would go to the Deputy Minister, out to the Regional Director General, studied further (read: delayed) until a new incumbent was appointed, and the process started over again. Finally, that was overcome, and the GMIA has flourished and grown.

In New Brunswick, there are many cases of similar 'control' by the senior bureaucrats over the less knowledgeable and not as skillful cabinet Minister. **The elected MLA, appointed by their elected Premier to their ministerial role, typically wants to manage their portfolio responsibly and make progress on the issues of the day**. When success is lacking, usually it is the less than necessary capability that is their shortfall, and in turn their government.

Paradoxically, the more capable amongst the cabinet seem also the most likely to consult with the public. Such paradoxes are apparent in many workplaces. The most reliable and higher performing employees tend to follow prescribed best practices processes and use the quality tools in place; whereas those at the other range of performance tend to do otherwise. The leaders who care the most, exhibit active listening skills, and take feedback, tend to hear the most criticism and receive the most complaints; hardly pleasant but it exists regardless, so they also are more aware and effective.

Responsible government requires responsible voters. Responsible politicians require responsible mechanisms. Fundamental for an educated electorate and modern society is a governing mandate that is measurable in quality and quantity; followed by a winning governing party that acts and reacts responsibly guided by that mandate, or commission as has been written.

And, many would say, the government should be held in check by the potential of a re-call referendum regarding support for a governing party that sways beyond its mandate. In the case of the latter, the Lieutenant Governor (Governor General federally) either can direct the governing party to govern accordingly, demand that it replace its leader, or ask the opposition leader to form the government to the end of the current four year fixed term.

The problem we have is responsible government can acquiesce or abdicate within an insufficiency of accountability and the over centrality of control, in our colonial Westminster Parliament model heritage. And, there often is need for a balancing of what the electorate wants, or thinks that it wants, and the difficult decisions that an informed government must make. It is wrong, morally and electorally, to deceive the voters in order to win an election, even if many still consider this 'winning politics' for which they confuse with 'good politics' and 'good governance'.

The bottom line is that we should not allow public policy to be decided by the biggest voice, or largest corporation or association, or noisiest special interest group. Nor can any of these, or the public at large, be treated as a bypass. We need facts, good communication, and leadership to have a steady and trusted hand at the wheel.

"Good governments do not allow mob rule.
They seize control of the agenda,
they communicate, they make decisions
and they lead.

Frank McKenna, Premier N.B
(2014Oct See Appendix)

So what are some specifics of good governance in government? Governance at all levels includes a number of characteristics, as the www.goodgovernance.org advises local governments govern better when:

Good governance is accountable
Accountability is a fundamental requirement of good governance. Local government has an obligation to report, explain and be answerable for

the consequences of decisions it has made on behalf of the community it represents.

Good governance is transparent
People should be able to follow and understand the decision-making process. This means that they will be able to clearly see how and why a decision was made – what information, advice and consultation council considered, and which legislative requirements (when relevant) council followed.

Good governance follows the rule of law
This means that decisions are consistent with relevant legislation or common law and are within the powers of council.

Good governance is responsive
Local government should always try to serve the needs of the entire community while balancing competing interests in a timely, appropriate and responsive manner.

Good governance is equitable and inclusive
A community's wellbeing results from all of its members feeling their interests have been considered by council in the decision-making process. This means that all groups, particularly the most vulnerable, should have opportunities to participate in the process.

Good governance is effective and efficient
Local government should implement decisions and follow processes that make the best use of the available people, resources and time to ensure the best possible results for their community.

Good governance is participatory
Anyone affected by or interested in a decision should have the opportunity to participate in the process for making that decision. This can happen in several ways – community members may be provided with information, asked for their opinion, given the opportunity to make recommendations or, in some cases, be part of the actual decision-making process.

Drawn up for municipal or local government, this encapsulates in everyday language what one would expect should 'good governance' be in place.

While 'governance' may have many definitions, be elusive in definition and application, be ambiguous according to some UN (United Nations) documents, be measurable and accountable according to the IMF

(International Monetary Fund), be applicable to governments of all levels, and to corporations for profit or not, boards and groups of all kinds, it has evolved with our society.

Today, good governance is a cornerstone of successful, incorrupt, effective government and includes Clarity and Truth, Transparency and Openness, Representation and Consultation, Accountability and Trust.

The issues of governance also have taken on a global concern for the 21st Century. Arguably, even as 20th century governance institutions that are still in effect today were being created, it was in the minds of late 19th century persons and expectations. With the lone extraordinary exceptions of people such as Eleanor Roosevelt, the visioning, dealings, negotiations, and structures, were of the males, the aristocracy of the old world and the wealthy members of the new world.

Hierarchical structures, command and control, central visioning without sufficient input of the millions or billions for whom these governments were apparently created, are adequate no longer in a more educated, emancipated, speed of thought communications people.

Citi Research has written that in the global world, national governments alone can't address international risks facing the world economy. However, the current international organizations are "poorly prepared to manage, mitigate, and govern 21st century risk," according to Citi. Global institutions were created during a different time, and they have not adapted to the new world order. When the UN was created in 1945, world GDP was $7 trillion and there were 2.5 billion people alive. Today, world GDP is $71 trillion.

In New Brunswick, on the other hand, our population was smallish pre-Confederation, and with occasional small upticks from an influx of immigration it tripled over the past 150 years to the 750000 level. Still, we are a very small population relative to our geography, dispersed into many small communities. This creates many benefits, and many realities and risks, to what we now define as 'lifestyle', or our 'prosperity'.

Chart 1: Population of New Brunswick

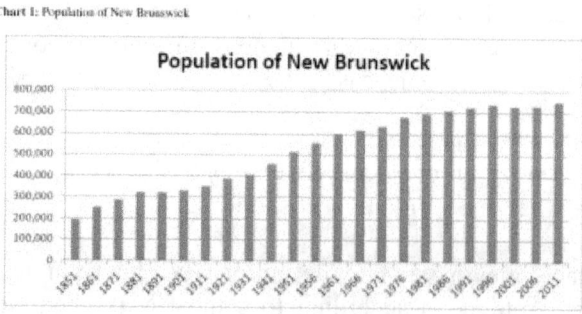

Source: Statistics Canada

It is this 'lifestyle', including the social support systems that contribute significantly to what we have come to expect, that is at risk in New Brunswick. Every option, including the status quo, is a risk.

The risks a people are willing to take are best determined on good data, clear communications of the facts, and sincerity of feelings and of desires. As the emotional quotient (EQ) has been acceptably paired with intellectual quotient (IQ) as a determinant to success, one might regard the intellectual and the emotional aspects of good governance, too, inevitably are paired.

Samara's Democracy 360 Talk.Act.Lead. is a self-described "report card on the state of Canada's democracy, and, focuses on the complex relationship between citizens and political leadership". It highlights that "Only 40% of Canadians report that they trust MPs to do what is right and only 42% of Canadians place some trust in political parties." More can be read at *http://www.samaracanada.com/research/samara-democracy-360*

Recent comments by a western province's former finance minister suggest this is applicable in all the provinces and territories as well. Local media commentary, as well as individuals in conversation and online comments, indicate many people in New Brunswick would agree.

Good governance begins with what it is that our government exists in the first place, and why a specific government is elected for a period of time. The 'agenda' for a government should be an explicit mandate given by those who elected the winning party based on the specifics presented during the election period. There is an implicitness and explicitness in good governance. When it is absent, or a clear choice of leadership not amply determinable, a topic seemingly rises to the top to fill the void.

Of course, it is up to the voters to make informed decisions about provincial affairs. However, it is unfortunate, that driven by a level of frustration and in the absence of a distinguishable differentiator, that a large enough number of voters lean toward a parochial topic or situation that it turns the issue into a strategic one. We have had recent provincial governments determined by a single issue that became a tipping point—highway tolls, NB Power ownership, and fracking of natural gas.

The Premier, as our leader, is first amongst Ministers, Chair of the Cabinet, and as will be noted perhaps a misplaced co-role as President of an Executive Council. Regardless of the terminology it is not without its problems. We do not have a 'president' role or function. Constitutional and legislative expertise aside, this is an important point for the roles that our elected officials, contained to four year mandates, should have in tandem with a professional civil service that provides us continuity of service.

Governance at the Ministry level is a continuity of the macro government level—the board level and not the executive level. In British Columbia, as we read from the government website, Ministry of Finance page:

"Governance encompasses the roles, responsibilities and accountabilities of the Legislative Assembly representing the public, and the organizations and management of government. Governance is the structure and processes that support the realization of overall objectives and the strategies to achieve them. It is concerned with the development, communication and implementation of government policy, and in monitoring performance with respect to standards. Governance includes ongoing risk assessment and management in the general course of delivering programs and services.

"The governance process starts with setting objectives, then providing direction and funding, establishing performance measures, and from then on measuring performance, resulting in redirection when necessary, or a change in objectives or performance measures as appropriate. While objectives are primarily the responsibility of the Legislative Assembly, and performance measures that of senior management, they need to be developed in concert so that objectives are achievable and results are as intended."

Continuing, in "Section 1.3 Policy, subsection 2, we read: Ministries must ensure that:
~expenditures are within limits approved by Treasury Board;
~their management focus is on outcomes, achieving service plan goals, reporting performance and being accountable for results; and that Treasury Board is notified and corrective action is taken when extraordinary circumstances may cause a vote to be overspent, and informed when a proposed policy or operational change will have significant financial implication."

While this begins with the general principles of governance, followed by more detail with regard to finances specifically, it provides a good overview of the British Columbia model of governance. Does this guarantee results, or outcomes, for service levels or policy initiatives? Although this does not, it does set the tone and expectation of clear outcomes with measurable and unencumbered reporting to the Legislature and to the people of the province.

Governance results in effective policy and program implementation and accountability if it is inextricably woven into the working culture, when the structures are in place, and the competencies of strategy and execution are available. We do not lack the broad strokes or broad policy statements, nor the gestures. We lack the explicitness of specifics of governance, and it seems the sincerity required, along with the requisite competencies.

Osborne and Gaebler, in the highly acclaimed national bestseller 'Reinventing Government', in 1993 were "bullish on government" as long as it was recognized as a government as facilitator, planner, policy maker—not a deliverer of service. [9]

Correspondingly, Crown corporations and agencies, when and if still required, need Boards that should be fully accountable to the Government. While these are typically established to keep at arm's length of politics, nevertheless these are owned by the people of the province and therefore are accountable to the government. Consider a hybrid of appointments (government, board, stakeholder group) and a clear reason to exist (mission). The government should establish with the agencies annual measurable outcomes and expect quarterly reviews, and make public all financial and performance reviews.

In all bureaucracies, senior managers and executives typically are concerned with their role and power within the larger organization. They know how to 'raise' the levels of their direct reports, or the number of staff, or the budget allocations, as this raises their personal profile by extension, and likely level of power and of compensation as well, all without appearing self-serving.

In government, executive civil servants also know how to prolong decisions, as has been earlier imputed, when it is in their personal interest, by sending back to departments for studies, etc., outstaying their respective minister, or Premier, long enough that upon arrival of a new master the loop begins all over again. When the managerial expertise of the civil service is more sophisticated than a Minister, or a Premier, then without appropriate governance, the civil service can quasi-run the province (or the country).

Financial governance means it is imperative to set targets that are financially linked to outcomes, performance criteria – and cost accounting. Every department, particularly the large and sprawling departments, as well as health authorities and hospitals, and school authorities and schools, need department by department full costing and accounting. (It is not clear if, even in 2015, every department in every hospital is fully cost accounted.)

In the defining of our values, Governance was accompanied with Civility. Most would agree, that there is a tarnish, even much lacking, to civility in our politics and amongst our politicians, at least in public. Some blame the cameras in the legislative rooms and yet it seems to pour out into the media as well. Some would say that it is "just politics" and that the opposition has a role to be critical of the government.

Surely, there can be a civility of working relationships amongst the politicians of such a smallish provincial community as is New Brunswick. If ever there was a time in which we need our political servants to transcend above the fray, collaborate and work together, in the best interests of our province, then it is now.

The opposition members can support good legislation and good change when it is developed together, and still play their vital role and disagree with certain government decisions or nuances of implementation. Should subsequently this prove to make it more difficult in differentiating themselves to the voting public come election time, well then they need to become more creative and recruit more superior candidates. Our parties are of such close range of philosophy, and general application in the political range anyway that relevant party platforms in actuality have only minor differences, and it is the team that becomes the biggest decision for voters to make.

The Institute for Civility in Government declares that "Civility is about more than just politeness, although politeness is a necessary first step. It is about disagreeing without disrespect, seeking common ground as a starting point for dialogue about differences, listening past one's preconceptions, and teaching others to do the same. **Civility is the hard work of staying present even with those with whom we have deep-rooted and fierce disagreements.** It is political in the sense that it is a necessary prerequisite for civic action. But it is political, too, in the sense that it is about negotiating interpersonal power such that everyone's voice is heard, and nobody's is ignored."

> "Civility is claiming and caring for
> one's identity, needs and beliefs
> without degrading someone else's in the process."
>
> Tomas Spath and Cassandra Dahnke,
> Founders of the Institute for Civility in Government

Good governance also allows good collaboration, not just consultation. This brings a level of civility simply in the act of working together for a particular purpose.

Good governance means that Ministers and other MLAs should not allow themselves to be caught in situations where local contractors ask about work distribution. The system should be totally transparent, with quality, quantity, cost all well-defined, and the bidding system open. Fortunately, we have come a very long way since even the 1970s and 80s.

It is peculiar, and perhaps questionably appropriate, to have musings by an Auditor General on how pensioners *might* feel or how Lepreau *might* have saved money with a couple of more tenders, and so forth. The Province's accountants and auditors and chief officers should work, report and comment within their areas of expertise, and leave the conjecture and speculation to the politicians.

Likewise, other 'Chiefs' in the employ of the government need to work within their mandate and not stretch or push the boundaries beyond their appointed duties. The senior medical officer, for example, may make a reference to health and air quality relative to 'climate change' theory, but to expend an extreme amount of energy in an activist role should be, at a minimum, on her personal time, not the public time for which she was hired.

As a final note on civility, most people would not be aware that the United Nations Universal Declaration for Human Rights was finalized using the framework and guidelines from the 1940 Rotary International Convention in Havana. Also in the 1940-50s, the world's first service club, Rotary International adopted Rotarian Herbert J. Taylor's Four Way Test, and the inspired words were authorized by the author for Rotary International to copyright.

> Of the things we think, say, or do:
> Is it the TRUTH?
> Is it Fair to all concerned?
> Will it build GOODWILL and BETTER FRIENDSHIPS?
> Will it be BENEFICIAL to all concerned?

The Four Way Test
Rotary International © 1954

This Four Way Test is in use every day around the world, in a myriad forms and forums, to encourage personal and business ethical practices. From a personal or collective perspective, the Four Way Test is a good guide to accompany good governance. In the end, is this not all that we ask of our elected officials? Wouldn't this be the character of a government, representative of the people, 'social license'? Voters will certainly recognize it when they see it.

Sailing directions are vital tools to accompany charts for planning and assisting in navigation—with information that cannot be shown on a chart. As with civility, governance is of attitude and aptitude, it is emotional and rational, as well as implicit and explicit. **Good governance in a 21st century society is not a matter of tacking to the right, or tacking to the left—politically—but tacking as a way to move forward toward a destination that creates and sustains the appropriate place of our province, our people.**

Strategic and Operational Decisions

Strategic direction and decisions are the responsibility of an organization's Board. Typically, a Board will include a Chief Executive Officer (CEO) as well as some other C-suite executives. As well a Board will determine some broad policy priorities and direct the CEO to develop the details and present back for final approval, with a President executing the policy.

A Premier and Cabinet, as with any other Chairperson and Board has authority through responsibility of governance. With a focus on Mission and Values and Vision to enable outcome-oriented governing systems, there are annual or tri-annual renewal plans.

The Deputy Minister, as with any other Executive, is to be accountable for outcome-oriented, organizational values-based delivery to fulfill the mission of the organization—the commission of their respective Ministries. This role is one of a Chief Operating Officer equivalent, as there is not a president in our government, nor a CEO. Notwithstanding the titles, the Deputy Minister as the COO has the vested leadership and authority for strategic execution and operational outcomes.

Strategic decision making cannot be delegated by the Board, or the Cabinet, but must be made by the Cabinet as is predicated by those who elected them. In the world of Boards, presentations are made at Annual General Meetings and motions resolved on strategy proposed. In the world of government the quad-annual election should serve as a similar situation. Unfortunately, we fall short in this.

Strategy is a key component of good governance. Along with the renewed interest in governance it is not a passing fad, and it is not new. Respected consultant and author John Carver writes that "...*the secret to the new governance lies in policy-making, but policy making of a more finely crafted sort*". [10]

A summary of Dr. Carver's key points would include:

1. **Ends:** The organizational 'swap' with the world. What human needs are to be met, for whom and at what cost.
2. **Executive limitations:** Those principles of prudence and ethics that limit the choice of staff means (practices, activities, circumstances, methods).
3. **Board-Executive Relationship:** The manner in which power is passed to the executive machinery and assessment of the use of that power.

4. Board Process: The manner in which the board represents the 'ownership' and provides strategic leadership to the organization

In New Brunswick, government reference to the Cabinet is used interchangeably with Executive Council, at least among government folks, elected and appointed. Note that from a governance perspective, the Board delegates to its Executive. Let us consider that one of our difficulties in this province's governance are the misunderstandings of roles and titles with perceived expectations of Ministers. As members of a Cabinet, referred to as an Executive Council, no wonder Ministers think of themselves as executives more than members of a Board, which in politics is called a Cabinet.

Removing the word 'executive' from use in and by our government could add clarity to roles and identity. So, replacing CEO with COO, the following can be applied to government not just for title but role as well.

"Manifestations of lax corporate governance, in my judgment, are largely a symptom of a failed CEO. In the end, a CEO must be afforded full authority to implement corporate strategy, but also must bear the responsibility to accurately report the resulting condition of the corporation to shareholders and potential investors."

Alan Greenspan, Chairman, U.S. Federal Reserve
To the Senate Banking Committee 16July02

With the roles of Ministries and Departments to be addressed in the next section, clarification of these important roles will now be introduced for context of more in-depth discussion on strategic and operational decision making.

Minister has a Ministry. Deputy Minister has a Department and the departmental staff to fulfill the reason for which the department exists. The government, as the political party in power with the 'confidence' of the Legislative Assembly, is led by the first Minister, the Premier, and a Cabinet.

The Government and its Ministers establish policy and expectations (outcomes), and should not manage departmental staff, as that is the role of the Deputy Minister. The Ministry strategizes, establishes outcomes, and legislates policies and programs. The Department as well as ensuring the appropriate outputs, must also attain the outcomes set by government.

A challenge, as previously identified, is how to ensure government decisions are implemented. The foundation necessary begins with Government having a clear understanding of the Province's values and mission and vision, and the subsequent outcomes, and then communicating these effectively. One would suppose this would be directly from the mandate given to the government when it was elected, and augmented and detailed in consultation with the respective departments.

Strategic planning should cascade to business planning (financial, program, policy and project legislation and implementation), then cascade to tactical initiatives. There are priorities at all three levels, influencing priorities as the 'cascade' occurs. Irrespective of the level at which an MLA or a senior civil servant or an administrative staff member works, **all tasks at all levels have but one end outcome—fulfilling the mission, and the values and vision, of the Province of New Brunswick as the government commits at election**.

It is accepted, and best practice, to have long ranging objectives, with 3-5 year goals, that are trackable with annual goals and action plans. These are complete only if all are stated with outcomes, not outputs, have due dates, and have an accepted ownership at the board level, or Minister. To expand upon the old saying that a goal is a wish with a due date, it also is not much more than a wish without ownership and when lacking metrics.

With four year goals, the fixed term of our government, well-defined, metrics in place, quarterly updates and clear communication, the government and its civil service and the citizens at large, would be better equipped to initially agree with the strategy, and subsequently review and assess performance and success.

Business Plans are not Strategic Plans, as are too often misguidedly regarded. Strategic decisions, associated with the mission and mandate, aligned with the vision and consistent with the values, are the responsibility of the Premier and Cabinet. Strategy cannot be delegated; to do so is an abdication of responsibility as well as of ownership. **With a government there is an implicit covenant of ownership for strategy, and that strategy should have been shared with the people prior to their electoral decision**.

> "Things which matter most must never be at the mercy of things which matter least."
>
> Goethe

Business plans and implementation are expected of the Departments and dependent on the delegation authorized. During the strategic planning and decision making processes, a Board would consult with its C-officers for their expertise, knowledge, process advice, research, and so forth. However, at the execution stage the C-officers are hired or contracted managers and professionals, with departments, and execution and implementation is their responsibility and expertise. These executive level staff want to take ownership and they should be held accountable.

This symbiotic relationship, and authority delegated as appropriate, is key to ensure the most important directives are not pushed aside for other choices. The electorate has mandated the government, and the government delegates to the departments, organizations and officers.

Career Deputy Ministers and their most senior staff, aside from some changes due to political appointments, tend to have a longevity in office that outlasts Ministers. This continuity of department 'memory', knowledge, skills and expertise, provides a stability to the governing of the province, and administering of programs and policies. The importance of this cannot be overstated. At the same time, while recommendations are made and options put forward by these professionals to their respective Ministers, it is still the Premier (and some Ministers) that establish direction and are supposed to make the overarching decisions, and ultimately held accountable.

Not many of our elected officials have senior management or executive experience. This likely accounts for the apparent lapses in 'executive' decisions, errors in strategic execution, and failures in programs or policies, at least as observed by experienced executives from the outside looking in.

Most people feel that we are in a race against a debt time bomb. If tax increases are to be avoided, or at least minimalized, then big cuts are required. In a 'scarcity' world that may be the only solution, as old style negotiators consider a zero-sum approach. No one wants either of more taxes or cuts, although many suggestions have been put forth for both. The preferences tend to be areas that affect others mostly, a sadly selfish approach much as NIMBY (Not In My Back Yard) is to development.

> Strategy is our racing plan
> based on wind, wind shifts, and current.
> Tactics involves implementing our strategy
> and dealing with other boats.

> Performance Racing Tactics by © Bill Gladestone

Values and vision invoked strategy shapes the circumstances that can lead to creative solutions. There is potential in exploring with an 'abundance' world philosophy whereby creativity is expansive beyond arguing over how to cut a pie in half. To do this, we must be clear as to the destination so that we can steer toward it together.

To best benefit from a diverse and representative Premier and Cabinet, we need to have in place a more explicit governance as well as strategic decision making and execution structure. Additionally, a broader orientation and training for all MLAs, particularly Ministers, appears as an area worthy of attention.

Ministries, not Departments

Across Canada, at the provincial level, the term Minister is used for the position of a person appointed by a Premier to lead a specific portfolio of duties. In some provinces, such as Alberta and Ontario, the Minister leads a Ministry. In other provinces, such as New Brunswick, the Minister is the leader of a Department, as also is the case as we see it at the federal level.

Thus, in some jurisdictions the use of department or ministry is not an inter-changeability of the two words. Good governance would have a Minister as part of a Cabinet of 'Chairs', with the Premier presiding over the Cabinet as the Chair. In turn, the Minister would chair a Ministry, which may include departments, agencies, officers with specialized roles, and special projects or programs.

In Righting Our Ship we need to face the fiscal breaking waves about to engulf us and the reducing integrity of programs that are expressions of our values. **We cannot avoid these waves, we must 'turn' into those waves. Our government has a serious strategic direction to set, and it must be compelling enough to engage our citizens, to unhesitatingly embrace a tsunami of change in how we govern, provide services, and be prepared for opportunity and crisis.**

A past tsunami of change for our province is captured in this passage by Lisa Pasolli:

"New Brunswick's first elected Acadian Premier, Louis J. Robichaud, came to power in 1960 determined to move the province into the 20th century socially and economically. By Robichaud's own estimation in 1969, the province had, prior to his election, "been dealing with its difficulties on a piecemeal basis, achieving only limited industrialization, its people in many areas underemployed and undereducated, unfairly taxed and over-governed." Robichaud's Liberal administration had ambitious plans for reform, but the bureaucratic capacity to manage and implement those plans was lacking. Above all, New Brunswick needed personnel and leadership to expand, professionalize, and modernize its civil service." [11]

A half-century later, we are once again overdue, this time to move our province into the 21st century. And, once again, a complete overhaul of our service structures as well as a modernization of our cabinet and committees, and our civil service delivery model. Only a tectonic shift from "piecemeal basis" with its limited success (to paraphrase LJR) to significant changes from the mid-20th century that Premier Robichaud pulled us into, to the 21st century.

We do not need an oversized Cabinet, rather the opposite can be more effective. Two successive premiers have begun the downsizing of Cabinet to more realistic numbers. We cannot afford a bloated bureaucracy which unlikely would be able to provide the significant increase in capacity necessary for what needs to get done. We need an updated governance model.

Each Cabinet Minister is the head of a *Ministry*, and in the 21st century ought not to be considered or act as the Department Head. This does not remove any responsibility or accountability of a Minister. Rather, more effective governance would reflect a refined definition of the mandate in which the person is commissioned. An updated, modern relationship and covenant between Minister and Deputy **Minister would result in more efficacious government. In the 21st century, one would expect our elected officials to lead ministries and delegate to competent deputy ministers who are in effect operations executives, or as above are commonly referred to as C-Officers from the C-Suite.**

Ours is a country that has evolved into a decades-long established, globally respected government with a professional civil service. In our province, a Deputy Minister leading the *department* for the *ministry* is in effect a Chief Operations Officer equivalent. More than semantics, a government understanding the nuance of roles would better prepare its Ministers.

From the British Columbia government website, in the subject area of Organizational Structure we read: "The BC Public Service is divided into ministries. Each ministry is responsible for a specific area of public policy, government function or service delivery."

It also reports that Service Plans provide an overview of every ministry and associated entity, including how they intend to achieve their service goals and how they support the direction laid out in the Government Strategic Plan.

In our Province we have three branches of government—legislative, executive council (with the Lieutenant-Governor), and judicial. And, we have a civil service which is responsible for public administration. As previously noted, the former group is meant to establish strategy, policy and programs that are effected through legislation. The latter group executes, implements and provides programs and services—in essence delegated to make things happen.

In many ways, our biggest strength is what should be a clear boundary of responsibilities and powers as it is intended to prevent undue political interference in the machinations of government. Concurrently, it can be our biggest weakness where a Minister, even of an assertive and high expectation sort, can be politely side-tracked or thwarted by very talented senior civil servants.

Politicians should not be doing, they should be deciding, legislating and delegating. The real weakness then, is most persons in the role of Minister do not have the competencies requisite to oversee at an executive level. As a result, for a number of governments now the Deputy Ministers are appointed by and have their loyalty to the Premier's office. **Direct appointments by a Premier overcome the restrictiveness of Ministerial selection only from MLAs. However, the reporting relationships of Deputy Ministers only signify the weakness of delegation skills in our politicians.**

"Any attempt to combine governing
with 'doing' on a large scale,
paralyzes the decision-making capacity.
Any attempt to have
decision-making organs actually 'do',
also means very poor 'doing'.
They are not focused on 'doing'.
They are not equipped for it.
They are not fundamentally concerned with it."

Peter Drucker
The Age of Discontinuity, 1968

Evolving beyond a 19th/-20th century legislature and civil service ethos would include taking full advantage of an educated and professional civil service, and modified and modernized working relationship. There likely are Ministers who understand their role and have the skillsets to oversee departments, allowing Deputy Ministers and other Officers in their COO roles. Some may even act as Chair of their own Board of Deputy Minister and Assistant Deputy Minister and senior Directors. A comprehensive orientation would include explanation, skills development, tools, and so forth that a Minister should have to be effective and efficient in their role.

We should not hear a Minister refer to "My Department"—more pertinent, it is "My Ministry". It is the Deputy Minister's Department and

Staff. By extension, the Minister is the Chair, the Deputy Minister is the Chief Operations Officer (COO) of the Department. Each Department should have as its leader a Deputy Minister / COO, with more descriptive position names by department, and each compensated commensurate with qualification and competence according to their profession.

Ministries and Departments make great things happen when the leadership of both groups have sufficient attitude and aptitude to respectfully 'partner' in the execution of strategic and operational priorities.

Premier with Ministers

In a province of only 750000 people, we are smaller than the large cities of this country. While there is a minimal Board (Cabinet) and management structure required to administer and manage any province, even the larger provinces are over bureaucratized, from the Cabinet to the civil service. Likewise, New Brunswick, as small as it is, is over bureaucratized at the political level as well as the civil service.

A Premier's task to create a Cabinet doubtless is always a difficult one. Traditionally, a Premier may attempt to 'balance' geography, language, gender, etc., in the formation of the Cabinet. But when compiled overly so it is weakened when competence is compromised for political balance and reciprocity of loyalty or party work. A good party member, no matter how deserving of reward, does not necessarily make a competent minister.

Practicably, at any given time, there are not sufficient elected members with the competencies necessary to delegate the responsibility of cabinet posts. (Although, at the time of writing, the new federal Cabinet appears to have had sufficient depth in the governing party's caucus to 'reflect the face of Canada' and still have a reasonable mix of talent, of which time will tell.)

It seems that not all that often is there a candidate for MLA nominated by his or her party with an eye on the nominee as Cabinet 'material'. Likewise, as the various party nominees compete for the electoral vote, with one of them winning their riding, to become the MLA, discussion as to their resume or c/v is frequently no more than one hears when these same people are given an introduction for an after dinner speech.

The Legislative Assembly is best when it is serving the Province with a healthy diversity of gender, regional interests, language, and other elements of the New Brunswick social and cultural landscape. It is not an imperative that all MLAs necessarily are Cabinet 'material' as there are different talents and competencies and perspectives that need to be represented.

Frankly, we don't need as many Ministers, as has been in many of our governments, for a small province anyway. Over the past several governments and cabinets, consider all of the first 'core' of Ministers, and you will see people who managed difficult portfolios and performed well, or well enough (except when assigned beyond than their capability).

The remaining, non-core ministers, elevated purely for political regional balance or good party loyalty reasons, were of no consequence to the Premier's success. Regrettably, these MLAs, sometimes in positions beyond their capability many times caused difficulties that had to be corrected; on occasion embarrassing their Premier. The result was a cost to taxpayers without corresponding value, and a cost to the Premier in time spent 'defending' as politicians are prone.

It is ironic, campy, and verging on disingenuous, that the month prior to a provincial election a member in an opposition party, perhaps as the department critic, criticizes staff, sometimes specifically, in a department; and then a month following re-election, this time in the government party, becomes a Cabinet Member defending the same staff.

A similar phenomena may also occur in municipalities. In truth, sometimes, in some situations, one has to wonder if the Councilor was elected to represent the voter/taxpayer in their ward, or the staff in city hall. Our elected officials must always be mindful of whom they represent.

Don't Dwell
As a skipper you should take charge.
Never mind how we got into this mess
-let's focus on getting out of it.
(Besides, more than likely it was your fault.)

Performance Racing Tactics by © Bill Gladestone

The move, by the current and past Premiers, to smaller Cabinets was mostly due to cost reductions and optics of sharing in the burden, the same as government workers were being asked, for which we should commend.

As many Boards and their Chairs have discovered, and many executive teams and their CEOs have experienced, ten or twelve is a large enough group for diversity and decision making power, while small enough for productive collaboration and communication.

The very large Ministries may be well-served to have a second MLA assisting, as an assistant minister, or Legislative Secretary, of sorts. This role can serve to provide additional expertise as well as share the workload with one of the portfolios within the Ministry. Or, provide a linguistic skill set in the official language that the Minister does not possess. Also, it provides a training opportunity for the MLA, and a testing ground for the Premier to observe.

While salary considerations, perhaps $10,000 on top of the MLA salary, is an additional cost, well-defined performance expectations on the relative projects assigned to this role would create value for the people of the province by using skill sets of certain members who are not Ministers. Perhaps, someday, a Premier may even appoint an MLA of another party to such a role, as was done in the 19th century.   This allows a Premier to take advantage of the best talent from caucus, and the Legislature. With perhaps 3-5 'Legislative Secretary' or 'Associate Minister' positions, with delegated specific projects or portfolios within a Ministry from a Minister, other MLAs have contribution and personal development opportunities.

A Cabinet of ten, including the Premier, is compact, nimble but appropriately staffed to govern, particularly for a smaller province such as ours. In addition, this saves money, consolidates Ministries and Departments, attrition will take care of surplus DMs, or reassignment to appropriate duties. Less positions lessens the challenge of competency requisite to be a Minister over 'balance' of geography, language, etc.

With all due respect, and with no particular reference to a current or past caucus, there is a lack of legitimate competency for Cabinet roles. As many have observed, beyond a core group of competent ministers, usually no more than five or six, while the MLAs may be excellent representatives for their home ridings, it does not necessarily extend to being a Minister.

It is time to focus on the governance and business of running government, not the politics. Now is the time because of our desperate situation. Now is the time because, well, it is time.

A premier and the governing party of MLAs are elected to govern. If the elected officials elevated to Cabinet by their Premier are to chair a Ministry, not manage a department, an updated organization model is needed. This includes a Deputy Minister as the Chief Operations Officer or equivalent of the department within that ministry.

The co-title, say Deputy Minister and Chief Financial Officer, is a signal toward a modern role. Some of the twin titling may be disputed, with suggested alternatives for some like Chief Legal Officer. Regardless, the new COO title equivalent should cause a review of mandate, metrics, and reporting relationships. This role, as is the case with a CAO (Chief Administration Officer) in a larger municipality is a unique management position, and is unlike a corporation. However, unlike a CAO who reports to a Council, a Deputy Minister is supposed to report to one Minister.

Ministers have a public who elected them as MLAs, customers who use their services, and politics of life that also affects a Deputy Minister, that a corporate equivalent does not experience. Ministers should focus on reforms and policies and fully expect the Deputy Minsters to follow through and execute plans approved to achieve the government's outcomes.

With regard to critics, there may be many. The purpose underlying this topic of governance, and a variation on the Cabinet, is to consider a modern, strategic and operational groundwork, relevant to our small province early in this 21st century. With this concept the following was developed and put forward as a starting point of discussion.

<u>Ministry</u>	<u>Department</u>
Premier	Deputy Minister
Chair of the Cabinet	/ Chief Strategy Officer
Intergovernmental Affairs	
Federal/N.B. Aboriginal Liaison	
President of the Executive Council	
Finance and Administration NB	Deputy Minister
Financial Reporting and Budgets	/ Chief Financial Officer
Crown Corps, Lottery & Gambling	
Payroll, Benefits, Pension—Civil Service	
Board of Management	
Central Procurement & Supply Systems	
Operations & Systems	
IT Services	
Economic Environment NB	Deputy Minister
Business Environment Support Systems	/ Chief Economic Officer
Tourism & Hospitality	
Regional Support for Development	
Employer/Employee Coordinate	
Culture & Sport & Festivals	
Economic and Trade Initiatives	
Immigration Support Systems Coordinate	
Education and Development NB	Deputy Minister
Early Childhood Care & Development	/ Chief Education Officer
Primary, Secondary Education	
Post-Secondary Education	
Labor Training & Development	

Health and Wellness NB
  Health, Hospitals, Healthcare Centres
  Seniors Nursing & Care Support
  Wellness & Preventative Health Care
  WorkSafe NB

Deputy Minister
/ Chief Health Officer

Justice and Law NB
  Attorney General
  Consumer Affairs & Protection
  Public Safety

Deputy Minister
/ Chief Legal Officer
Deputy Attorney General

Infrastructure NB
  Transportation, Roads & Ferries
Oversight
  Engineering & Architectural Services
  Government Land and Buildings
  Schools & Hospitals Buildings &
Property
  NB Provincial Capital Commission
  Provincial Parks

Deputy Minister
/ Chief Engineer

Social Support and Services NB
  Social and Income Support Systems
  Seniors Support Systems–non-Health
  Non-profit Social Services Support
  (Food Banks, Single Parents, etc.)
  Status for Women
  Status for Ability Challenged
  Family Services
  Poverty Reduction Directorate

Deputy Minister
/ Chief Social Services Officer

Community and Environment NB
  Regional and Local Government
  Emergency Measures
  Environment Protection
  Aboriginal Affairs Municipal Liaison
  Human Resources - Government
  Contracting: policing, protection
services

Deputy Minister
/ Chief Community &
Environment Officer

Natural Resources NB
  Forestry,
  Mining
  Oil & Gas
  Agriculture
  Aquaculture and Fisheries

Deputy Minister
/ Chief Resources Officer

It really is a matter of trust. Trust, as dealt with earlier, also is a trust of capability. Simply put, there are not enough people who run for office and get elected, with sufficient competencies to these most senior positions of responsibility. It is not that we need every elected person to be of a high level of competence to be a Minister of a portfolio, know how to lead a Ministry and 'direct' a senior civil servant with a large number of employees.

To be representative of the people of New Brunswick, diversity from the citizenry of New Brunswick is important. However, we also need a more diverse set of competencies to lead and oversee than what is needed to fill the Cabinet for a competent Executive Council.

The trust level then becomes two-fold. On the one hand there is the 'trust' in whether or not those going to the polls 'trust' the potential Premier and potential team of incumbents capability—competence—to do what they claim they can and will do. On the other hand, there is the matter of can we 'trust' you not to then turn (as so many have) to not doing what you said, make self-preservation your priority, and be secretive rather than open and transparent.

We need Cabinet Ministers, and Deputy Ministers, with skill sets for a modern governance. These include:

~Attitude and aptitude to collaborate across Ministries, to enable cross-departmental streamlining of government priorities, to implement cross-functional projects.

~The proficiency to, for example, as a Minister chair a meeting of MLAs, Deputy Ministers and Directors, to determine broad outcomes with senior health and medical staff, senior education staff, and so forth.

~Collaborate with the senior staff to detail the pragmatics of actual goals, timelines, execution strategies, etc. In strategy the Board and Senior Executive consult (for input). But, when it comes to implementation, there must be a collaboration with those who know how to get the work done.

~Negotiating and influencing skills with the variety of groups that exists in our provincial government to move forward priorities

~Understanding and managing Ministerial oversight, and Departmental oversight, rather than management

New Brunswick has benefitted, federally and provincially, when certain Ministers knew how to perform their role, develop a working executive relationship with their deputy minister, setting the tone of what had to be accomplished and effectively delegating and following through on expectations to ensure success.

Most professionals, including lawyers and accountants and doctors, are easy to admit that they may have their professional training but they never learned to be a manager. Similarly, there are many people elected as MLAs who may have their own credentials but lack the experience or the knowledge to be a Minister. **Without the experience of managing at senior and executive levels, one is relying too much on the Deputy Minister, and therefore either abdicating responsibility or ineffectively delegating.**

Others who are elected, having experienced volunteering on community boards and chaired committees, and are managers or business owners are better prepared and equipped for their elected roles. In all cases, there should be specialized executive management level training for Ministers. Orientation may be sufficient for Ministers to either learn or refresh themselves of their role and responsibilities, and those of their Deputy Minister, and other officers. Governance has an implicit element of delegation that is crucial to effective and efficient assignment of duties and authority.

Delegation and delegating authority is often a misunderstood concept. Research has shown that to some to delegate means that it is now the receiving person's responsibility. While to others, it means that it remains the delegator's responsibility. Effective delegators know that it is relative to the task at hand, and to the person. Should a task regarding normal course of business delegated to a person of an appropriate competence and experience, then a report back that it has been completed is sufficient. If that person is of lesser competence and/or lesser experience, then an additional step or two of 'touching base' is appropriate.

When there are times of unprecedented circumstances and/or tasks that are unprecedented, then it is appropriate for the Ministers to keep closer contact and more frequent updates, and perhaps collaboration. A Premier with a new Cabinet applying these same fundamentals, in early on situations, with each individual Minister, is able from the results to establish the various levels of delegation for each Minister. Not all individual, managers, executives, or Ministers are to an equal task in their capability, execution, nor their timeliness or accuracy. Good delegation skills can prevent big errors being made by Ministers. Likewise, successful Premiers working via Ministers.

In their own Ministry, the Minister applying the fundamentals of delegation should competently facilitate smooth delegation of authority and responsibility—and the basis of good governance. Governance cannot be delegated but it can be cascaded. From Ministers to departments, agencies, crown corporations and on to municipalities and Region Service Commissions.

As guaranteed in the Canadian Constitution, the Provinces have powers, with governing to the elected party, inclusive of governance over all provincial jurisdictions. These jurisdictions include the municipalities. Municipalities spend a lot of their energy fighting this, individually or collectively with their associations, with the provincial government. The to and fro of authority and responsibility is healthy 'testing' of contemporary approaches, but considering the small population consolidation of services and programs make sense, and will take leadership to facilitate change.

Governance cannot be delegated and it is wrongful and irresponsible when it is abdicated. Compared to government departments, outsourcing and privatization and Public Private Partnerships (P3) optimize our resources results in a higher level of accountability for quality and customer satisfaction.

Lack of quality or service level, or any other metric failure, by a privatization service more than likely is related to a lack of governance by the elected officials and their professional staff. Most often it could be traced to insufficient skills in oversight. Ineffective contractual agreements due to lack of competency, or perhaps to facilitate expediency by the staff or their politicians does not make privatization 'wrong'.

When the water disaster in Walkerton, Ontario occurred, the subsequent hearings reported the incompetency and negligence of key managers in the Walkerton Public Utilities Commission that allowed the tragedy to occur. The directors of the Board, and Mayor and Councilors should also have been rightly criticized and put on notice for future projects and programs. Many journalists and politicians were quick to jump on the bandwagon of anti-privatization, citing this as the poster child for such mistakes.

The accountability is, as it ought to be, to the politicians who set up this commission, as it should be with the case of any commission, or outsourcing or privatization model. Appropriate outcomes, accountabilities, reports and audits, as a minimum, should have been clearly identified and followed through.

In New Brunswick, we have been lulled into a sense of security by Boards which have members of the public appointed and elected officials. Even many of the elected officials who are appointed by their municipal council to these boards defend this practice—not because they are covering up anything, but because they believe the boards are accountable. There is a 'break' in the governance over these authorities because it is either delegated away, or inadvertently abdicated by the elected officials.

Across the province, in municipalities and unincorporated areas, there have been boards of solid waste commissions, sewer commissions, water commissions, and the like. As well, we have many community boards for recreation, community centers, wharf authorities and parks—without direct accountability to elected officials under the scrutiny of the public. Fortunately, the migration to the Regional Service Commission model has corrected the situation with solid waste facilities and rural planning commissions now reporting to the Boards of Municipal Mayors and Local Service District Chair/Presidents.

Just because a Board or a Commission is compiled of members who have been elected to a municipal council and then appointed to the board; or chosen by the Minister of Environment and Local Government from a community to represent the interests of their area; does not mean that it is accountable. Once on the Board, these members become an authority of their own, electing a Chair person, as well as the Executive Director or General Manager. There is an 'indirect' line accountability, at best, to the elected officials.

Judging by the leadership elections of our traditional parties, the Progressive Conservatives and the Liberals, the chief criteria for a Premier, is the capability to speak in both of our official languages. Of course, we want a Premier to be representative of the people. There is nothing inherently wrong with proficiency in both of our official languages being one criteria; and certainly mostly everything absurd with it being the only, or even main, criteria.

Leading our government requires a capability that transcends a singular competency of say language skills. A Deputy Premier, with appropriate latitude, can team with a Premier, as an American Vice President does with the President.

> "A straight oar looks bent in the water.
> What matters is not merely that we see things
> but how we see them."
>
> Michel Eyquem de Montaigne
> French Renaissance Statesman and Author

It would be an interesting election, potentially precedent setting in itself, when a Premier candidate signals during the election campaign whom will be their Deputy Premier, and maybe even two or three other key Cabinet posts. While there are no guarantees as to which candidates are ultimately elected, the voters would have more clarity as to team, and a better indication as to which team they think is most suited for the forthcoming four years.

Of the competencies necessary to be a successful Premier, or Cabinet Minister, communication skills is important, and that would include language skills. Yet, if language is the most significant criteria, we rule out other competencies necessary, as well as two thirds of the potential leadership talent—in our already small pool of 750000 people.

Strategic design, followed by social mapping and business planning, then tactical decision making is the approach to success. However, once it goes 'strategic' the politicians and senior decision makers go into platitude mode then static frigidity, little of consequence or nothing happens, and we are back to spending more money but not fixing anything for anyone.

We need to diffuse the 'who do you want to have a beer with' as a criteria for holding a high office. I do not care if the Prime Minister or Premier is someone "I want to have a beer with"—I just want the most capable leader; I do not care if the surgeon is someone I want to socialize with—I just want the best attending to me; I do not care if the special care person overseeing my mother is a great dining partner—I just want my Mom receiving empathetic and professional care.

The way for change is for New Brunswickers to wake up, look past what they like to see and like to hear, and support politicians with the skills and aptitude and willingness to lead our province.

> Every morning in Africa, a gazelle wakes up.
> It knows it must run faster than the fastest lion
> or it will be killed.
> Every morning a lion wakes up.
> It knows it must outrun the slowest gazelle
> or it will starve to death.
> **The moral:**
> It doesn't matter if you are a lion or a gazelle.
> **When the sun comes up,**
> **you better be running.**
>
> Jungle Saying. Unknown

The evidence is ample that New Brunswick is at a juncture in its history to warrant a comprehensive review of our governance with a plan, and implementation and adjustments, within the current term of government, across the province. This would be best served by a Standing Committee on Governance, reporting to the Legislative Assembly, separate from the Standing Committee on Procedure, Privileges and Legislative

Officers. This also is an opportunity for a model of a different kind with co-chairs from the two major parties, and all committee meetings open to the public without restriction.

We are in a time without precedent to compare. Normal course of business is not sufficient. Ministers of a 21st Century government require a higher talent, competence, qualifications, experience—and representation of the people of the province. Undoubtedly, the Ministers to get us there do as well. In the 21st century, we expect our governments to be representative and to competently steer the ship. And, a lot of very hard work–every single day.

Chapter 5

Re-creating

a Nouveau New Brunswick

As we consider the earlier expressions of mission and values and vision for New Brunswick, recalling the legacies of the great strides we have made with a few great leaders, there should be an optimism of what we can do together. Over the past century and a half, we have taken bold steps to become part of a confederation, transformed the way we govern ourselves to pull ourselves into the 20th century, and then capitalized on a homegrown modern technology to create thousands of non-traditional jobs.

Each of these significant changes was not without criticism, of either the change or the leader. Great changes, even with opportunities mean leaving some things behind. While the status quo is being challenged and changed, it is also being defended and opportunities missed. However, we are once again past the time of having to do something, and for this we must gather ourselves and move through unchartered waters.

Paraphrasing an earlier passage, we can make this happen with a collective understanding of what our reason for being, our raison d'être, our mission, is as a province. We have to set our direction and find our way, and reinvigorate and do for ourselves rather than wait, cap in hand, for 'top ups' of federal transfers and politically motivated policies.

A mindset and willingness to govern differently, to steer rather than row, and to make changes in our governance structure and in what we want our professional civil service to do is a major shift that is transformational. The focus has to be on the delivery outcomes of the services we require and not on the organization delivering those services will be transformative in itself.

To endure, as a self-sufficient province, not dependent on support as we are, we must stop the need for increasing federal government transfer payments before these are further slowed or stopped without our input; decrease our annual deficit to a balanced budget state; and reduce our overall debt. This is not a matter of if it has to be done; it has to be done.

But, this does not have to, and will not, be by cutting and curbing alone. We can modify the way we govern in this province, change to oversight from operations, and recreate New Brunswick into a 'Nouveau' New Brunswick.

We are, in many ways, right now, ready to make significant change. We know that change must occur as the status quo is far less than adequate. To survive we will have to stop wanting and stop listening to what we have to this point wanted hear. To thrive, and to endure, we will have to look outside the box and we must look inside the box

Time to Look *Inside* the Box

For successful organizations, success can come from looking *outside* the box, being innovative, creative and willing change makers. Some governments look outside the box. In the past few years our governments have reconfigured the structure of hospital boards and some support services seeking to find a more sustainable way to deliver health services to New Brunswickers. This may or may not have been looking outside the box—we do not know what innovative changes were adopted and adapted from elsewhere, or whether it just was tinkering and cost savings motivated.

These initiatives were starts to change, upheavals for some, some savings and efficiencies, and yet not nearly enough, as here we are again at it. Of course, any organization whether profit or not-for-profit or government, if it is responsible and accountable is diligent in its continuous improvement in all things.

Some government departments have had the internationally recognized continuous improvement approach of six sigma introduced to improve processes and services, and cut costs. To have a lasting effect, this will need to be continued as well as expanded and become woven in the work culture to achieve the performance levels that New Brunswickers deserve.

Looking outside the box is important, and the government will surely continue to look for innovative and creative ways to increase service to New Brunswickers either by adopting best practices or even by finding new ways created here by our people. But, will it be enough and soon enough?

There are provinces with better practices than ours in some areas, and there are others looking at the Service NB model. Yet there are 25+ years of documentation and reports on US states, municipalities and agencies adopting all sorts of best practices, creating improved ways of delivery, removing bureaucratic process blocks, while increasing service delivery quality and decreasing costs.

There are provincial health care and education structures much bigger than ours with data base systems and other information technology infrastructures that we do not have. Outside the box would be to explore these and negotiate terms to have them provide the same service to our province.

It is good news that currently the three Maritime Provinces (perhaps, Newfoundland & Labrador), are working on reducing 'red tape' and work together on common processes. These costs are in the form of barriers, labor intensive paper work, and hard costs. Regulations and laws ensure safety, security, and integrity, but as they become a growth business of their own, some of the burden outweighs some of the benefit. Movement and business development and free trade across the Maritimes should be seamless.

Osborne and Gaebler write of **"Scraping the Barnacles off the Ship of State"—the dead weight of accumulated rules, regulations and obsolete activities."** [Note: Presidents Reagan and Clinton were of like minds on this.] "Government needs some rules, of course. The ship of state needs a coat or two of paint; if we take it down to bare metal, it will rust. The problem is, most governments have acquired several dozen coats of paint and layer upon layer of barnacles. The goal of deregulation is to get back to one or two layers of protection we really need—so the ship can *move* again." [12]

We also have to look *inside* the box. Look *inside* ourselves. We need to loose ourselves from the entanglement of it must be done here in the New Brunswick way. The biggest barriers that we have are ourselves and our perceptions, deeply sunk by decades of politicians telling us that certain services were values when in fact they were programs. We can be successful if we have the willingness to look at the outcomes we want and expect—the services and the service levels—rather than necessarily the civil service delivery of programs.

We need to choose our direction, and make the right decisions. We need to look at the data, the facts of our situations, so that we can put the right plans in place, take the right actions, solve our revenue problems and decrease our inefficiencies and expenses, and increase our effectiveness and efficiency.

All of this makes for a very tall order. But we know that we have to make it. Some of what we do may be without precedence. Some does not have to be invented here, as it has been done elsewhere. In all cases, it is with belief, perseverance and much hard work, that this must be undertaken.

Inside the box, not everything is pretty, and much is messy. Beginning with outcomes expected, facts, data and measurable performance assists in sorting through it all. As Dr. W. Edwards Deming, the famous American statistician and father of quality gurus, said, "In God we trust, all others must bring data." We must share the data. Not all the data is shared, we know that.

A lack of openness of government, by politicians and public sector workers, has to be reversed The 'secrecy' is real, partly due to the cumulative centralization of power, partly because of the protective secrecy inherent throughout both halves of government, and partly because one of the secrets is that not all important outcomes are measured. More concerning, the measurement aspect is not welcome by many. Errors are perceived to be embarrassing to workers and to politicians.

As addressed in the Transparency and Openness section, transparency should and can be the best friend of a politician. And in time, the public sector workers will find that theirs can be a work place with a better atmosphere with transparency. **Outcomes are defined with more clarity and metrics create a focus for performance, and all of this is shared electronically with the public, their taxpayers and customers**. Some may find this frightful at first, but will come to realize how it can actually reduce stress and increase work satisfaction.

Looking inside the box, begins with government, then civil service, and being open and transparent to the public. Naturally, employee private and confidential matters are protected, as are some other areas of governing. But, the secrecy is shed, and the optics are with openness.

By way of the example in Chapter 4, hospital wait times and other statistics made widely available may be an outside the box idea 'borrowed' from elsewhere, but even more needed is inside the box thinking or a mindset that patients—customers—should be provided such information.

"All we need is a key,
and the decision to swing the door open.
There is only one key,
and it is called willingness."

Twelve Steps and Twelve Traditions

We have to look *inside* the box to observe the outcomes of the services and programs provided against key measurable performance metrics, and renew and revise the policies, methods, procedures and processes. This can be taxing and even exhausting on the civil service and so will need to be managed, and supported, with some situations requiring propping up with external support, as short timelines are essential. Public service workers know how to work hard, and are as aware as private sector workers that continuous improvement is continuous, and never ending until the day after retirement.

As a province, we have to look *inside* the box, and inside ourselves to be honest with each other and take ownership for what we have to do. Few will disagree that we have services and programs that are eroding, and vulnerable to further erosion from reduced spending support. Nor argue with the reality of a debt that has to be brought within our control, and then decreased as a percentage of provincial GDP, followed by real dollar reduction. We have an annual operating deficit and we need to bring into line our expenses with our taxes and fee revenues.

These are areas we should have not let get out of control, and now have to get under control, just as each of has to do with our family budget or our business budget. To not look at the reality of our debt situation, and to fail to be honest, or to not really understand that there is a crisis that must be dealt with if we want to maintain our health system and better our education outcomes and have a competitive environment for jobs so people can work here—none of these are questioned. We know this is our current situation, even if we do not like, even if we do not like the prescriptions.

It may be what we want to hear, but 'hope' is not a panacea or a solution. A political leader is being forthright only when taking a clear stand on the significant issues facing our province, or providing an alternative way to steer and govern our province. Hope might be a four letter word that sounds great in speeches, but it is hollow without substance as to direction or destination, disposition or design.

In not fully reporting the facts of our financial situation with comparatives to equal form prior year reports, quarterly and annually on the website as shareholders (citizens) rightfully expect; or the realities of the benefits of the multiplying factor of job creation in our resources sectors; a political leader shows only that in the 2010s they don't know where to look outside the box and they don't know how to look inside the box. The best that can occur is they skirt around it, trying to sound positive, avoid dealing with the sometimes horrid facts, and not state what they will do eventually, if they even know, as it might make them to not be liked.

Yes, our Province has looked outside the box, occasionally, as a government, as employers and employees. New Brunswick entrepreneurs have made strides in diversifying our economy by adding large numbers of knowledge workers and service workers. Our Province has historically done its best to prosper from our natural resources—our fisheries, our forestry, our mining. Now we have modern, new technological ways to continue benefiting from our natural resources for new jobs and to grow our economy, and be environmentally sensitive.

From natural gas, to oil pipelines, to newly discovered minerals— each of which has 'spin-off' benefits as well as direct benefits—to modern forest silviculture and harvesting to aquaculture, we should

continue to benefit from our natural resources. Balancing protection of the environment with jobs and profits is a modern society's choice of stewardship, where no special interest group 'owns' this concern.

As we look inside the box, it is clear we need to do things differently. At least it is clear to most New Brunswickers, and it is clear to most politicians. The challenge is to make decisions, first strategically, then tactically, moving those who seem to remain silent or continue to think otherwise on board with real change.

Government Revenues and Expenses

It goes without saying that government revenues from taxes of the income and property sorts, along with fees and licenses, and royalties on natural resources, are necessary for general program support and for specific services. Let it be suggested that it is when those revenue sources are regarded with one accord, as if all revenues are created the same, the onset of unconscious ambivalence prevails.

Although not alone amongst contemporaries, **In New Brunswick, the co-mingling of revenues, is entrenched in our government, to our detriment**. One only has to observe the economic cycles of our wealthier-kin provinces and see that royalties streams ebb and flow with the tides of global commerce and commodities prices. The only difference, as with a rich person, is that poor financial planning and management results in more zeros on their deficit and debt numbers. Throwing all the money in one big bucket is not accountability.

Aside from income taxation, and many other general taxes unilaterally taking money from citizens, the 'big bucket' feeds the size of government while failing to improve services. It is the position, or perhaps simply the fall back position once in office, taken by political leaders of weak policy and incapable oversight.

Ridiculous statements are made by otherwise bright people, politicians and non-politicians, about the government revenues we call taxes. To state, with all authority and indignity, that a reduction to taxes is an "expensive program" is absolute nonsense. Reducing a tax, any tax, may reduce revenues to government, and to some may be considered a costly policy, but it is not an expense—it is a taxation or revenue reduction.

For anyone to claim that revenues were decreased without also coupling it to taxes decreased, is a shifty way to lay blame. The decreased percentage of the tax rate often is offset by the growing dollar base that is taxed. The trend to reducing taxes, at federal and provincial levels, was recognition that people should be able to keep more of their hard earned pay, and, with an offset coming from a larger dollar base due to a growing economy, government revenues can maintain the level requisite for expenses.

Troubles set in when the growing economy does not grow, or the growing population stops growing. Some economists have differing perspectives on our decline in revenues coinciding with increased service costs. Whether or not our annual deficit is 'structural' or 'cyclical', it seems that we have become accustomed, in good times and in bad, to it always being there, like an overdraft that cannot be covered.

The discussion on revenues is a good example for the governance aspect of Transparency and Openness. Financial statements, accounting practices and audits are not of the most interest to the majority of citizens and such details are left to the professionals who perform such duties and to those who provide the scrutiny on our behalf. However, this does not mean that the broad stroke numbers should not be shared and discussed openly, and explained.

Royalties is a good case in point. Why is it that citizens were never made aware of the revenues to the Province, from all sources including from Brunswick Mines during its decades of operation? (Other than a single line item total with comparison to the prior year.) Or not made aware of what the depletion and eventual closing of Brunswick Mines cost our provincial revenues?

Knowing these dollar values would provide a level of insight to citizens as to how and by how much one revenue stream is contributing to our province, and when it decreases toward the closure of facilities and ultimately when operations cease at depletion that it needs to be replaced by other revenues.

Unlike people who always will be around to tax, revenues from non-renewable royalties have a horizon. Just as a call center needs to replace a lost or expiring contract with another new contract in order to keep revenues and jobs, the province needs to replace expiring royalty streams. To replace the lead/zinc mines royalties, how much natural gas royalties are required, or tungsten mine royalties, or pipeline payments?

Informed citizens make informed decisions. Disclosures and discussions with New Brunswickers would reflect respect of citizens, and a regard for their deliberation on situations. Openness of government is about removing the secrecy; transparency is about showing of information and ensuring understanding of the workings of a government by its people.

Fees and licensing income for the province really are a fee for service or 'retail' sort of revenue source, mostly transacted by Service NB points and website transactions. Regular incremental increases, although an irritant to the clients, is a relatively simple method for the government to increase revenue. No doubt increases are preceded with inside discussions as to which are 'easier' to increase. More fitting, does an audit for value analysis ever occur for more appropriate market-driven pricing?

Good business would consider revenue collection, netted against costs of collection and distribution, as an amount available to pay for government costs of operations, services and programs. In addition, streamlined, automated, and best practice applied processes reduce the 'costs of goods sold', thus further increasing the net revenue available.

To leverage what little economies of scale we have in New Brunswick, inasmuch as is possible, taxation collection ought to be centralized in the Ministry of Finance. Irrespective of the sub-jurisdiction within the province, whether taxes collected belong to municipalities or agencies, studies should be completed as to the benefit of centralized collection. The province could collect, tally and electronically deposit monthly or quarterly payments contingent on the item collected—with minimal delay to the appropriate body. Initially, this may not be popular, but with appropriate study and discourse, it could prove to ease the burden to municipalities, leverage available economies of scale, and only be implemented if factually proven to provide net benefit (dollars) to the taxpayers. **In the end, there is only one taxpayer—everyone says this, yet actions show otherwise.**

New Brunswick may be the last jurisdiction without a policy for hotel levies to fund local tourism and hospitality promotion. Municipalities wish the province to pass legislation allowing them mandatory collection of hotel room levies, with each determining what formulae is used within their municipality for general promotion or for use by the hotel association.

There are costs to collecting, so a hotel room levy should be streamlined and centralized. Legislation, preceded by consultation with the municipality associations and Regional Service Commissions ought to include a standard levy, province wide, of say $2.50 per $100 per room per night, collected by the hotels and remitted to the N.B. Finance. Of this amount, 80% could be disbursed to the applicable region, and the remaining amount to the provincial Tourism & Hospitality promotional budget.

Municipalities, or Regions, would determine if the levy is higher within their boundaries, with that portion accruing to them, and the agreed formulae allocation retained by the Province. Every step could be electronically transacted, from the accommodation desk collection daily total transfers, to electronic deposits monthly by the province to the region/municipality. (With the Regional Service Commission model, more strategic, forward looking would be directing to regional pools of tourism promotion funds.)

Compared to federal government transfer payments of $3billion, and provincial government taxes of $4billion, the balance of $1.3billion from all other provincial revenues represents the smaller portion of New Brunswick's total $8.3billion revenue. Consequently, while we need to optimize the net of non-tax revenues, it is tax revenues that have the biggest impact on our availability of funds to spend.

At the same time, with an awareness of total royalties collections, past and present trends, and future projections with or without certain sources such as gas, minerals, etc., an educated electorate can make up their own minds as to their preferred choice. For example, faced with $x increase in HST or $y increase in personal income taxes or $z increased revenues from royalties streams of natural gas, voters are enabled to make more informed decisions.

With regard to taxes, the Province's financial statements leave all sources lumped in one sum—nearly three quarters of the revenue is not further broken down. At a minimum of disclosure, it should be identified on the statements as personal income taxes, corporate income taxes, harmonized sales tax (provincial portion) and if there is a balance, other. These figures may be available elsewhere, but that makes it too difficult to find, and transparency is meaningless without ease of understanding or access. (Other sources indicate $1.5billion personal income taxes, $1.1billion HST, $481million real property taxes, $251million corporate income taxes, etc.)

By increasing our population and growing our economy all tax revenues can increase, without further increasing the percentage burden on existing taxpayers. New jobs in the civil service is not job creation unless directly attributable to further value add to the taxpayer. The latter is something rarely witnessed as evident by vast increases of funding to health and education coincidental with falling behind and to last place in our federation.

With our births barely replacing our deaths, increased population will need to come from out of province and out of country immigration, as well as new jobs created that attract others to migrate here for employment. The net benefit to the province will result from the taxes generated and economic growth being more than the increased health and education and social services costs. It is only the net benefit that produces the wealth to pay for our 21st century government organized services.

While small business makes up the largest number of businesses, the hard facts are that many entrepreneurs and other folks have, by choice or by circumstance, created only a job for themselves. It is from professional services and bigger businesses that the creating of most of the higher paying jobs with better non-compensation benefits packages result.

Naturally, all amount of attention given to revenues, net revenue, cost savings, and expanding sources of revenue streams, is secondary to reducing the costs to taxpayers while increasing the value of services provided. The bare truth is that we have to do it all.

Revenues can and must be increased, as much as possible with minimal further tax burden to our citizens and our businesses. Cost containment has to be realized. It is possible, but we have experienced underwhelming success so far. We are in our second government, of different political parties, trying to do just this by searching out every efficiency to cut costs.

If revenue sources cannot be secured, and should incremental revenue increases with incremental efficiency improvements continue to prove insufficient, with a deficit of chronic scope, then increasing the HST will be the only option to bring in significant revenue. Many say that in the absence of significant current fiscal year progress this should have been done in April 2015 to avoid a year wasted without any substantial progress.

As to the other half of the income statement, expense control is equally as daunting. School closures, courthouse closures, and health care line-ups are causing grief to the communities involved, the people of New Brunswick. By centralizing services, in some cases it may only be a matter of time until these are further centralized again.

Likewise, cuts to certain health services to feed the wider system, while causing distress to the affected is helping to keep other services in place. Priorities have to be established and acted upon. Triaging services has kept all sectors of our civil service busy. For what headway?

In all of this, while politicians are fully aware that there is only one taxpayer (they too are one, so they are not removed) and yet the full cost to New Brunswickers appears beneath the radar. When many kilometers of highway are left in a 'raw grid format' for weeks until surfacing is complete, the tire wear and the increased gas consumption is a cost to New Brunswickers. When a court house is moved and police, lawyers, witnesses and defendants and families all have to travel much further distances, more gas and maintenance costs are out of pocket.

It is clear and practically inarguable that we must cut costs. All the same, does anyone in government account for the *real total* costs of these changes? This should be considered as the many cuts that are being exacted for our expenses to be sufficiently covered by our revenues. On the other hand, has sufficient creativity been applied, other jurisdictions checked, for alternative options? If so, these have not been reported, or taken to the community hall meetings for a more collaborative approach, or at least a more citizen informed consultation process.

One size does not fit all. We hear that from all corners, at least on occasion. Does even one of these locales include all of an old school, an old community center, an old court house, a closed service point—old buildings, inefficient energy probably, and on too many lots? What of a newly designed building, front half the school, backed by a combination of the other buildings, with access controlled between? A potential Private Public

Partnership, land owned by the Province, other properties sold to apply to the debt?

For politicians, more worrisome than the NIMBY of cuts and reductions, is the sheer difficulty it seems to control costs in the big areas of education, health and social services, never mind reduce them significantly. Federal government pushback on the percentage increase of annual increases for health transfers was predicated partly on the trend that more money was not getting better results, anywhere.

> "You gain strength, courage and confidence by every experience in which you really stop to look fear in the face."
>
> Eleanor Roosevelt

Once again, reading the words of Richard Saillant, "The inescapable reality is that the New Brunswick government spends around three-quarters of its program dollars in three areas involving hard-won social gains: health, education and training, and income support and other social services. It is in these shark-infested waters that New Brunswick politicians will continue to have to swim in search of savings."

One of the significant factors overlooked, Professor Saillant highlights, is that "the provinces, more than federal or municipal governments, have to absorb the full impact of aging." The professor also maintains "That the Maritime Provinces spend relatively more on public services therefore has little to do with profligate spending on social programs that richer provinces cannot afford. The reality is more prosaic: these provinces are spending more and growing their spending faster than the Canadian average mainly because they are aging faster." [13]

This finds us at a crossroads of real and formidable challenges. We somehow have to contain costs *and* increase health care for an aging population. As the former and current Premiers have rightfully expressed, we need Ottawa's help. But, we are always *needing* Ottawa's help, always putting in requests for buoys to be thrown to us. Yet, there is a potential solution and, as expanded upon below, it requires both inside the box thinking and outside the box thinking.

A recurring premise as various government services are examined, is the pervasive lack of knowledge and information on costing and cost accounting. Over two decades of observing and asking questions of the most senior public servants has made clear this shortcoming. In turn, this has been shared with the most senior of ministers, of both parties, in this province.

When line items are 'rolled up' for financial statements, it should come of little surprise that it is likewise for everything down the lines from there. Hospitals are unawares of department overhead allocations and true costs of each unit. In Local Service Districts (LSDs), district engineers cannot provide actual costs of road maintenance and snow removal. These same LSDs receive annual financial reports without the roads budget, and for everything else only year to year budget comparisons—there are no actuals, only roll-ups to provincial totals.

Any operation, government or business, needs more than the financial statements of profit & loss and balance sheets. Cost control and cost reduction cannot be competently managed unless managers can figure out the costs of products and services, and consider all factors including fixed and variable costs, and period-over-period variances as well as contributing factors to success.

Taken further, consciously or unconsciously, this is an undercurrent to some of the public service animosity toward any provision of services other than by government sector workers. The whole picture is not available or made available for a Minister to come to a fully informed conclusion to make a recommendation to Cabinet.

No wonder then, there is a conviction among many that the only way to control costs in government, is to give it less money, less tax dollars. Governments that lower taxes are in effect giving less money to Ministers and Deputy Ministers to spend. The misspoken notion that lower taxes, because it lowers revenues, is "spending surpluses" is either from lack of understanding or it is deliberately misleading.

In a related context, it is not a question of whether or not the civil servants are working hard enough, as they work within the system. Even when there is a public servant or group recalcitrant to the party in power, they are still following their working orders. As in any workplace, anywhere, there are various levels of performance, aptitude and attitude.

Nor can one fault another person accepting a job in the civil service. It is honorable work with competitive pay and better than most health and pension benefits. Moreover, savvy managers in a bureaucratic hierarchy, public or private sector, know how to increase their reach by performance outcomes and by increasing their staffing numbers.

It seems like we live through one stroke forward and two strokes back when it comes to preventing civil service growth. And, we hear of statistics as to how our growth has outpaced other provinces in numbers of positions in nursing, teaching, and so forth on a per capita basis.

Still, one questions as to how citizens can make informed opinions on the size of the civil service when so many different sectors are totaled together. As discussed in the section on Clarity and Truth, we need civil servant government numbers separate from health and hospital care employees, separate from primary and secondary teachers, separate from NB Liquor, NB Power, Community Colleges (and separate professionals from administration.

Telegraph Journal   Greg Perry

Additionally, transparency would be providing such data available on the government website, clearly detailed and easily located. Comparative data to the provincial average of the largest provinces and the average of the smallest provinces would facilitate reference points. Openness of government would manifest in a desire that information is available so that reference by either side of the Legislature is neutralized, at least as far as the facts are concerned.

The public, generally speaking, does not pay much attention to or know that Keynesian economics actions are what drives deficit. Nor may they want to understand how Hayek influenced economic democracies usually fare better, nor do they particularly care. **What people do care about are the quality of services, line ups, or whether or not to be concerned about the big costs of government including salaries and wages.**

To previous generations, frugality and moderation was a noble philosophy. Waste not want not. Take care of the pennies and the dollars take care of themselves. Austerity, on the other hand, describes more of a hardness, even meanness and coldness of leadership. The United Kingdom public is dealing with this, as did Canada's electorate in 2015October, and New Brunswick's senior citizens' backlash.

Cutting the size of government and maintaining taxes can be considered frugality or austerity, or responsible management. Or, it can be considered a means to right size the economic balance of our province and return to an economy where government steers and not rows. But, we do not have to accept that as cost reductions occur so do cutting of services, in either quality or quantity or both. Nor without options or even conversations to explore alternatives to the taxpayers affected.

As a case in point, the pan province district engineers' budgets reduction for the snow plowing and grading of rural streets and roads with less than three houses. Since these budgets are no more than total equipment, fuel and salary costs, all that was known from the savings was it would save some amount. But, the question should be asked: What was the actual cost of each affected street or road?

If a street is in a small unincorporated hamlet or village-like community, it is not the same situation as a house at the end of a private road out in the country. Irrespective of location, what is the cost to snow clear that street/road while the vehicle is dispatched? Why is that cost not offered to the homeowners so that they at least have the option to pay for it rather than lose it? A private company would not have overlooked such opportunities. And, the affected homeowners would have had an option, likely less expensive and more reliable than individually trying to source and pay a contractor.

The circumstances of the budget reduction and the decision is not one made by the district engineers, or even their directors in Fredericton. It is more of a philosophy and an approach of government, and it is an ideology that must be changed if we are to have any semblance of success.

Other areas where poor decisions, from lack of good governance, sound cost accounting, and citizen centric consideration, could be overcome include: secondary and primary road maintenance and snow removal; Information Technology; school bus ownership and staffing.

If Government is to steer, then it is there to provide the services but not necessarily the delivery of those services. This will not occur until our government looks inside its box, has the senior civil service executives look inside their boxes, and then be prepared to look outside the box for best practices in other provinces, other states, and other countries.

'Leave no stone unturned' to reduce costs and efficiencies does not continue with 'but...' It does not stop at our borders either. There is no embarrassment to not knowing everything, while there is satisfaction in discovering new ways and new ideas.

Even smallish areas like the various cards issued by the province has potential for increased convenience to citizens, cost savings to the province, and plain old common sense. In British Columbia, one can get one card that includes the Medicare number on the back of the Driver's License. Consider the streamlining for even those without a Driver's License, as they can now obtain a picture ID card.

By going into a Service NB location a citizen could obtain one picture card that serves two purposes, an ID / Driver's License and a Medicare Card combined, with one five year expiry date. Plus, the province has as an improved control system for relocated citizens as most jurisdictions require at some point a locally issued driver's license. Thus, at the expiry of the driver's license, the renewal of the Medicare card is not automatic. And, every citizen has an ID card easing the problem of photo identification at the election polls.

There is nothing complicated to most New Brunswickers, jaded by the write-offs of hard earned tax dollars lost to loan defaults or guarantee executions, in expecting **no more loans or loan guarantees given to business. Period.** This alone could be an election winning promise. The return of the economic development staff to the private sector would further save money on this unpopular pastime of politicians assuming power.

"They think that the cure to big government
is to have bigger government...
the only effective cure is to reduce the scope of
government - get government out of the business."

Milton Friedman
Big Business, Big Government

Finally, it needs to be noted that a truce must be called, in the name of civility in government, to desist all exaggerated criticism of Premier, Ministers, and senior civil servant expenses. The meanness of austerity is not in Ottawa alone, and with expense claim guidelines that are less than the federal ones, and less than even many large businesses in our own province, outrageousness over expenses when within guidelines is just plain wrong.

When all of the non-governing party folks, righteous in their own eyes, judge of all, mocked-in-shock and played the media to the limit (which can be done) in the matter of a federal cabinet minister spending a ridiculous amount of taxpayer dollars on a glass of orange juice, it was front page news. (See Chapter 2). In New Brunswick, let us just agree that if the office of the

Auditor General reviews, and is satisfied with the explanation of a claim over the prescribed amount, then it should be left as it is.

If not already in place, let the Legislative Standing Committee on Public Accounts attain all party support on a policy with regard to Premier and Minister and other MLA travel for various reasons and events. If one already is in place, then let us invoke the same aforementioned civility.

We have fiscal challenges, but being mean and chintzy (as more than one former Prime Minister has noted or inferred regarding the decades of 24 Sussex grossly inadequate maintenance) when it comes to our most senior politicians called upon to travel, is by media or opposition simply gratuitous. Our Premiers of the 1990s onward have been responsible and respectful of this province's finances.

The Premier is our person on the control deck of our ship, so allow them to travel as leader so we are not embarrassed, provided within the guidelines. We have an unprecedented task ahead, let them get on with the task.

Oversight *of Operations and Quality*

We need to redefine what we mean by 'big government'. For sixty plus years the term grew from school systems to health and social services, being marked by government buildings everywhere. Thus, the described externalizing of our values. Now, with the trepidation spurred by some of those buildings disappearing or being closed, people are even more concerned with the services and access to the services.

Government funded services are here to stay in a modern democracy, but the 'big' no longer can be government owned bricks & mortar and abundant resources. If it never should have been, it no longer needs to be now as our private sector has expanded so much, the geographic reach has been extended so far, and expertise is available virtually around the clock.

With a transformation from doing to oversight, government funded services can still be provided in a continuously improving environment. **The new 'big' is 'comprehensive'. Comprehensive government works on ensuring quality of services to its citizens, not necessarily doing the delivery of those services in all situations.**

Compass Group Canada, which runs Chartwells, is the food-service management company that operates some 100 cafeterias in schools in New Brunswick. In a corresponding arrangement, Les réseau des cafétérias communautaires operates 25 out of the 36 cafeterias in the Francophone South school district. Having two separate contractors is a prudent approach to outsourcing or privatizing. (But let a local parents committee have input.)

Separate contracts allows the oversight by civil servants with a comparison of benchmarks, quality checks, regulatory and safety compliance, and outcomes success. It also prevents being held 'ransom' by a sole contractor, and with appropriate performance clauses, arrangements could be made for a temporary contracting of the other party.

However which way the government decides to proceed, along language lines or geography or some other means, a minimum of two contracts in the province should be mandatory. Exceptions may be reviewed by the Executive Council with a special resolution brought before the Legislative Assembly should all party consensus not prevail at the **Legislative** Standing Committee on Public Accounts.

In the arrangements with the cafeteria contractors, it appears that any issues that arise are within 24 hours reported to the Education Department, an action plan is undertaken to resolve concerns, and the school board is worked with closely to implement. As well, all cafeteria supervisors must complete a provincially recognized food-safety training course when hired, with the training renewed every three years. Six full-time staff employed by the company regularly visit the schools.

It is very likely these contractual arrangements are more 'iron clad' and with more oversight than the previous staffing approach. That is to be expected as a client-supplier relationship carries with it a higher expectation and a more business-like, performance driven relationship. What needs to be transparent is the appropriate level of oversight by the province to ensure quality and safety for our children including government website reports on oversight checks for each school cafeteria.

Our provincial government, whether by outright privatization, P3 (Private Public Partnership), sub-contracting, or de-regulation, is freeing up capital. In some situations, the buildings and properties are no longer holdings of the province, and in other instances it is a matter of getting government out of running things it either never had the justification or capability to do, or should no longer. **Disposing of buildings surplus to our needs, and perhaps land in some cases, can be ways to free up funds to either build new, modern and efficient buildings to house multiple government services, or to pay down the provincial debt.**

Regardless of one's perspective of the foregoing, the services remain the responsibility of the government. In some situations, the ownership of the land beneath is still the property of the province. In my previous financial career, it was a learning point to discover that major financial corporations frequently own the land their buildings are upon, but lease their required portion or the whole building from a property management company.

The government cannot abdicate its responsibility when it makes a shift of the provision and delivery of many services away from direct

delivery. Likewise, there may be certain services best delivered by public employees. In all instances government must play a role by maintaining its responsibility and accountability for all of its publicly funded services.

It seems that most times a change is made, the party in Opposition is against it even if they were favorably inclined while in government. A new governance and civility will by necessity bring on a more constructive and creative way to fulfil this important role in our democracy. In an age to which we have evolved where little differentiates the two main parties, and governments seem to turn over on wedge issues of the day, it is the alternative team of leadership, confidence and choice of sub-mission that will determine elections.

Most developments affecting our natural resources can be expected to be greeted by protests of doom and disaster. **Responsibly transparent and open government communicates better, informs more effectively, and meets with people and deals with issues**. Environment is everyone's concern and no one has a monopoly on caring about it. We need to stop the incessant, and insulting, mantra of how this will hurt our children and grandchildren. This is tired tactics, serving only to get people alarmed and try to own 'family' and 'caring' values.

There is a huge transition we are embarking upon, either thrust upon us by inertia and outside forces taking us in one direction, or by our choosing monumental means to overcome what we can longer deny. Our quality of services will continue to deteriorate and our deficits and debt load will continue to sink us unless we deal with both.

In The Financial Post 2015-Jan27 column by Tom Velk, Director, North American Studies, at McGill University, is this warning:

"So-called "generational accounting" shows that governments have over-extended every variety of future spending promises. Economists measure true debt by asking two questions. What is the present value of future committed spending (pensions, welfare, housing, medicine) and what is the present value of future revenues (tax, excise, license fees)? Subtract excess spending from inadequate revenue and the resulting negative number measures true debt. Thus measured, debts are gigantic, unsustainable and—unless promised spending and threatened taxing plans are radically rewritten—guaranteed to end in repudiation, inflation and crisis. …have enormous unpayable debts, and even have… large net generational imbalances."

Sadly, in New Brunswick this is more like us than any other province in the nation. For whatever reason, we are still in a fog of denial, knowing this is true, but hoping we can somehow get out of this mess. Like many fellow Canadians, many New Brunswickers do not like the negativity of it and we are drawn to the positive messages of hope. This is not the dilemma of choice, though, hope versus change. The dilemma is how the change will occur, in our control or by others.

Over many years of consulting and training, at all levels in the public sector, there has been a noticeable steadfastness in civil servants being convinced that private companies can neither do a public service task as well as government workers, nor do it for less than can be done in-house. And, even when they can, they are making a profit, and that it just isn't right.

> In my experience, most senior civil servants cannot bring themselves to believe that private enterprise, because it makes a profit, can deliver for less, and even better. This ideology is harmful to our best interests.
>
> *cfs*

Commentaries by heads of civil service unions, nursing unions, bus driver groups, and others, are frequenting our provincial newspapers. These are not the workers and professionals themselves speaking. These are the hired hands, self-preservationists who rarely are concerned with the performance outcomes of those whom they are paid to represent.

In a reference to the new government's Strategic Program Review summit in his Times&Transcript column 2015-05-23, W. E. (Bill) Belliveau wrote, "Many of their spokespeople are paid, professional communicators. They are not paid to give away what they have gained or to suggest that members of their cause want to diminish their circumstance."

So, if the status quo is not working and almost broken from insufficient funding and underperforming systems, and changing the way we deliver services is not considered, then what are the alternatives? Those hired professional communicators do not seem to present concrete solutions rather than repeat the merits of their public service union members.

Funded services never should have been considered a public service, but a publicly funded service, in some instances delivered by public servants. Perhaps we would not have evolved to the point of public service monopolies and oligopolies. As well, the reasoning for alternative delivery methods is more than saving money. It also is about systemic changes that will bring about enhancements in both quality and quantity of service levels. This should not be taken as a slight on the civil servants, teachers and healthcare professionals, for they do want to do their best.

Frankly, the P3 fights picked by unions are primarily of the bogus variety. The union bosses have to come clean: their reason for being is to represent their workers and protect their workers, with everything else down from there on their priority list. There are failures here and there in the landscape of publicly funded services, so to point out a few P3 cost overruns does not tell the whole story. There are cost overruns in publicly funded hospitals as well as shortfalls on delivery. Of the few P3 hospitals cited in some commentaries, did these meet their delivery quality and quantity metrics? Metrics? Chances are the P3s have more metrics as part of their contractual obligations than their public counterparts in the first place.

The full argument on funding of patients, with cherry picking of the lower cost patients by the private facilities, "burdening" the higher cost patients on the government is a most ridiculous statement as all patients are funded by the government using our tax dollars, ergo the costs will be there regardless.

Bill Belliveau, in the same column continues, "Perhaps more importantly, we have to get rid of the French-English rancor that blinds us to reality. There is no room in a bilingual province for segregated school buses. There is no room in this province for urban dualities. There is no justification for 24 hospitals to serve 750.000 people. There is no rationale in a just society that permits a predatory attach on somebody's lifelong savings. There is no need for a $477 million deficit. We need to get out of this box. It's stifling." Clearly, we have to do things differently, because indeed it is stifling. Equally as clear to the citizens affected is this should be accomplished, where it has to be done, while minimizing the drawbacks. The province's larger urban areas will be the least affected. Tweaking will bring about some cost savings, efficiencies, and maybe even some improvements in service.

So, then the questions become first, which services? And second, what delivery methods? To the first it is whatever government does not need to be doing and can be provided by non-government providers. The second depends on the services under consideration.

For services that are easily identified as having potential alternative deliveries, the province can use an authorized Request For Proposal (RFP) process. Consideration should be given to exploring what is known as the best practice jurisdictions in Canada, USA and UK, to determine if refining of the RFP approach is appropriate. Decisions need to be made as to those eligible to bid, within the Province, within the Maritimes, across Canada, or North America, in accordance with agreements.

The RFP process should never be compromised by opinions that only certain businesses are capable, and therefore only those are advised to bid. Entrepreneurs may decide to partner, or merge, or reach out of province for joint bidding, so excluding potential contractors is not responsible as well as not fair. The monopoly given to the not-for-profit corporation for hospital laundry services was an exclusive process. Senior Management at FacilicorpNB determined that none of the private wholesale laundry companies could handle the volume. It was not until after the awarding of the contract that this same senior management was made aware of at least one businessman who was contemplating purchasing a large competitor and would have bid had the hospital contract been made available to bid.

Rather than government managers who are not business people making decisions based on uninformed opinions, an openness in bidding would in the least have provided competitive comparisons of pricing, as well as all other terms and conditions. The taxpayers lost. Additionally, the opportunity of having two providers, one for Moncton and north/northeasterly, and one for Saint John and northwesterly. This provides the above indicated ongoing comparative benchmarks, and an alternative in the case of under performance by one or the other.

An interesting federal example is the initial Canadian Food Inspection Agency foray into fees for services. Projection of revenues looked great as the new spin-off from Agriculture Canada launched into its first fiscal year. With one particular service the farmers, who previously had options of certain services on individual cluster/grouping, historically preferred the individual testing. With fees introduced, including individual and cluster/grouping, it was the latter with its lower per unit cost that was the overwhelming choice. The result was, along with a number of other pricing presumptions (not assumptions), CFIA revenues were much lower than anticipated.

It is apparent that the knowledge, experience and skillsets are not the same in the worlds of big government and comprehensive government. The traditional civil service worker was hired and works in a different environment, with a different context, and different set of performance expectations in big government.

A widely used method of sourcing and determining potential suppliers is by Request For Interest (RFI). One use of an RFI could be issuances over the broad spectrum of many different government services including those provided by agencies, as a means to determine what capabilities are available. For a government, this also provides a platform to estimate the success rate of provincial based businesses, and to determine if it wants to recommend to the potentially qualified respondents further things they should prepare, or partnering with each other to better qualify, etc. (This will be explored further in Economic Environment, below.)

An RFI allows a government to explore opportunities that may not otherwise come to mind. An RFI should be publicly promoted, attracting private enterprises, not for profits, and government departments or groups, for submissions and proposals. Examples could include:

~consolidation of smaller services that have potential for outsourcing
~elimination of services (ask the question: if this didn't exist would it really matter?
~support services, to health and education and community colleges and all parts of government, including janitorial, snow removal, road maintenance, etc.

It is possible that a wide range of interested potential contractors and suppliers may suggest any number of potential areas that they wish to make a proposal and bid. Additionally, this would enable the government to take advantage of attrition, demographic or other, and review if those positions have an optimum timing best for employees and to costs, to establish a relevant RFP.

The Province has positions with roles that may be fulfilled by private enterprise, with competitive driven private sector wages, benefits and pension plans. This should be addressed honestly, not coated in politically correct euphemisms, not speaking of it as if it is not a reality. As some USA states and municipalities have experienced, opportunities may arise whereby there is competition, head-to-head with departments/divisions and private enterprise. Not everything is necessarily a matter of P3 or private enterprise versus government, but everything should be looked at with open eyes.

The government also has a need, from time to time, in different departments for additional assistance. Over the years, independent contractors have been hired as stop-gaps, or to provide a temporary skillset or knowledge base. While costs of consultants can be difficult to control, there are ways to fix contract costs.

Should significant changes occur in local government, the Environment and Local Government professionals and other department colleagues, once decisions are made, likely will need additional short term staffing to expedite any changes so that full benefits can be accrued quicker. Rather than the typical law or consultant office billable hours, one wonders if arrangements could be made, at a much lesser hourly rate in segments of x-hours, for a contract that recognizes the benefit to the firm of experience gained, and reputation built from such an assignment.

The art and skill of managing consultants is an imperative for any business and most particularly a government. The listing of consultants and consulting contracts that go over budget, take longer, and the almost inevitable many unexpected 'unknowns' occurring, may seem endless. This is a major factor in scaring off the concerned and prudent civil servant, perhaps even more than the risk of job redundancy.

Those executives who have the knowledge and experience, know how to manage the consultants from even before the contract is awarded. This includes clear qualifying criteria, demonstration of capability and satisfactorily concluding projects on time and within budget. Firms with a track record of their principal lead consultants with a primary concern of the foregoing, rather than extending billable hours and extending time at the project site, are the most trustworthy—in capability and integrity.

All of this to say that we find ourselves in a world of senior management (not Ministers) at the helm, and union leaders (not managers) guiding the oars, all of whom have been recruited and groomed for their methods. What they are doing is what they know and what they do best.

It is with this awareness that a Minister might request the department staff to examine alternative delivery opportunities such as privatization, outsourcing, P3, and various hybrid options. When analysis and comparatives are prepared for their Deputy Minister, followed by a recommendation to the Minister, there must be assurances that all components, variable and all applicable fixed expenses, are included. It is questionable, given some of the opportunities side stepped, if this is what occurs.

Returning again to Dr. Peter Drucker, who wrote nearly 40 years ago in his book *The Age of Discontinuity* that what is needed is:

"...a government that can and does govern.
This is not a government that 'does';
it is a government that 'administers';
it is a government that governs."

Peter Drucker
The Father of Modern Management

Government has a role to play, of great importance and relevance. Jeffrey D. Sachs, in his book, 'Common Wealth, Economics for a Crowded Planet' writes, "At every stage of development, and for every sector of development, the public sector and private sector have mutually supportive roles. Public sector capital—roads, clinics, schools, ports, nature reserves, utilities, and much more—are essential if private capital in the form of factories, machinery, and skilled labor are to be productive. Economic development is a complex interplay of market forces and public-sector plans and investments." [14]

The transition from big government to comprehensive government, requires a new kind of political leader who embraces their role in the strategy, design and capital provision, not the building, operating and employing. Government that governs sets the direction, appointing Ministers to steer. Oversight requires clear deliverables, metrics, timelines, and scrutiny by those Ministers and their senior management and professional staff. This is a government that administers, and executes and controls the sails, not delivers the services.

The oversight and scrutiny should be macro at the Minister level, more focused at the Deputy Minister and Director level on actual administering. Consistent with best practices, this would include project 'gating', a common term for reviews, certain next step approval points, checks on risk, and so forth. These are critical in the delegation process to ensure control of the outcomes.

It will take more than a Premier to waive a magic wand, get their Cabinet on side, their caucus to buy in, and the voters to elect them. A Premier who has the capability to fully embrace, communicate, and oversee with 'chairperson' acumen, is a good proposition to govern effectively. The professional executive staff, when given outcomes and expectations, know what to do, and those who do not should be reassigned so that the brightest mindsets and best skilled workers are implementing the government's new order agenda.

If a Premier needs a Cabinet of Ministers with the competencies for a new order of governance, the Ministers need Deputy Ministers with the competencies requisite of a civil service for a new century way of managing things to move forward, not yesteryear. **For comprehensive government to supersede big government, it must be preceded by a philosophical shift by government, followed by ensuring the right people are in the right place.**

A government has the obligation and the responsibility and the right to establish purpose, and then have oversight of the quality and quantity of policies, programs and services to which it is entrusted by its electorate. Citizens, as the electorate or otherwise, have a right to agree or disagree; complain or influence. Respectful of the public, Ministers need to present clear objectives with well-thought through plans, and be prepared for discussions that explain, then listen, and then make the right decisions, and then execute.

Ministries of NB

Economic Environment NB

Business growth and diversification, jobs and opportunities, can be impacted by the role of governments, positively and negatively. Federal and provincial governments have their respective roles, each often overstretching the reach of their capability and influence always has consequences.

A modern government will come to terms with its role as a public sector funder of infrastructure and social programs as the above quoted Jeffrey Sachs statement disentangles, leaving the private sector to business builders.

In New Brunswick, it is clear—at least to most citizens, after decades of financial carnage, that **economic development and political class lending is an oxymoron of which few will argue.** Business development needs to be left in the realm of, well, business people, and investors of the private sort. It is time to put an end to a department of economic *development*, by any name or logo or status.

A Ministry of Economic Environment is not a Department of Business Development, or jobs creators, or any other situation of choosing winners to 'invest' tax payers' monies. For the majority of New Brunswickers the message to governments has been clear and consistent. Get out of funding and running businesses.

As with each Ministry, a strategy contributing to the overall mission and values of the Province is the starting point. Consistent with the format ascribed, the indicators of success would be understandable, measurable, and allow work plans to flow up to achieve it. The umbrella description:

Value: Our Way of Life

Economic Environment NB Key Indicator of Success:
   A provincial economic environment conducive to opportunities in business, jobs, innovation and global competitiveness

Perplexingly, along with the politicians, some citizens due to the acute need and want for jobs particularly in economically depressed regions, are beguiled by government creating jobs. Like Peter Pan seducing the children to his Neverland, the destiny only rarely is as is hoped, and too often what is required to escape is not without its complications.

That is not to say political intercession is never appropriate, particularly under ripe conditions, and chiefly on a coordinating level, as will be explored. In addition, federal government decentralization of offices out and away from Ottawa, not only as the right thing to do in fairness and in lessening cost of doing business, is a good economic contributor. As is provincial decentralization when practicable.

Overseeing the economic environment of a province should not include funding, nor running, businesses. Choosing winners has not been a particularly successful strategy or tack of this province, or any other province. Several loans in recent as well as longer memory, each in sums of tens of millions of dollars, have been poor decisions by our province and for our province, and almost always against the tide of professional opinion.

There may be some merit, in sometimes, to some businesses, providing what is referred to as 'payroll rebates', whereby after the job is filled the provincial portion of the income tax deduction is 'rebated' back to the employer. This also is government employees choosing winners, but at least it is not lost money. At the same time, although the new companies may not be direct competition to other employers, they still accrue unfair compensation benefits.

The true costs of any of these methods of 'job creation' is much more than the income tax rebates, or the grants, or the bad loans. The staffing and administration and other fixed costs have to be factored in. Full disclosure (transparency) would divulge the per capita overhead costs be allocated to each job created. One is left to muse as to whether this even is done internally.

Financing is critical to business start-ups and growth, but when personal investments, outside investors, and financial institutions are not willing to risk certain situations, it is hard to understand how provincial employees would have better insight when tax payer dollars are at risk. Even if some of these are former bankers, theirs is a skill of financial analysis, not running a business or raising one's own money. Besides, timing and market are much more important to success.

Consider what Bill Gross, Idealab CEO and founder of 100+ companies from PetSmart to Duron Energy as well as co-founding PIMCO, the $270Billion Total Return Fund, said at a TED talk 2015-03-19 in Vancouver.

"Timing accounted for 42 percent of the difference between success and failure, while team and execution came in second, followed by the idea itself. The company's business model and availability of funding had the least significance. (That part makes sense. "If you're underfunded at first, but you're gaining traction, especially in today's age, it's very, very easy to get intense funding," [15] Gross said.)

Add to this, "To stimulate the economy, we need to give entrepreneurs the means to create wealth. We need to put in place the best possible conditions to allow the private sector to become more productive: by curtailing public spending, cutting taxes and signing free-trade agreements. Growth and progress depend on more economic freedom," commented former federal Minister Maxime Bernier, National Post 2014-02-26.

New Brunswick needs an Economic Environment oversight to ensure that the environment is ripe for entrepreneurs and investors to create jobs. That is an environment with competitive tax rates, reduced red tape, removal of unnecessary regulatory inhibitors, and continuous development of transportation and other infrastructure.

Our challenge in New Brunswick is to establish the best possible conditions in our province at its jurisdictional level, including ensuring an environment conducive to job creation by the private sector, attractive to investors, and being pro-actively diligent in inter-provincial free trade. The latter is only possible with provinces of like mind.

Like minded, mutually beneficial, two way trade, for example, would see partnering with Alberta as much more compatible than with next door neighbor Quebec with its regulation, union run sectorial oligopolies, and other protectionists measures. Maritimes initiatives have on occasion gotten close until the expanding to include the less similar Newfoundland. Hopefully, none of the difficult routes were intentional to pre-empt free trade by any of the provinces with the others.

With this in mind, concurrent with the Maritimes initiatives, New Brunswick should negotiate with British Columbia, Alberta and Saskatchewan to join the New West Partnership Trade Agreement, , if they would allow us to join. Another suitable action could be New Brunswick partnering with the federal government and Irving Oil to proactively seek out potential contracts overseas so that this reliable and significant corporate enterprise has the business case to expand its refinery capacity for Alberta crude oil when the Energy East pipeline is complete.

What has to be avoided, when a jobs loss threatening situation arises, an unfortunate frequency given the state of our economic morass, is the point where a Cabinet finds itself considering 'support' to maintain existing jobs. The Premier and Cabinet, united, has to pull back. Approaches other than loans, that a non-interventionist (and financially destitute) government might have the capacity to do, must be considered. It cannot be said in too many ways, nor overstated. Provincial tax dollar risks to prop up businesses is proven folly, so no more loans or loan guarantees to business. Period.

> "True wisdom is to know what is best worth knowing,
> and to do what is best worth doing."
>
> Edward Porter Humphrey

There is many a quandary in this province relative to seasonal industries, chronic unemployment in some industries and in certain areas, lack of employees available to other industries and in other areas. **A value-add role for government would be in the interfacing and coordinating of labor activities to match opposite seasonal employers and employees.**

The first area to come to mind is the fisheries and processing industry, of substantial presence in New Brunswick and of some considerable impact to our economy. Workers are needed in the primary and secondary businesses, or the catch will not be brought in, and more worrisome the processing will go elsewhere, as some of it has already. The employment situation is more complex than the far-removed federal politicians and their bureaucrats acknowledge or respect.

The contradiction comes in the circumstance of local workers, unemployed and residing in the same areas of higher employment as fisheries, and agriculture, are not working at those jobs that are vacant. Allowing the focus to turn repeatedly to statistics as to how many weeks a year those plant workers can expect to be paid, and how many are without work a good portion of the year, and whether not any of this is 'fair' or congruous to an employment 'insurance' plan rather than an employment and employer 'welfare' policy, adds little constructive toward a solution.

Rather than the merry-go-round which is everything but merry, the government needs to use its resources, and perhaps its access to federal resources, for a role in coordinating employee and employer supply and demand. Those workers available for seasonal work in the spring/summer/fall weeks relevant to their industry, and not be on Employment Insurance, what jobs can they then transfer themselves to other weeks/months so as to have full year employment?

In the Rocky Mountains of British Columbia and Alberta many workers work the ski hills in the winter and other seasonal outdoor jobs in the summer; or offset the seasonal work of their preference with a hospitality industry job in a restaurant, bar or hotel. As with the farmer who spends the winter logging, these are industrious folks with skillsets transferrable to other jobs.

Not surprisingly, some who quality may also go on EI for the balance of whichever is the off season for them so that they can indulge in skiing (winter) or hiking or kayaking (summer). There may be even more of these workers than our Maritimes fisheries, yet the stigma does not attach itself to those provinces. While the feds should stop their condescending and co-dependency behaviors, according to their tendencies, toward the Maritimes all the while auspiciously looking the other way in their own backyards, this would not be of help to our economy.

If those of the sort who are willing and able to work in our fisheries or agricultural sectors are either encouraged or are to be encouraged to work the balance of the year, and not be reliant on EI, there must be jobs for them during those off-season weeks for which they are qualified. We need to spend more time being creative here, more time spent by the so-called labor and economic experts on the federal and provincial civil service payrolls, and in political positions, working with the private sector employers to make this problem an opportunity.

This is another of many examples of a duty to look inside the box at our attitudes and shortcomings and missteps and habitual activities, and then outside the box to find a solution of more value and of longer lasting duration. An analysis of an area's industries and businesses should be able to ascertain the offsetting seasonal jobs and should a matching of pool of worker availability be established.

Next, using professionals in the relevant job recruiting specialties, consider what additional job skills need to be cross-taught, and which groups of workers would be inclined to apply themselves. Alternative opposite-season jobs could, with some creativity, arise from applicable seasonal employers who may expand to the area; contact center contracts that may leverage offsetting seasonal requirements with employees inclined toward those contract situations. Finally, skills instruction, and where applicable numeracy and literacy upgrade classes, may be required.

There may always be those workers who spend part of their year unemployed. To those of whom this is a lifestyle choice, the free ride should end, as it serves no purpose to society nor is it fair to others, and the rest should bear no guilt. For those with physical, intellectual, or other abilities not sufficient for offsetting season work, the provincial and federal governments need to develop and agree on a nationwide policy of EI and welfare blend to subsidize a dignified lifestyle.

Lastly, job persuading payroll rebates, in situations where justifiable rationale supports the practice, civil servant involvement should be reserved to what their skillsets may include, a coordinating of resources role. Business people, with 'skin in the game' as employers in this province, are far better equipped to make business decisions and hiring decisions. The Province should establish regional boards comprised of entrepreneurs, accountants and lawyers, with small to medium sized business experience and acumen, to review the province's job subsidy and applications. (See the section on Community and Environment NB.) A local regional development officer could chair this Board of five business persons (without personal conflict in the situation) put together on an ad hoc basis from a pool of twelve. Payments for meetings, similar to Regional Service Commission Committee participation in meetings, would be appropriate.

The ad hoc board would assess the financial success of the venture, advise the department as to competitive conflict with employers in the region, and provide an opinion as to the benefit of the applicant to the regions. The payroll 'rebate' should be more to year two and less to year one to better reflect longer term jobs. The employees, union or non-union, must sign on for a portion of their payroll, say 5%, being deducted and paid into a provincial jobs subsidy bank account at the time of each payroll. New property taxes related to the new or expanded venture, accruing to the municipality, ought to have a portion allocated to the costs. All community stakeholders would have 'skin in the game'.

The announcement of further expansion of the nb+ digital lab and open data initiative may be reflective of economic initiatives by government, if the private sector has 'skin in the game'. Hopefully, the outcomes are well defined, the metrics in place, and the best balance of government employees and the private sector partners' work is defined. To this point, if these are established, the open government data part of the collaboration does not seem to include this on GNB website.

The Premier's Office announced this "is the next step in the partnership previously announced between the provincial government and TechImpact, which represents the province's technology sector. The partnership brings together expertise from the public and private sector to act as a catalyst to engage and attract some of the best and brightest in the information communication technology sector to New Brunswick. It is intended to accelerate job growth and investment in the sector while achieving savings for taxpayers."

Hopefully, this is not in the same vein that many of us pushed back, and lost, when the Province helped a group of trainers with the inside track on business and on subsidized deals. If people in business cannot get business, i.e., sales, on their own, they need to sharpen their skills or partner with other business people, not secure government assistance.

There is widespread agreement that older, obsolete and irrelevant, or newer red tape and needless inhibitor or expensive or time consuming, barriers to doing business need to be removed. With representatives, one from each of Finance, Economic Environment and Infrastructure, and one business owners from each of the regions, a committee, armed with recommendations received from numerous sources over the past few years, should be able to make quick progress toward a list of recommendations.

Along with the positive sounding progress of a recent Atlantic Premiers meeting, our province should finally be able to remove red tape, reduce or consolidate regulations while maintaining regulatory safety and security.

Correspondingly, a committee, comprised of representatives from the professional associations in the province, co-moderated by a representative from the existing Departments of Local Government and from Justice, should be charged with a mandate of within six months to recommend changes to the legislation to acts for the associations. Included would be to remove any provisions for professional associations' unilateral control of members thus ensuring all associations do not have barriers to a business starting and growing, as well as to consumer competitive pricing and choice.

Each of this initiatives contributes to transitioning toward a more open economic environment, while reducing costs to government and to business. **More open borders in the Maritimes will provide more opportunities to business, increase the competitiveness in the region, benefiting everyone**. Far from an exhaustive list, there are many more.

An even more significant impact can be made on government capital tied up, funds released for debt pay down, improved service delivery, as well as business opportunities. That is by getting this province out of running businesses. Just a cursory glance reveals many situations where taxpayers would benefit from government getting away from the oars and specializing in the steering, its real reason for being.

There are so many businesses for this province to get out of running. It must get out of operating, for the poor or negative cash flow, for proceeds to pay down the debt, for the quality of service and customer service. There is a time when pragmatism and practicality are the drivers, not ideology.

Highways, ferries, and most other transportation related infrastructure may need to be public sector capital supported, as Jeffrey Sachs wrote above, but do not have to be built and maintained by government. This will be addressed in some depth in the section of Infrastructure New Brunswick.

In the case of some provincial businesses and services, to either citizens or internal to government, it is a matter of the most profitable method to back out of operations, followed by paying down the provincial debt with net proceeds of sale of land, building and equipment. And then, collect by taxes and royalties, leaving private enterprise to run the businesses. Yet, ideology can fog the analysis, debase the decision making, and stay with the status quo; consciously or subconsciously.

The latter was the case, in the opinion of some, of the aforementioned **FACILICORP** decision to maintain the centralized Information Technology (IT) services. When so many corporations outsource IT and security related issues, then governments ought to as a first consideration follow suit. Even when IT security architects are in-house, the biggest corporations in the world, including the IT companies amongst them, hire external security consultants to test and secure.

Previous comments on laundry outsourcing by hospitals describe how, even when outsourcing occurs, mismanagement due to ideology may not have resulted in the most favorable of conditions, economic or quality.

Likewise, with the imminent, at least at the time of writing, outsourcing of food and cleaning services to the same corporation. Again, one contract, and in this situation, two completely unrelated services. Again, our civil service is getting us bound to a less than prudent arrangement.

Not only is it a shame that so many politicians and civil servants refuse to believe that outsourcing can and usually does save money, they miss out on the expertise gained that is not available within the civil service.

There are provinces, states and school boards across the continent that refrain from the costs of self-operation of school bus services. Schools are in the business of education, not busing. And to tie up capital in equipment, and time in supervision and payroll, when quality controls and oversight can still have a school bus program, should not be ignored. It is done elsewhere safely and it should be able to work effectively in New Brunswick as well. If every stone is to be turned over...let us consider what 80% of the nation is doing.

We have to stop going further into debt, continuing to borrow to finance our annual government operation and services. The alternative is those assets which are not directly part of government should be sold, with net proceeds applied to the debt. The federal governing parties did just that as they disposed of Petro Canada, CN Rail, Air Canada, and other assets, each of which has thrived as publicly traded private operations.

From some sources, the **NB LIQUOR CORPORATION** valuation may very well be $1.2billion if it is sold in its entirety. We should be advised as to what the cash value is for other options, and the Province needs to find out and determine the best option other than running a retail system.

Moving forward on what seems to be a feared zone of politicians, an almost untouchable, this government owned and operated alcoholic beverage monopoly cannot and does not need to be secretive. **One option is to sell off NB Liquor completely, and henceforth to only collect HST on sales. A second option is an NB Liquor that is scaled back to central purchaser and product distributor, collecting prescribed royalties and fees, which would continue a larger stream of revenue in addition to the HST.**

The third option does not even suit a free enterprise nation, the status quo, but this is what all governments heretofore have perpetuated. All that this does is maintain a workforce which has an artificial competitive salary and wage model, and other than a desire to perform well, in the absence of competition it has minimal creativity and is void of competition for prices to consumers.

Supposing the government and its ministers and the CEO of NB Liquor are completely forthright with the people of New Brunswick, the choice becomes one of the first two options, and certainly no longer the status quo.

As with every other sale of a business and property, the covenant with New Brunswickers must be to use net proceeds to pay down the provincial debt.

Once either of the first two options are followed-through, then the Province could work with the governments of Prince Edward Island and Nova Scotia for a Maritimes central purchasing and delivery Crown Corporation. This would increase buying power, and by centralizing in the road and transportation hub of Moncton, lower warehousing and distribution costs.

Ontario and its succession of governments are hardly worthy of consideration as to financial best practices, particularly when it comes to Crown corporations, let alone liquor, wine and beer. Alberta, on the other hand, at least on the alcoholic beverages case, now has years of proof of benefits to disposing of the Crown corporation retail model, and the increased customer service, selection, and competitive prices. As with many things, there are experts elsewhere, one does not have to start from scratch, or invent at home, to progress.

Many will recall that the independent NB Liquor Agencies did not always exist. The concept was adopted by the Province at the time the alcoholic beverages monopoly came to the realization that it was losing money on many rural outlets. Politics as it is, people claimed they had a right to an outlet in their community. That they thought so may sound laughable, but they had every right to request access to a government service.

> "A thought which does not result in an action
> is nothing much, and an action
> which does not proceed from a thought
> is nothing at all"
>
> Georges Bernanos (1888-1948)

Of course, it is difficult for anyone of sound mind to believe that beverages are a government service. Government revenues can be generated *and* the Province can get itself out of running the business, both retail and distributorship. The choice to be made is the model for the procurement and distribution aspect. It may be to create two or three or four and sell those concurrent with the sale of the stores, thus avoiding a monopoly. Together, the new owners could have a consortium to work together for volume purchases, thereby taking over the existing relationships with producers. But then each will determine their own pricing from whichever stores choose to buy from them, and likewise with restaurants and bars. The free market will determine the outcomes.

SERVICE NEW BRUNSWICK was a leap forward for all users of licensing and payment of fees and fines in this province when it was launched. SNB was an innovator that was copied and has even made sales of its software. The new premises, whether owned or leased, are a pleasant retail atmosphere, indoors, unlike the left over post WW2 re-purposed buildings where long line-ups would continue on outside in weather of all sorts. The quality of premises and the access that extends to website purchasing, payments and registrations, is very good.

The licenses, registrations, fees and fines collected from the public on behalf of the province is a revenue producer, and one would assume a profit generator. However, when fees are set, there is likely little attention, nor likely has there ever been, to the gross profit generated by each fee for the service rendered. Rather, it was a tax by another name, perhaps on occasion with cost recovery consideration. Pricing and fee increases, from time to time, have been based on a sense of value to the citizen, and to some degree supply and demand in the case of certain hunting and fishing fees and licensing.

The Province's fiscal situation, resulting in considering potential consolidation and closures of offices, is now seeing some SNB offices closed r folded into wider area central offices. People, naturally, do not like less convenience. And, in rural areas it is another sign again of government buildings leaving their community.

It is timely to consider options for the provision of services by SNB. One option would be to privatize the entire enterprise and apply the proceeds to the debt. A second option would be to franchise the retail operations. While a third option would be to outsource to a third party of credible circumstance and with a culture of confidentiality.

A practical choice for SNB, and the easiest transition would be to a network that exists in rural and urban New Brunswick—the Credit Unions and Caisse-Populaires in the province. Not only would this be more popular than turning to the large banks, these secondary financial institutions have a community and folksy reputation, and many have the physical capacity to expand their services. The additional revenue source would also contribute to a more stable institution and perhaps prevent further closures.

The first response by the senior civil service may be that Service NB cannot be privatized due to the confidential information to which it has access. The answer to which is that this information is of no more a private nature than what banking and insurance institutions have and there it is held in confidence and security. Confidentiality agreements, if not presently fully applied can be easily augmented and signed on employment, reviewed annually and signed upon departure of employment.

The logistics would need to be worked out, the fee structure comparison to the existing SNB retail network analysis undertaken, some transitioning of staff to the new retail outlet, etc. This unique arrangement would be beneficial in many aspects. SNB Online would be maintained by Finance NB, and ancillary services and non-retail services could be housed where government regional offices are established.

The economic environment of the Province would be positively affected by this new arrangement. In the partnering with these community based institutions, a collaboration of creativity and expertise could result in future enhancements. As examples, development of onsite terminals for self-serve online application for Drivers License / Medicare Card, vehicle registration, traffic act fines, and other streamlining of services payments.

Infrastructure NB

Real property, with its sea access, rivers, lakes and overland routes, and of all of the inherent rights and interests, is the original infrastructure of New Brunswick. As governments built roads and buildings were constructed, the provincial holdings of real property and real estate grew. Public buildings were and are required for government workers, roads and bridges are necessary for a modern transportation network, and funding by the government is critical to all of this.

While funding the infrastructure for our province is an important part of the equation for accessibility and a progressive economic environment, continuing on an earlier point, it does not by extension include the actual building and operations, or even ownership of anything other than the land itself. As long as the land is retained by province, and responsible stewardship prevails, the people are secure in perpetuity.

Strategically and pragmatically, infrastructure, whether public or private, is a product for the government to leverage economic benefits. Royalties and fees are earned from forests, minerals, and all sorts of land uses. At the same time, environmental regulations are in place to ensure appropriate use and stewardship of our land, waters and air.

As with all of the Ministries, there are a number of indicators of success for Infrastructure that are 'marks' which can be referred to determine if value is being provided. Regarding infrastructure with respect to travel, we could say:

Value: A Safe Place to Live

Infrastructure NB Key Indicator of Success:
   **Professional oversight of our roads and highways and byways and
   trails and waterways for safe travel and economic progress**

Premier Frank McKenna's talents needed a 'product' to enable his
accomplishments. His vision of a safe passage and economy enabling
highway system required a government funded project on provincially
owned lands, with private sector expertise in construction and subsequent
operations. Likewise, it was NB Tel vision, technology and investment,
along with a critical mass of bilingual workers that was his 'product' in
successfully creating and growing a new industry for New Brunswick.

**We need out of the box thinking with regard to all of our
infrastructure, from freeing of funds to apply to our debt, to reducing
costs and increasing revenues.** One threatening situation is Crown lands
from which our forestry companies harvest wood, process and export
product, and the Crown fees thereof, that is at the root of recurring
grievances by American competitors. Of course, the complaints occur
conjoined with a sinking Canadian dollar exchange rate relative to the U.S.
dollar.

The Province, as has been suggested to the government, should add a
supernumerary stumpage fee, tied to a set Canadian/American dollar point
($.95?) so that the monies go to provincial accounts and not to USA duties
and penalties. After all, it is the lower Canadian dollar that obviously
exacerbates the conditions to the point of the American competitors
complaining to their government. The New Brunswick supernumerary
stumpage fees could be reviewed quarterly and should the loonie recover for
the full three months, then for every 1% exchange rate upward reduce the
stumpage fee a corresponding amount. One would expect that goodwill
negotiations with our lumber companies is possible since they want the
business, as we want them to do business and provide good paying jobs.
This fluctuating portion of stumpage fees would end most of the advantages
of the currency exchange while not affecting what already is factored into
the downside of a higher Canadian dollar.

Public roads and bridges may be built by the private sector and operated
by the private sector, but of course the land ownership can be retained by
the Province. **While the operations of the road system may be by private
concerns, the government remains fully responsible and accountable to
its citizens and voters for the safety, as well as the efficiency, of the road
network regardless of the number of operators. This is accomplished
with 'oversight'.**

Already, there are two privatized major highway systems in New Brunswick. One, the infamous MRDC Operations Corporation, from River Glade to Fredericton, the contract of which was to be for a toll highway but subsequent to an issue-winning platform, the toll booths lasted only a short time. Although we may not know the true and full costs to taxpayers, to fully understand what this contract does for road travelers in New Brunswick, it is worth quoting directly from the company's website.

MRDC Operations Corporation is a private contractor responsible for the maintenance, operation and rehabilitation of the 195 km four-lane divided highway (RAD 120) which is located between the cities of Fredericton and Moncton in the province of New Brunswick.

MRDC was developed in 1998 by their shareholders; Miller Paving, Vinci Concessions, Dragados Y Construcciones and Fomento De Construcciones (FCC), as part of a 30 year term Public Private Partnership (PPP) with the province of New Brunswick.

This highway, known as the Route 2 Trans-Canada highway, was designed and constructed by MRDC, and opened to traffic between the periods of 1998 and 2001. Each year, since the opening of the highway, MRDC performs Summer and Winter maintenance services with most of the services completed by the MRDC workforce. The staff, fleet and facilities for providing these services are housed at four depot sites located at strategic locations along the highway.

Routine Summer Maintenance services generally include activities such as; line painting, asphalt repairs, slope repairs, crack sealing, detailed inspections, patrolling, grass/brush cutting, guide rail repairs, hydro-seeding, illumination & sign repairs, and traffic control. During the Winter months, MRDC performs patrolling and snow & ice control operations, such as plowing, 24 hours per day, 7 days per week. Winter operations generally include anti-icing, de-icing and snow removal operations. The website also indicates that its quality is guided by the standards outlined under the ISO9001:2008 Quality System.

What the costs are to taxpayers is not known as details have been held in confidence, i.e., 'secret', since the dismantling of the toll system and toll booths. However, where the transparency of government might fail the test, expectedly the performance of the company outweighs the provincially maintained highway stretches, as most road warriors would attest. As alluded to earlier, as a benefit of a business contract compared to an employee service, provincial engineering staff are more driven by holding a private contract to a higher level standard without as much regard to the providers' morale, or their budgets. That is human nature, and it is an easier role to fill.

The other significant P3 highway contract is with Brun-Way Highways Operations Inc. As it states on its website, it is "responsible for the operation, maintenance and rehabilitation of 275 kilometers of highway from the Quebec Border to west of Fredericton, and between Woodstock and the US border, until 2033." The Brun-Way partners, SNC Lavalin O&IM, "head a team that includes a number of New Brunswick companies that are involved in a range of design, construction, operations and maintenance roles."

When it comes to our provincial portion of the Trans-Canada Highway, the worse of the taxpayer subsidies situation is regarding trucking firms, using our province as a free drive-through to Prince Edward Island, Nova Scotia, Newfoundland, and the USA. Once these trucks transit out of our province, into any of these jurisdictions, they pay bridge, highway and ferry tolls. Of course, they will balk at paying, and warn of dire consequences to our economy, but they can pay here as they do everywhere else.

Wear and tear causing all sorts of highway conditions for the smaller wheel-base vehicles to navigate, and additional maintenance costs are naturally more than that caused by smaller automobiles. Still, provincial recapture of some costs can be attained, and tolls do not have to be the sole solution. As suggested to the government, the existing weigh stations could be used more extensively by increasing both travel fees and weight load fees to recapture what the requisite tolls would have been collecting.

> "The problem with public projects is that the costs of delay don't create existential problems for the public sector, as they can do for private firms. Most of these "external" costs are borne by ordinary citizens."
>
> William Watson, PhD,
> Former chair of Economics Department, McGill University

To continue from the highlighted quote of Professor Watson, regarding the Irving Oil shutdown, the project is being "self-financed" (which does seem unlikely, hardly anything in Canada" being self-financed), it's going to cost $200 million, it will employ 3,000 people and it will be done in 60 days. That last bit is what's truly shocking. Almost nothing in Canada gets done in 60 days."

"The difference between Irving's project and the multi-million bridge, sewer and highway projects we see slouching their way toward completion is, of course, that Irving has considerable skin in the game. And it's not artificial skin grafted onto projects by means of fulfilment contracts that provide for penalties if projects come in late and which may or may not be imposed, at the discretion of a regulator." [16]

'Skin in the game' is influential on operational quality, effectiveness, and customer service. It is evident from the maintenance and ongoing rehabilitation of the two sections of TC Hwy in this province that these are operated by private companies. In contrast, provincial government employees maintained highways and roadways, by admission go longer before repair. And the quality of the overall job usually is not to as good a level of quality overall. Witness the mess of loose asphalt left behind rather than swept up or over to the gravel sides, and left to be spun up by moving tires onto vehicles.

Road construction costs are not just for the actual contract—there are the costs that the taxpayer has to bear as well. So that a highway with several kilometers of asphalt removed ought not to remain with 'grooved' conditions for months while 1000s of vehicles wear out tires and consume more gas—it might not show on the expense line to the province but it is an expense nevertheless to the citizens and other travelers.

It is a certainty that due to geographic location, N.B. highways are a benefit to our province as well as contribute significantly to inter provincial trade. The two largest, best maintained highways in this province are the two managed by the private sector, presumably with oversight by the provincial engineers for quality and value for the taxpayers.

As will be repeated, this is not to point at the provincial workers, rather to the system within which they work and the 'whys and wherefores' of decisions made in that system. **Provincial District Engineers are allocated resources and mandated expectations in a different philosophy than they would experience in private road construction companies.**

In all regions of the province there are road construction and maintenance companies that could bid on road repair, maintenance, and snow removal for a defined geographic area. The recommended area would be coinciding with the Regional Service Commissions which be conducive to competitive and comparative contracts over a number of providers. Additionally it would afford the potential decentralization of the Regional Engineer Offices to the Regional Service Commissions, with continued co-funding.

The first recommendation is to outsource, using the processes for Requests for Proposals to the provincial road builder companies, all of the other highways and roadways in the province. Our provincial engineers and staff costs would be reduced and at the same time those staff with the skills who remain would provide the quality and value of oversight for the Ministry. Responses to RFPs would be premised on the Province providing a well-defined work relationship as well as measurable expectations and clear outcomes. All equipment currently owned or leased by the Province could be negotiated to be purchased or assumed as part of the winning bidders' contracts. Regional maintenance sheds could be leased, or replaced at their expense by the contractors to non-political locations such as the nearest highway side industrial parks.

The second recommendation is that projected toll revenues could be substituted with increased fees at the various Truck Weigh Stations in the province, near the same strategic locations at border crossings and significant interchanges. The infrastructure is in place, and the premise of more wheels and more weight should bear more cost to trucks only makes sense. N.B. trucking companies, operating and paying taxes in N.B. could have partial offset costs with a reduction perhaps as a corporate tax gross up deduction. If the tolls are going to be introduced, then the costs will rise for trucking regardless. The Weigh Station fee approach collects the revenues from the most appropriate sources, avoiding expensive contract renegotiations with the highway P3 partners.

Should revenue from tolls for all vehicles remain a convincing move by the government, the toll booths ought to be erected in proximity to the weigh stations, and the entire combination enterprise go to RFPs for building, maintaining and collecting tolls and weight charges. Land would remain in ownership of the Province, all else to the winning contractors. Full online access by Provincial officials to the software used would allow monitoring and audit of commissions retained on tolls collected by the contractor.

From a financial perspective, it is unfortunate that a government mandate was won by promising and following through on removing fully justified tolls that were no different than the tolls for the Cobiquid Pass, Nova Scotia highway, except lower charges in New Brunswick. To add further expense to the voter-politician fiasco the same contractor for the toll booth buildings was then paid to tear down those new constructions.

Most will recall, that it was a small group of disenchanted people who could easily have used the alternate old TC Hwy route post-toll installation, who began the strong and long demonstration against the tolls. The 'movement' gained momentum with uninformed opinions and untruths-- including the oft mentioned free Hwy 15 Monctonians had to go to Parlee Beach, when in fact it was a highway built to serve PEI traffic and a level of 24/7 commuter traffic to Greater Moncton significantly higher than even that of the TC Highway near Salisbury would ever experience. The mob rule warning of a former Premier was not heeded by the incumbent government.

For economic development purposes, these two recommendations would provide a level of competitiveness for our home-grown trucking companies, off load expenses and debt from the Province to the private sector investors, increase revenues, and increase service.

Another component integral to our highway system is the connector ferries, across fresh waters and across salt waters. As with roads and bridges, ferries are another subsidized transportation system within our infrastructure. There is a cost born by the province to provide the various ferry services, just as there are for roads and bridges, but in some instances the users pay a fee.

A critical mass of ferries in the Fundy is helpful to maintain costs, and one would expect the efficiencies and improved flexibility of a combined workforce, as has been reported. Still, at a contract of $13.8 million annually for the Fundy Isles, as with other government contracts, the details are not available. There are a number of considerations in this service.

First, consider full disclosure as to how much (only the $13.8 Million contract?) subsidy is provided to Coastal Transport for the ferry service to Fundy Island communities. As with all government services, publicly or privately delivered, transparency is expected.

Second, consider allowing permanent residents to buy low cost fare packages (say, 6 one way, 10 one way, 20 one way, etc.,) which they can then submit their receipt to Service NB for a partial refund. Rather than an annual pass which is unlimited and only serves high multiple crossers, this would provide some financial relief to lower income and seniors who only travel to the mainland for medical or occasional other trips, as well as more frequent travelers, but not tourists and other occasional ferry users.

Third, **the Province should not own or lease ferries, or any other equipment, and as a matter of policy should negotiate to sell to the private operators.** This cost to the government will be reflected in any annual subsidy that forms part of the contract. Ferries from Yarmouth are privately owned and operated, as an example.

Municipalities tend to have the same proclivity toward ownership of businesses as the other levels of government. Frequently, the costs borne due to the bias of municipal worker operated businesses are higher, in spite of the evidence that indicates these should be contracted out. Unfortunately on occasion opportunities are missed as well. A large municipality in Atlantic Canada, with a municipal worker transit system, lost an opportunity to add a rail line transit option into its system because it would not consider subsidizing the train if it were privately owned. And because it could not afford to make the purchase outright, it allowed a unique opportunity to slip.

Municipal transit, bus or light rail train or shuttle, does not need to be owned by any municipality. It was not always the case, and is not now in many jurisdictions in North America, the UK, and elsewhere. The provision of public transit is for a variety of reasons, including for those citizens who either must have or desire to use a public transit system, as well as for traffic and environmental concerns. And where there may not be a business model, most particularly for smaller centers such as in New Brunswick, where such systems can be self-sufficient on fares, then subsidies are the norm. Subsidies, however, is not the issue.

As with ferries and the Province, a municipality or metro-region resolves to what extent they are willing to subsidize their transit system. In fact, most have determined this already and reflect this in the fares charged and the routes either kept, replaced, or eliminated. The Province, because there is only one taxpayer, should use its resources, partnering with the municipalities, to establish a process for full contracting out of all transit systems—perhaps to one provider should savings be proven. The net cash proceeds to the municipalities could be applied to their debt, or to other capital projects.

The municipal transit system would need to have an evaluation of buildings and equipment prior to an RFP process and reported on the publicly accessed website. As well, the fares for the period of the contract duration would need to be clearly outlined. The RFP bid submissions would require a component determined by the operator as to the amount of annual subsidy its bid includes. The winning qualified operator would purchase the entire infrastructure and equipment of the existing municipal system, with the net funds to the municipality.

In some other jurisdictions, the bus workers / union have been provided guidance, or pointed to a suggested partner, so that they could, if desired, submit their own bid. This is an option for consideration.

Our Province can reap the opportunities of off-loading capital and operating expenses, applying net proceeds to debt, in addition to establishing higher quality metrics for customer service. And stick to the business of government which is administering not doing on behalf of its services to citizens—its customers.

"The single most important thing
to remember about any enterprise
is that there are no results inside its walls.
The result of a business is its satisfied customer."

Peter Drucker

Community and Environment NB

The Emancipation and Democratization of Rural New Brunswick

The struggles of urban versus rural, English versus French, incorporated areas (cities, towns, villages) versus unincorporated areas (Local Service Districts) are all negative tensions that can be turned into opportunities of positive tension that spur transformation of our province. The occasional outcry and media headline aside, there is far more of which we agree and experience, than we disagree.

A Minister of Community and Environment New Brunswick would focus energies on the overarching and unequalled dual priorities of intra-provincial relations and good governance for the people of this province. Since Local Government forms only part of this important mandate, the change of name to *Community* establishes an important context consistent with our values and reflective of our citizens. The *Environment* is a more far-ranging reference than many consider, encompassing noise and other elements within community, as well as enjoyment, conservation and protection of the environment.

Picking up on the topic of local government governs locally better than provincial government, a broad outcome could be:

Value: Governance and Civility

Community and Environment NB Key Indicator of Success:
Supporting regions and municipalities in providing local government that is accountable and trustworthy in policy, action, and outcomes, and fiscal responsibility

The Local Government reorganization that included The Regional Service Delivery Act legislation and the establishment of Regional Service Commissions has brought a belated post-20th century governance to this Province effective 2013 January. Decades earlier, and long overdue, saw the transcendence of provincially funded services over the county system in Premier Robichaud's reforms and overhaul of outdated and inequitable systems. Now long overdue is the subsequent inequities left from the removal of local decision making in the unincorporated areas of the Province.

When construction waste sites, gravel pits, asphalt plants or other controversial developments within unincorporated areas, too close to houses or schools, without local or regional oversight, are applied to and then recommended by bureaucrats in Fredericton and signed off by a Minister, the people are angry, when eventually they find out. A Ministry of Community and Environment should not have the current centralized power to make decisions, predominantly without the input of those unincorporated LSDs with active Advisory Councils to the Minister as per the legislation.

The Regional Service Commissions, as devised currently but more realistically reduced in number to a group of seven or eight regional Boards reflecting population and geography, overseeing their respective areas, should then be partnered with and mandated to complete the evolution to localization of government. The historical county boundaries have over the years become less relevant as compared to the RSC areas.

The residents of the 200+ unincorporated areas have a right to direct representation, and to participate in local decision making in matters that affect their daily living. As well, with regard to finances, to establish a fairness and sensibility, this also must coincide with appropriate responsibility for payment of services rendered.

All accounts show the costs to be inequitably borne and unjustifiably evenly applied to property owners, and, at a sizeable deficit to the Province. **Depending on the source, the province's unincorporated area total net costs for services over property taxes collected amounts to a $60million to $100million shortfall annually.** The source who is most knowledgeable and reliable pegs it at the higher amount. It seems that many of the LSD residents are complaining about the level of services for which they are not even fully paying.

(Locating details of LSDs on the GNB website is restricted, from an ease of access viewpoint, to rambling legislative files, long on 'legalese' and maddeningly short on understandable descriptions and clarifying situations. As a manifestation of another failure in transparency that also is understandable to people, it is easier, and to the user of more interest and friendly data, in a logically laid out table, to go to https://en.wikipedia.org/wiki/List_of_local_service_districts_in_New_Brunswick.)

Notwithstanding that we are a more affluent people in the 2010s than we were in the 1960s, with a now aging population and out migration of our rural and northern areas a return to a less equitable services model would be contrary to our values. **Of course the larger urban areas will have larger and more hospitals, schools and other services, but the balance must be had in the service level accessibility and quality to all New Brunswickers, fundamentally because we cannot be contrary to our principles.**

Given the frustrations of unincorporated area dwellers, and the overall shortfalls of taxes collected by the Province to pay for services (significantly contributing to the annual deficit in this province), we need to complete the transition to direct representation. The current situation of the Minister of Local Government as, by job description, the 'mayor' of each and every LSD is preposterous from all of a democratic, governance, bureaucratic and pragmatic perspective; and non-value add on the time of the Minister.

"A general legislature which manages the private business of every parish (and in New Brunswick the townships are still traditionally called parishes) in addition to the common business wields a power which no single body ought to have. Local assessments and the application of funds arising from it should be entrusted to local management." So wrote Lord Durham in his report on Canada for the British parliament in 1839. [17]

Regrettably, even in the aftermath of the great reforms of the 1960s, this still is the situation of those residing in LSDs today. Some of these areas are significant in size, population and property tax assessment rivalling the base of large towns, yet receive the same level of inadequate service as those in smaller areas whose taxes do not come close to the actual costs. With a density of population the taxes collected are far in excess of the services.

Nevertheless, there will be areas of the Province that may need subsidies to subsist, and in our Canadian way, most citizens would be empathetic and supportive of the Province maintain some equilibrium for those communities.

In any event, guidelines, not subject to political positions and posturing and government changes, need to be established. **Critical to full disclosure, the property tax assessments should have a line showing the credit back reflective of the subsidy to those property owners.**

For a frame of reference as to how off balance our incorporated and unincorporated areas are with regard to representation and services, it only takes an example to illustrate how 1839 is not much different than 2015. In the South East Regional Service Commission area alone there are several LSDs larger by population and tax base that are *each* larger than the combined five smallest villages. **Moncton 'Parish' is one LSD at 9345 population (up 550 in 3 years) with a 2015 tax base in excess of $734million, is larger than every incorporated area in the Region except the tri-community metro municipalities. Yet, it is without direct representation and for all intents no more than a 'ward of the state' of a removed, and by all regard uninterested, Department and its Minister. Tinkering will not fix this.**

"A computer cannot be fixed at a typewriter
repair shop, just as 21st century problems
cannot be governed by 20th century institutions"

the Citi report

Returning to recent movements on local governance, the report commissioned by one government resulted in the action plan of Jean-Guy Finn in 2008 that had a vision but the steps included provincial government initiated amalgamation, a non-starter for the government of the day as it would have been for many governments. Mr. Finn had hoped that his comprehensive report would not be thrown on the pile of the 25 other reports that since 1971 had studied the situation.

The subsequent Regional Service Commissions inception, after a most extensive consultation process by the succeeding government's Environment and Local Government Minister Bruce Fitch, provided the next major phase.

The final phase will require an able and willing communicator as Minister, providing the Department's resources, and collaborating with the RSCs. **The opportunity is to leverage what critical masses of population we have and economies of scale, while introducing a three year transition period for property taxes to adjust to the cost-recovery level, and subsidies where warranted determined and indicated on the property tax assessments**.

A process will have to be developed for communities and residents on streets to make decisions and come to agreement where they may wish to obtain service upgrades, including 'community hall meetings' and a relevant plebiscite of those registered voters. Where significant increases in population occur, by-elections will be required.

The benefits of the RSC model are many, despite what a minor smattering of members on a couple of RSC Boards are voicing. We are at a juncture where regions can move forward due to the anticipated outgrowth from the greater cooperation within the regions as the RSC model continues to mature, relationships are developing, and best practices are shared.

Next for the provincial government would be pan-provincial and pan-regional compliance to consistent and best practice methodologies, processes and reporting. Successfully accomplishing this, by necessity of expertise and time, calls for full collaboration with the RSC Executive Directors and the elected Chairs to whom they report.

Community restructuring is necessary to motivate, inspire and compel communities to merge—because it is in their best interests. Fear of change and lack of information on property tax allocation regarding budgets for administration, policing, roads, etc., are two major impediments to community restructuring. No one wants higher taxes and everyone wants better service, thus sensitivity and full disclosure of details is a precondition.

Community matters to people. Sensitivity to this is important as it is not simply a matter of a line on a property tax bill or movement of boundaries, it is a matter of people. This is why the conviction of both Premier and Minister is critical, as it was for those who trail-blazed prior significant reforms.

Monday June 22, 2015

If not vested in the success of the communities, the people, and what is best for them, transcending all the ambiguities and entrenched beliefs and habits, collaborating with the RSC Boards and their Executive Director teams, the ugliness similar to forced amalgamation can surface. A lot of energy and political capital may need to be expended, and the person to lead this needs to have the mettle and the belief in the outcomes.

Perceptions are people's realities, so goes the saying. On occasion, between some communities, less than friendly relations, sometimes animosity, on land uses, fees for the other's arena, property lots here and there amalgamated to the incorporated community by a Minister without regard to the unincorporated community, and so forth, cannot be pushed aside. Some families have been in the rural area for generations, others recent arrivals. The case must be made with tangible, rational evidence and facts, but also with appreciation for the emotional attachment to historical community.

It is easy to underestimate the value that came from the introduction of full and direct accountability to the democratically elected officials in each Region by the solid waste commissions, planning commissions, and the like. While each of the predecessor boards were appointed, and typically included some elected local government representatives; and while each of these boards worked in what they considered the best interests, and often altruistically so, of their community; the realities that have come to light since the onset of the RSCs indicate that better budgetary, strategic decisions and operational decisions will now be made with full accountability to the RSCs.

Finally, the modern democratization of rural New Brunswick is on the cusp of proceeding; and while there is much effort and resolve required, it is not an exaggeration to state that within the next three to four years we could see the **Emancipation and Democratization of Rural New Brunswick**.

If a government cannot find itself wanting to move forward, then the only responsible step it can take, at a minimum, is to establish a pan provincial legislated set of basic bylaws to overcome the anarchy that can be, and is, in the unincorporated areas. While this avoids conflict and patience-required community hall meetings and might be the 'right' thing to do for some politicians and bureaucrats, in the face of real progress, it really is the 'weak' thing to do. Completion of Regionalization is the right and proper outcome.

In open consultation and collaboration, now is the time to move forward with a strategic initiative by the government for modernization of local government and governance. The poor county days were put behind us by end of the 1960s, yet too much of the days of 1839 prevail still.

Key to the success of this emancipation will be presentation of a clear 'picture' and path forward, co-led by the RSC and the Minister, resource allocation by the Department, the decentralization of any remaining local services, and a transparent detailed property taxation billing system.

Change rarely is easy. Contrary to the oft repeated 'People don't like change', in fact people do like change. People change all the time—clothing styles, vehicles, houses, and more than ever in history, jobs. What people do not like is *being* changed. That is why non-consultative forced amalgamation is greeted mostly with aversion, and this is why collaboration is vital.

Establishing a clear path forward might be accommodated by beginning with a 'pilot' early adopter Region. The RSC Board's appointed committee can facilitate a macro conversation with their colleague mayors, identifying LSDs and nearby municipalities that are geographically and population centric with each other. Information and data important to this would include the full disclosure of what each community now has and will have post amalgamation. This includes property taxes current as well as projected rates as the $100million deficit for LSD administration is reduced and eliminated. Region by region, not piecemeal, is a method for success.

The TransCanada Highway and other primary roads and bridges should be tendered via an open RFP process, and contracted in regional packets, without the secrecy of contracts past. With many larger private operators maintaining and servicing the major highway systems, oversight is the responsibility of the Department as to quality and service. This is their job, as it should be for government. In addition, the presences of different private operators allows options of replacement by another operator for either a temporary period of time or the duration of a contract of an operator that is not meeting conditions.

Negotiations between the Ministry and the RSCs would determine the timelines of transition of secondary roads from administration by the government, and which would be assumed by road companies contracted by the enlarged municipalities. The regional engineers and a significantly trimmed down staff could report to the Executive Director, or directly to the RSC Board in their region, thus retaining skilled professionals.

Some of the larger sprawling low density population areas may require a continued subsidy for a period of time so as not to overburden the municipality and/or RSC as well as to ensure continued traditional service. Future developers of property in remote areas would be assessed with recovery cost rates, not subsidized as has been historically the case. Whether residential or commercial, the property owner will be able to make their decision based on the quote for providing services.

Providing support and keeping open communications by the Ministry with the RSCs toward a focus on ensuring success of RSCs may involve resolving misunderstanding, conflict and working through creative solutions. The existing process for the petitioning and meeting with the Minister is too lengthy for what could be straightforward, simple services, and it would be obstructive to constructive and timely decisions.

Completing the decentralization of activities such as the animal control officer, and the Regional Service Manager along with their administrative and contracting tasks to the RSC Executive Director office should be straightforward. The apportioned fees would be transferred to the RSC as well but the Province would have less administrative positions to budget.

A **transparent system of Real Property Taxation** and collection is also required and will take some work as well as upgrading of software. It is not sufficient that current tax bills do not provide a better breakdown of the tax allocations for servicing, police, emergency services, roads. Transparency with increased clarity on the 'Real Property and Assessment Tax Notice' will provide taxpayers an annual 'snap shot' of where their taxes are being applied, with a corresponding dollars breakdown.

This full transparency also would have the added element of providing a platform for elected officials and departments to be accountable. As well, better communication regarding real costs and tax apportionment as to where tax dollars are allocated means more informed tax payers, and a more constructive conversation when their assessments change.

Furthermore, additional line items need to be added to tax bills to enable flexibility. These lines could be used for an extra tax for recreational facilities, community bus, or even a lane residents wish to share costs, community or road improvements residents are willing to share in costs beyond the budget allocations, and so forth. (This sort of flexibility has existed in other provinces for decades.) One of the special lines could be used to indicate the aforementioned provincial subsidy in special case areas were the Province has deemed appropriate to justify financial support.

Assessment / Rate / Taxes
Local Government Tax Residential
Provincial Tax Residential
Public Safety and Policing
Fire and Emergency Services
Solid Waste and Recycle
Special 1
Special 2
Equalization subsidy (-)
Cost of Assessment

Irrespective of incorporated or unincorporated, large or small, the major apportionments of tax ought to be fully transparent. This ensures a two-fold benefit of the taxpayer being aware of what is being paid for what services, and the service provider (typically municipal or provincial or RSC) more accountable. This will be of particular assistance in the progression to elimination of all LSDs in the emancipation of the rural communities.

There has been some evolution on property tax disclosure, at least in the unincorporated areas, with the multi-year phasing of police and emergency taxes migrating from one 'box' to another 'box' on the property tax bills, for more appropriate cost identification. And, a slight, very incremental, reduction to 'second' properties that at least show a sign to future fair play.

Given our dire fiscal challenges and the unfairness of the provincial tax on 'second' properties, the Province may not be able to make much movement other than continue with small 'goodwill' incremental amounts, until the annual fiscal situation improves.

Until real change is made to our Province as a last holdout of 'non-resident' taxation, apartment owners and renters will continue to be unhappy, and many second property owners are looking toward a solution to eventually be implemented, but it seems more than likely that somehow the shortfall of eliminating this 'double' property tax (the last of its kind in the country) will need to be offset by other property taxes. Therein lies the real challenge of any government that takes on this widely regarded indefensible tax.

The days of unincorporated areas being amalgamated into a municipality, often with neither happy, with property taxes having to rise to the same level, and water and other services foisted upon the municipality-edge residents, are gone. Yet, most people understand this still to be the way these things must occur. **The incorporated Rural Communities have multiple property tax levels when they are created from an amalgamation of many LSDs since there are different service levels. Municipalities do not have to have a singular rate**.

Some communities, such as the higher density LSDs, may find amalgamation with their municipality neighbor relatively easy with minimal or nil property tax increase. Choices on increased service levels may add to the assessment.

> "Nobody said it'd be easy.
> They just promised it would be worth it."
>
> Dr. Seuss

Over the past five years, the Department staff of Local Government staff have completed a lot of the groundwork for sound decision making that would support the proposed initiatives in this section, if the political will is with change. They were tasked to draft a local governance and planning framework under the auspices of reviewing and modernizing the Municipalities Act and the Community Planning Act and revisiting previous commissions and reports. The department has the accompanying data, investigations of other regions in Canada, and the benefit of input from stakeholders across New Brunswick having reached out for input.

Many viewpoints have been provided to the Department's Legislative Renewal & Legal Affairs Branch. There is justification for some areas of jurisdiction to continue with a compliance to provincial legislation as ours is a population that in total is less than large cities. Areas such as transport and transportation systems, and safety and protection of people and property, and other areas, seem to make sense with a province wide compliance.

Legislation should protect the citizens and taxpayers from local government colloquial definitions of efficiency, a habit that occurs too often and costs tax dollars and energies. It should also ensure protection of community interests, providing flexibility in some areas by those in the local municipality. Many of the challenges of jurisdiction are due to lack of full transparency by municipalities and by the current versions of departments of Environment & Local Government and Transportation & Infrastructure.

No longer tolerated, rather put to an end, should be the current smoke and mirrors of budgets but never actuals by the Province's regional Local Services Managers of the LSDs. Add to this the state of affairs where no budgets exist to be shared by Transportation & Infrastructure to the LSDs. Even that minority of citizens who attend every annual general meeting of their Local Service District are unaware of the unaccountable and non-transparent use of their tax dollars.

The Local Services Managers and the Local District Engineers are conscientious workers for their respective departments. They work up their budgets each year and forward them to their Directors in Fredericton. However, in the absence of 'actuals', it is difficult to ascertain what the actual costs are for each LSD. These are the amounts that the Departments must ascertain and share with the RSCs so that real costs can be analyzed, RFPs developed and contracts signed.

A provincial planning policy in a province of only 750000 people, the same or lesser size of major cities in this country, is only common sense. This is a strategic approach, one in collaboration with the Regions, which a Ministry of Community and Environment could sponsor.

A community plan should cover municipal/incorporated, rural/urban/unincorporated, again more readily accomplished by the fully municipalized province. As with the consistency of profit and loss, budget, business plans, etc., the community plan template should be legislated for mandatory use by all other governing bodies at the local government level. **Compliance and consistency of streamlining increases efficiencies and enables performance and other criteria comparatives**.

Obviously, smaller municipalities would not use all the 'input lines' in the reporting that a larger city may need. At the same time irrespective of size, compliance allows comparisons between various bodies within the province including local governments themselves, ministries, cabinet. Additionally, all of these can be posted on the Community and Environment NB website as well as by the individual governing bodies on their own websites.

Matters of public and provincial interest should include, but not limited to:

~protection of drinking water;
~management of agricultural land including protection of farmers from 'urban creep' forced affected changes;

~preservation of heritage sites and structures with a provincial/federal fund for support;

~flood risk planning, preparation and reduction in rivers and tidal waters areas;

~social housing – provincial policy, not municipal (does a city need/want to administer social housing)

~mining and subsurface activities, related areas such as oil, shale gas, pipelines, etc.

Two issues are apparent, to which 'open minded' attention must be given: Streamlining and Alignment, and, Land Use Governance. These are areas of significance that should take precedence over the growing list of ideas the two recent governments have gathered to either save costs or increase revenues. The positive response by citizens to the current and past governments' consultation for input indicate that an annual promotion of this online, and perhaps biannual town halls, is worth the while. This should extend to a formal annual exercise within all parts of our public sector. Yet, it is a list of unrelated, tactical ideas without strategic connection.

A provincial interest framework is needed that has 'teeth' to it, no matter how difficult it may prove to ensure a respect of all governing bodies, including our 'major' cities. Individuals, corporations, interest groups, the Province, and Local Governments need to be held to a framework that protects our broader interests.

Much of this can be accomplished within the planning of the prescribed Regional model. It also will be useful for comparative purposes provided a common reporting and methodology is adopted (legislated) as described above. Every Ministry, all departments, and all corporations crown or agency or private, need to comply. We cannot have provincial parks, for example, breaching generally accepted environmental practices albeit with 'approval' of the Minister, while private persons and groups are charged with lesser offences—hypocritical and offensive.

Strategically, a best practice approach of a 20 year vision updated every 4 years; a 10 year set of key broad objectives with measurable and annual reports; a 3 year detailed strategic plan fitting within the term of a government. Once the Province has established these three strategic accountabilities, the Regional Service Commissions, local governments, and other bodies, then can work on their own with the broader framework that is in the best interest of our Province.

Effectively allocate these timeframes, establish the outcomes and results we want, and use the most appropriate means to provide services to citizens is a modern world approach. Some outside assistance may be needed. A

Minister and the Deputy Minister need to have mindset and experience and skills to manage consultants as well as civil service.

Despite any pressure otherwise, the Deputy Ministers cannot waste time and money mapping and documenting existing processes. There is no need to measure and document everything the way it is now, as many process improvement consultants assert. If a transformation is to occur then establish what the best practices are and who is doing them, emulate as much as appropriate, apply to the New Brunswick context, and proceed.

> The only time to look back is to learn;
> to dwell longer is to wallow.
>
> *cfs*

Land Use Governance is a contentious issue and potentially an ongoing controversial topic. A Land Use Act should be developed within the aforementioned principles and parameters, beginning with provincial properties and crown lands, and then regional and local governments. There will be disputes, and when occurring these must be transparently dealt with and openly documented on the government website.

Dispute resolutions can be adopted from the voting process currently in use by Regional Service Commissions—the 2/3 - 2/3 formula. For regional/local disputes, a panel of representatives, one appointed by each of the RSCs, could adjudicate a dispute, presided by a senior official with the relative expertise from the Community and Environment NB department.

Statements of policy should be broad statements only with the exception of those areas by law or environmental practice need to be detailed. Statements should be supportive of sustainable development, with 'sustainable' defined to include economic, environment, public benefit, and other criteria. Climate Risk ought to be included in policies and statements with a pre-empt of politicizing this by not using terms such a 'global warming' or 'climate change' or whatever may be the next special interest group moniker.

In all of this, it must be recognized that the municipalization undertakings throughout the province will create larger municipalities than now exist. Thus, with democracy coming to rural New Brunswick, the many very small municipalities will also become larger, with a critical mass to better leverage economies of scale and quality of services.

Existing cities will also enlarge in population and geographic coverage. However, the last area of significant trepidation by those who believe that the previous era of amalgamation should have included the tri communities of Greater Moncton, may have been eclipsed by the passage of time and the benefits accruing by the development of RSCs. Dieppe, as the de facto capital of Acadie, may very likely someday meet the borders of Sackville and those of the expanded Shediac. Riverview should be legislated to city status as it sprawls over more of Albert County. Moncton also will be enlarged, significantly with the appreciable populations of adjoining LSDs joining the city. A day may come when Moncton and Riverview decide to join.

These three communities, along with Saint John and Fredericton, are destined to remain our largest population areas, arguably with the three continuing to outpace the rest of the Province. In all regions, the RSC presence will continue to evolve to evermore regional benefits. If there are RSC Boards struggling for identity or purpose or to be more than a landfill board, then the Ministry has an obligation to become involved with its fellow politicians, as well as provide professional assistance to facilitate them through their unique challenges.

A Minister of Community and Environment would meet at a minimum semi-annually with a Council of the RSC Chairs (themselves the elected mayors of their own municipality) for issues of common regional and provincial concern. The Deputy Minister should likewise meet semiannually with a Committee of the RSC Executive Directors.

Much could be gained by gathering municipal and RSC treasurers/financial officers together, municipal and RSC planning commission managers together, municipal engineers together, and so forth, along with their provincial counterparts, to design and submit to the Minister of Community and Environment, the planning and financial and business plans as well as the other methods and reports mentioned previously.

Contrary to some, and in contrast to those in public work with beliefs tied to their own self-preservation, the foregoing actions would not create another layer of bureaucracy or more costs. **Consolidation of regional road maintenance contracts and other decentralized responsibilities; sharing of resources for large projects such as parks and arenas, commissions of police, fire, water and sewer; and the replacement by the full RSC model of the associations of cities and municipalities, would result in more direct responsibility and control of expenses.**

Natural Resources NB

The Ministry of Natural Resources is more than our oversight of the inanimate, as natural resources include also the animate. Forestry, Mining,

Oil and Gas, Agriculture, Aquaculture and Fisheries—all are resources of our land and waters. The relationship of industrial activity, food and fish harvesting, and safety of water and of land use, is one to which we pay more attention than in decades past.

Stewardship of our resources is more than those issues related to environment and conservation. Good 'stewardship' also is concerned with long term viability, such as harvesting and replanting of our forests, or fish farming that is respectful of natural wildlife. Exploiting our minerals and gas and oil in environmentally safe methods and economically beneficial payback also is good stewardship. And, recreational use, including non-damaging activity.

We need all of our resources providing the benefits our people can derive from them, and where evidence exists to support safe *and* economical use, the Minister must be responsible to facilitate private investments, and create revenue streams to the Province. To not reap the economic benefits of our resources, pay our bills and maintain our services, is not responsible.

Pipelines, irrespective of the proven, statistic based evidence levels of efficiency and safety over rail or truck, always will be opposed by some. Fracking for natural gas, the clean fuel for heating and power in business and household, no matter the reliable safety records of the modern drilling methodologies, will be opposed by some. Yet all those opposed join others who are not in favor of further cuts in our already dwindling quality and quantity of health care and social services.

> "We have to decide if we're going to sit around for someone else to look after us or are we going to take responsibility for looking after our own future. We can't refuse to exploit our resources and continue to pay our doctors, social workers and civil servants and maintain our robust social safety net. As long as people believe they can have it all, they will not face the hard choices that need to be made."

Former Premier of New Brunswick
Francis Joseph "Frank" McKenna, PC,OC,ONB,QC *

Continuing in the same interview: "Try to build a nuclear plant in Alberta, McKenna said, and you'd probably have enormous protests. By contrast, most Albertans are comfortable with fracking because it's been done there for a long time. "Familiarity is like sunlight – it illuminates everything in its presence. We need more illumination in the current shale gas debate in New Brunswick and Nova Scotia. More light, and less heat." [18]

We have other energy resources as well, including sunlight, wind and tidal action. We rightly are proceeding cautiously with these, as we cannot afford to be on the 'bleeding edge' or even the 'leading edge'. These require immense upfront capital investment, even with the costs lowering thanks to some other countries and provinces 'investments', and need huge storage, because none of them are 24/7 reliable due to the tendencies of nature.

Larger and wealthier jurisdictions have spent monies beyond our capability on subsidizing and developing the 'renewable' energies. And now Germany and other 'leading green' countries are backing off their fast move to non-fossil fuels because these are too expensive and less reliable. Oil & Gas producing countries have less reason to move away from O&G because it is plentiful and makes economic sense. If the European countries, and others, had the same access as the oil and gas producing countries they would be using O&G as much as we. That is the reality of the world, and of global agreements.

Natural gas as a clean burning fossil fuel is an area which we must move forward, environmentally aware of what are known to be safe extraction processes. Likewise, the Energy East Pipeline is good economically during the construction phase and then afterward for domestic supply, security and economic benefits. Add in the very important export potential to Europe for economic benefit and for our role in European access to safe, secure energy that removes reliance on thug nations, and Energy East is compelling.

As with most things in life, we need to strike a balance. Or nothing moves forward and everything will continue to weigh down our ship. **The stalemate that defines our status quo is not okay**. We cannot have it all, as former Premier McKenna says, and we are facing the hard choices now.

Living with the realities of the broader definition of stewardship, decisions and action consistent with our values could be based on:

Value: Governance and Civility

Natural Resources NB Key Indicator of Success:
   Pursuing optimization of our resources while safe-guarding our environment, providing economic benefits to New Brunswick, with social respect

The Ministry does require a department providing modern oversight and transparency of exploration, extraction, refining and transporting fossil fuels and potash and minerals. Also, the Minister needs expertise of advice in the sectors of agriculture, aquaculture, forestry and other areas of responsibility.

Highways, byways and bridges may be built by road building companies, but the land on which they reside is owned by the Province, as are the rights to all that is beneath the surface. The lands may be harvested for wood, or mined for precious metals and potash, or drilled for oil and gas, but the ownership for the most part remains with the Province. This is a big responsibility and an area of stewardship—economically, recreationally, and environmentally—in the best interests of New Brunswickers.

Health and Wellness NB

People should be empowered to manage their health, make decisions with the guidance of their family doctor and other medical professionals, take preventative measures for themselves and their loved ones, and count on the availability of facilities with capability and capacity.

Along with schools, the hospitals and related facilities are representative of the largest institutions in our daily lives that can affect us, positively or negatively. Health and education are major areas that should be atmospheres of empowerment to the end users. This is difficult when both are landlocked in old systems, methods and hierarchal inadequacies, regardless of the capability of the professionals, occasional renovation, new building or equipment.

As 'wards of the Medicare system' citizens cannot be empowered as they are left stranded with few choices or options. The costs are spiraling, if not out of control, reined in a bit here and there, and at an impact that is negative, failing and falling short on the quality and timeliness of service.

Medicare as the misplaced 'value' of Canada, as covered in Chapter 2, is a major hazard to transforming our failing system. This could be the singular challenge, if allowed to leave us without suitable motivation to change the course that within not too many years fills our ship with water until we do sink.

Even should a 'friendly' government in Ottawa open the taps a bit more, or collaborates in solutions for our aging demographic pressures on healthcare and budgets, we cannot use this as an excuse to delay fixing the problems. More proactive emphasis on prevention rather than reactive prescription and surgery, is known to be less expensive. Yet we have a culture of scarcity thinking and old ways that was here before the budgetary challenges. We react to 'must-do' and fail to proactively prevent.

We must be more open to what is best for us—the healthcare outcomes and expectations, not the programs. The right mix of deliveries, which is not bound to only government employees in

government owned buildings as the sole provider, deliverer, and decision maker of our lives and our health.

If the United States is the global holdout of the provision of universal healthcare, Canada is the holdout of integrated public and private sector health delivery, amongst the wealthier nation democracies. Where there is no competition, mediocrity sets in its place. Communism proved this, and state provided health care monopolies are proving this.

Some still wonder why at one time we could "afford" rural hospitals and ancillary health service locations. As with small schools with low paid teachers laid off each summer, hospitals of those years were not what they are now. Technology and medical care is of a level not even in dreams in the 1960s. Likewise so too are the salaries and wages, benefits and pensions.

We continue to be awash with rising expenses while our expectations of a modern health system expand, as we sometimes nostalgically look in our wake at the healthcare of decades past. As the earlier point regarding financial governance highlighted, particularly cost accounting, every department within health authorities and hospitals has to have full costing and accounting.

An agreed raison d'être and focus for the Ministry of Health And Wellness would provide a starting point for dialogue leading to decisions and actions regarding what we want and what we are willing to pay. A suggestion:

Value: Dignity and Well Being

Health and Wellness NB Key Indicator of Success:
Person and family centered, proactive on quality of life in wellness, prevention, and healthcare from cradle to grave.

The 2015 November announcement that losses related to hospital cafeterias will be reduced by closing many smaller cafeterias and scaling back on others was responded to by everything from surprise at the losses, to surprise and dismay for the closures, to lamentations by the unions. A health authority should be in the business of provision of health services, not operating restaurants or retail outlets. Revenues, not expenses, can be derived from leasing spaces to qualified responders to public RFPs.

The qualifier is 'public' RFPs. The rumors of **an outsourcing contract being awarded to a private contractor for both the cafeteria and the cleaning services should be of serious concern to taxpayers. It was not transparent**, therefore not all qualified applicants, including potential provincial companies, could bid. The contract bidding process should not be restricted to Authority wide, but by hospital, although bids could include multiple or all hospitals, for the best competitive pricing comparisons. The cafeteria and cleaning services should be separate contracts, although some companies may choose to bid on both for a discount due to volume of work.

Most troubling once again, is the habit of this province's persistent tendency to 'putting all of its eggs in one basket'. Contracts are needed of reasonable duration to attract the private sector, but not so long as to create problems of quality, or replacement should termination be necessary. **Oversight policies and processes need to be in place, civil servants with those skills sets need to be assigned, quality and quantity metrics well defined, and contracts inclusive of performance controls with penalties as well as potential termination where warranted**. It is the latter circumstances that dictate having contractors at other hospitals so as to provide options for a potential assumption of the terminated contract; that otherwise an exclusive Authority wide contract would not.

> "The goal of the delivery of primary health services,
> should result in making it easier for New Brunswickers
> to receive the health services they need
> at the right time, in the right place,
> and by the right provider
> to achieve the best possible outcomes"
>
> New Brunswick Health System Report Card 2014
> New Brunswick Health Council

Parking at hospitals is difficult, and expensive. While not as vexing as media reports on inner city hospitals in Canada's major metropolitan areas, business people likely would handle differently than civil service workers. Where land is owned, either historically or by acquisition, by the Province (not the Health Authority, see Infrastructure) private business could be contracted to operate the parking commission.

Without the capital cost, the RFP would be for the percentage share of profit the contractor is willing to operate with its own staffing, electrical and heating, snow removal and maintenance costs, based on a pre-established parking fee. Unlike the potential profit centers of retail stores, cafes, and cafeterias, parking for hospital patrons should be at cost recovery. Employee parking can be controlled by a number of creative means.

While we set up accounting systems that can measure and track, and we get costs under control, decreased or eliminated, we can simultaneously, with the health experts redefine and look to transforming our health care, from birth to early childhood to childhood to adulthood to senior ages.

The decade old splitting of health and social development has unnaturally divided the transitions of peoples' lives and the necessary interconnectedness of health and wellness services. The transitions of life needs connectivity.

The Executive Director of York Foundation in Fredericton, Ken McGeorge wisely states, "...I would redefine what we call 'hospitals,' leaving small communities with geriatric facilities with enhanced community health centres attached; the long term care and community health centre staff would be integrated into a coherent health-care team." Continuing he adds, "Properly done, health-care services in rural areas can be improved while removing what the public refer to as emergency departments and hospitals." ≈

Mr McGeorge would be in agreement that appropriate oversight, management of services, and deployment of technology is not probable in the circumstances we have today in our healthcare system. We have competent medical and support staff trying to work in a system that is overly hierarchical, disjointed, and institutionalized.

As with other Ministries, there is a need for streamlining and alignment, and that will take transformation and realignment. **If we are to reduce the number of full service hospitals, for decreased costs and increased quality of services, the level and quality of health services to smaller centers need to be addressed.** There are many questions, by patients, by medical professionals and by our politicians.

"The constant negativism that has engulfed health care is creating an environment in which mediocrity is too often accepted, excuses are too often accepted and professional pride and pride of performance is compromised."

Ken McGeorge, Executive Director, York Foundation [19]

What in other jurisdictions, where small populations at a distance away from urban centers, is done to provide reasonably comparable health care services? How do other universally-provided health coverage countries integrate public and private clinics and hospitals into their respective delivery models? Real political will for expense containment will be shown by a better mix of public and private delivery so that we can benefit from the expertise, customer service, and expense control of private clinics. One step could be to accept the ambulance workers recommendation to introduce advanced care paramedics. Starting with the remote areas would replace some service level changes.

How do we address situations to prevent a future occurrence of a well operated specialized equipment establishment is put out of business by a self-centered publicly paid medical professional team? How is it possible that the CEO of a Health Authority, in a small province as this, was not aware of all public and private significant medical equipment installations?

What are other provinces doing in the areas of health and wellness from which we can learn, copy, modify, or outsource to them? This could include the elusive electronic medical record system, annual healthcare use records for patients to audit; and private operating rooms of dental surgeons.

What are private hospitals of the approximate size of ours, profit and not-for-profit, functioning as to quality and quantity metrics, staffing, and costs? We can check Boston and Hartford, or the 'mixed' public/private health services of France, Germany, Sweden and Australia. And, the small cities of Maine and Vermont, as well as the budgets of Canadian small cities like Moosejaw, Prince George, and Brandon.

Ratings of hospitals in a variety of performance indices, should be easily accessed on the government website. This provides instant and cumulative feedback for those responsible for oversight of our healthcare system.

In the **UK**, particularly England, the National Health Service Trusts (hospitals) **have extensive pages on their websites for various procedures, and qualitative & quantitative customer service style ratings**. And, some private facilities also have operation procedures.

For example, if one has an interest in keyhole prostate surgery, this website provides hospital by hospital comparisons.
http://www.nhs.uk/Service-Search/Keyhole-prostate-surgery-(TURP)/London/Results/375/-0.085/51.511/1377/13136?distance=25
This is just one example. Go to the webpage, and scroll down—check the columns across and the comparisons vertically.

New Brunswick could apply some of the UK (and northern Europe) model under a 'pilot' financially supported by Health Canada for real change. On our own, the resources are scarce, but that does not prevent us from being creative.

Potentially a solution may be similar to how American hero John Glenn, the first US astronaut to orbit the earth, was able to go back in space nearly four decades later. Toward the end of a 25 year career as a US Senator, as the story is sometimes told, Glenn wanted to return to space. He was in great shape, had experience, but at 77 years of age NASA declined him. Becoming aware of the value of weightlessness on the testing of the elderly in space, and the comparison of an ideal person 36 years apart in space, he offered himself as a human guinea pig for geriatric studies. Having aligned his values with NASA's and a common objective, the still Senator Glenn went up in the Space Shuttle as the oldest person in space.

Our solution, if we do our preparation well enough, could be put the data and facts together, engage some national experts on the topic, **and propose to Ottawa the Province of New Brunswick as a pilot for transforming the approach and methodologies of seniors social and health systems in our country**. With a population the size of a mid-size city, a bilingual province with First Nations peoples, we are a microcosm of the nation. Even the distribution of hospitals and nursing homes in urban and rural settings is a to some degree a model of Canada, and with a geographic region that is small as compared to all the provinces west of us, it is a good test ground.

This is a legitimate opportunity to partner with Ottawa and Health Canada, with a proposal of transformative impact to us, and of timely importance for planning and action by the other provinces. This could be initiated by our Premier appointing a trio of Health Minister and two appointees of sufficient knowledge from each of the two major party persuasions, to first develop a conceptual framework, then arrange for an early 2016 meeting with the federal Health Minister for initial conceptual discussions.

For this to have any merit, both inside the box and outside the box thinking is necessary. **The focus has to be on a new framework for seniors healthcare, and concurrent with this a new framework for all of healthcare**. This will take time to plan, so meanwhile other initiatives cannot be held in abeyance.

Alberta, back in the 1970s, was mailing to all families an annual statement of usage of their healthcare system access, including doctor and clinic appointments, and hospital visits, stays and procedures. In New Brunswick we are still talking about it, likely because we want to create our own. Why do we not see what other provinces are doing, including Alberta, with their 2000s automated version, and contract them to provide this service to us?

Another suggestion passed along to government was the example of the nearly ubiquitous occurrence in the USA of pixel billboards along busy roadways that advertise hospital ER wait times for adults and children. For example, alongside of Highway 192 in Florida there are two different hospitals with live time billboards showing actual, up to the minute wait times. Naturally, this is due to competition, and people do realize that ER triage may complicate this, but this is no different than elsewhere.

If not pixel billboards in N.B, at least report on similar metrics and get into the view of the public. Use websites, tv monitors and billboards inside or outside each hospital indicating the local statistics as well as the half dozen other major hospitals. Provide full disclosure on the government and related hospital websites of 'certifications of hospitals' etc. for full transparency.

Transparency and Openness as an indicator of success within the value of Governance and Civility is an important aspect voiced frequently by many people in this Province. A government cannot be open and transparent to the public about the best way to address the fiscal and accessibility deficiencies (an indicator of Dignity and Well-Being) in the health and wellness of New Brunswickers unless it knows it has considered models elsewhere.

There are not-for-profit and for profit hospitals that are models of price and quality transparency. In California, the Hoag Orthopedic Institute is known for its posting of quality data on its website and its partnering with not-for-profit hospitals. This data even includes patient pain level pre- and post-surgery, return to recreation and sports, their use of anesthesia, quality improvement projects, and so forth. Other than the promotion on its website and its annual quality report, it never advertises.

Imagine our hospitals disclosing clinical outcomes such as readmission rates, surgical site infections, and other complications. Hoag does. And, it shows that transparency "can be done, not tomorrow or by the end of the decade, but today, if only physician leaders had the courage to put all of their data up on the web. [20]

High usage wait times, and other data is informative to the public, the oft overlooked reality of the customers who pay for these services with their taxes. These statistics could be posted simultaneously on the central website for each hospital board, with the combined listing of all hospitals enabling people can to make choices and decisions. Openness, transparency, and empowering.

Purchasing highly expensive equipment, at a million plus dollars or more, and then buying a second due to 'demand' for a hospital that operates these in a 0700-1600h schedule, is irresponsible. One machine running two shifts a day, and then three shifts a day, would be acceptable to people who knew the savings would be focused on other needed equipment or medical staff.

A recent study of hospital gown use in Canada revealed that a significant portion of patients should not be required to wear the gowns. It cites effect on dignity, the humbling place of patients in the healthcare hierarchy, and other side effects that are avoidable. **If over half of patients did not wear the gowns, that alone would save on laundry costs.**

More openness and responsibility can be shown by health care staff with Province wide mandatory 'standard issue' large name tags easily read by children and seniors. **Healthcare workers should be identifiable to patients and loved ones, by name and by role, and for a more personal atmosphere as well as accountability.**

Social services for seniors is in need of a complete overhaul. Seniors assessments and board decisions take six weeks or more due to backlog and lack of placement locations, except for emergency situations. For many, the wait is months. By re-joining Health and Wellness, streamlining should be more easily established and coordinating of these vulnerable patients and their families in a system that is more customer oriented.

Efficacy in hygiene and cleaning of premises is another area that would benefit from benchmarking metrics and transparency of the data by reporting. The pubmed.gov site in the US publishes research and reports on topics including audit tools for efficacy of cleaning, referencing amongst others studies in the US and UK.

Do our health authorities use standards that are best practice, and are corresponding metrics in the contracts apparently under consideration by the Minister? Such things are not transparent to citizens, the taxpayers who are the customers and the patients. New Brunswick hospitals are subject to accreditation. There is not a reason why there is not a policy and system in place that identifies standards, deviations, corrections, and by location, on its website.

It seems we are at the juncture where a 21st Century modern society ought to have its citizens with adequate medical coverage including health, pharma and even dental. The challenge will be the most economical, and the most effective and efficient way to facilitate this, not the most expedient political nor 20th century way.

We cannot have another social program of the same mold as the other current social programs that have us in desperate financial deficit and debt problems. That would be more insanity on top of our cumulative insanity on programs that are now not sustainable even in their shortfall of delivery and excellence.

Employees should bear the significant part of any pan-provincial plan, if it is to be legislated; for example 60%, with the employer paying 40%. This would ensure employees and taxpayers are fully cognizant of value for pay, eventual increases and proposed enhancements. (It also means that minimum wage increases beyond the incremental steps in place now would need very serious deliberations prior to any political or ideological leap; the medical/pharma insurance is an increase to the wage earner as it saves them the otherwise higher out of pocket costs.)

Concurrent with any new health/pharma or even dental plans (as all of these will be introduced eventually) should be a separation of the costs from taxes so that full transparency allows citizens to monitor what they are paying. Private sector suppliers would be mandated to prove changes to the senior bureaucrats who in turn have to justify to their political leaders who would now be tangibly accountable to the taxpayer.

While it may be too late to go to an Ontario or Alberta 'premium' separate from taxes for our basic healthcare, there is every reason why our current healthcare system should have full cost allocated for individual adult and child, rather than buried in income taxes. **The great giant bucket of taxes collected and doled out to big buckets of departments is way past its best before date and into spoiled and beyond continued keeping territory.** The 'phantom-premium', while not collected directly or separately, would allow taxpayers full disclosure as to cost of the system. Any increased tax dollars to the healthcare system would see this phantom-premium increase thus providing full transparency and holding healthcare executives and the government accountable.

A Ministry of Health and Wellness would be attentive to the holistic outcomes of the people of New Brunswick. To an insightful politician, concern is not with 'their' Department, as the Department is only one of many bodies accountable to the Ministry. Again, it is not 'their' department as that is the responsibility of the Deputy Minister. **Reporting directly to the Minister would be a CEO of a single Board of hospitals providing outcomes based care. This would co-exist with private clinics, medical facilities and medical technology service providers operating under the oversight of the Deputy Minister.**

A strategy with an execution plan that streamlines health care and aligns newborn to senior health and wellness services, with performance metrics, cost savings more than just reactive 'cutting' and bypassing preventative care, and a path to continuous improvement might, communicated in a manner befitting a major shift, be palatable and even welcomed by people.

Social Support and Services NB

The Ministry of Social Support and Services calls for a person of wide-ranging capacity and time for others as well as compassion to be its leader and political advocate. This is a Minister that should be 'out there' visiting the streets of the homeless and impoverished, the apartments and food kitchens of those on income support, the group facilities supporting the ability challenged, and the nursing homes.

Continuing from the previous section, there is a growing consensus that the care of seniors and the elderly should be part of the health care system to prevent a senior citizen being abruptly 'assumed' by the Social Services system. By retaining citizens in the health care system from cradle to grave, evaluations should be streamlined with better response time metrics, silos of bureaucracy would be minimized, and patients and their families will be able to better manage their lives.

As it is, assessment timelines of seniors are far too long, and regardless of which department is responsible, this situation has to be addressed in months rather than long term studies. We know that we have resource problems, primarily financial, but this is another problem where dealing with people's situations properly would save money. But, the proper methods are not within budget, and the reactive methods used have no choice but to activate and that is over budget and more expensive.

In the absence of the major decisions to be made in this Ministry, and its coordination role on behalf of people with other Ministries, consider:

Value: Dignity and Well Being

Social and Support Services NB Key Indicator of Success:
 Assisting people in sustaining their dignity and well-being through timely and appropriate access to lifelong social support systems

The social workers, like many other civil servants, are caught within a system and do what they can when and where they can for the people they see every day. No amount of empathy will move that elderly person to a placement that does not exist, help that single Mom with transportation to get her high school equivalency and then to a job every day and off social assistance, or deal with the myriad of support systems for children in need.

Only paradigm shifts in how we take care of people will provide solutions. If the senior civil servants on these tasks, and their political masters, are not up to it, then the first paradigm shift may be for a Minister to get Cabinet on side, and make the changes necessary including possible contracting of some functions. The actual social workers would be retained to do the people work in the homes and care centers.

The mandate of providing people lifelong social support systems as and when needed, from new born to senior citizen is a big task. The solutions are more complex than simply more funding is required. What is the most optimum back and forth 'hand-off' and coordination between Ministries of Education and Health and Social Support? The strategic decision is overdue, the strategy to execute and the social support coordination role are needed now for real people in real situations in this real world.

Education and Development NB

Politicians, like parents, business owners, commentators, and just about everyone else, have an opinion as to how to 'run the schools' and what teachers ought to do, or not do. What each of these does know is what they want from the graduates of the school system. Those expected outcomes should not be dismissed even if the suggested prescriptions are overlooked.

In any event, our educators, teachers and the superintendent teams should be student centric only. Theirs is not the buildings, or the grounds keeping and snow removal, or the transportation systems for the students. These are areas that should be the responsibility of the Ministry of Infrastructure and its engineers and department staff.

As with its counterpart at Health and Wellness NB, the Ministry of Education and Development should be streamlined and aligned to ensure the development of our young people from early childhood development to graduation from high school, and a preparatory foundation for community college or university or career development.

Good governance in education would equate to establishing the outcomes expected, some broad parameters, a general philosophy consistent with our values, principles such as inclusion, or second language immersion, physical and arts development), and funding. There is much to view on the Education portals of the government website, and it is informative as well as indicative of the knowledge of our educators. More is needed in the realm of tangible measures and comparative data within our Province and to other areas.

The Education & Development Minister, along with the Deputy Minister, as the Chief Education Officer for the Province and the senior staff, would determine the measurable achievements, appropriate benchmarks (international, national, regional) and the broad expectations for those outcomes.

The Ministry would then set out a mandate for the Deputy and the two School District COOs, all three of whom report directly to the Minister, to use their collective education expertise, the pedagogical experts and trained professionals, to recommend the plan of action for outcome achievements province wide, for 10 years, 3 years, and current year.

The Government has the right—indeed, the obligation—on behalf of the voters and taxpayers to set expectations for each Ministry, and Education is not an exception. However, governments, even in the rare situation where a teacher may be in Cabinet, have a track record of lackluster, sometimes regressing outcomes, and lack the wherewithal to make the best decisions to improve the situation of our students.

The recent submission to government '10-Year Education Plan' is a wide-ranging discussion paper, following consultation across the Province, by two co-chairs who provide a balance of qualifications and experience. We will have to hope that the government's chosen way forward is one of proven best-practices that create increasingly better outcomes in our student population.

It is far from a boasting point to have more students graduating 'on time' than any other province, when our subject outcomes are at the bottom of the pack. We have experienced that having the most educated teachers in the country does not automatically equate to "the best" as one Premier once said. When hours of instruction are 20+% less for the younger students in New Brunswick than the national average, maybe it is time for our early grade students to have more time in the classroom, not less, than elsewhere.

Vision statements for our education system have been postulated, but they are rambling, include many statements and unclear goals rather than something concise followed by goals of quality and quantity. A format that would be understandable, measurable, and allow work plans to flow up to achieve it, might be:

Value: Dignity and Well Being

Education Key Indicator of Success:
Students with the knowledge and skills necessary to have fulfilling lives

Followed by at each of specific grade levels, a student outcome defined with measurable knowledge and skill levels. The key bench marks of capability should be summarized in the broad expectations so that each parent and their child, each teacher and their student, each principal and their teachers, each school district and its region, can work together, transparently for the best education levels we can facilitate our children to attain.

	Grade	12	9	6	3	K
Literacy Reading						
Literacy Comprehension						
Literacy Writing						
Numeracy Arithmetic						
Numeracy Application						

While these may be the primary competencies to which we focus the most attention, there are the additional subject areas such as the sciences, history and geography, and so forth, which would need established levels to be attained by trimester and individual grade. National and International testing, or equivalents, should be administered to all students, not just a sampling, and teaching with a focus on those test outcomes.

We should expect that at graduation from Grade 12 a student is able to "___" and so be enabled as a "student with the knowledge and skills necessary to have fulfilling life." And, at the completion of Grade nine they are able to "___" and therefore be on their way to complete the next three grades; and at the end of Grade 6 able to "___" and be well prepared to go on to the next three grades, and so forth.

This is a 'strategic' approach. Along with complementary sets of goals and premises it should be understandable and straightforward for the politicians, department, teachers, parents and students. The pedagogical experts, in the department and districts need to more effectively consult with their counterpart experts who are with the students every day, the teachers, as well as the employers and post-secondary institutions to finalize the high level metrics. Then, the policy makers need to collaborate with the teachers to set the course as to how it will happen.

To achieve these, and be able to 'compare apples to oranges', we also need similar school resources, course timelines, exams, for each of the subjects and for all the schools, with English and French aligned as closely as practicable and where costs of materials can be justified. This would enable a province-wide compliance by grade and course for expected outcomes and the corresponding tests and exams. It would not supplant individuality of student for their personal learning progress, nor would it codify teachers who would still leverage their personalities and strengths to facilitate their students' knowledge acquisition and learning progress.

The government website does provide some outcomes expectations and metrics, but not at the depth for true assessment of student and of the school system. If these do exist, openness in our education system would have these disclosed, without names, for the public to view.

High school students in the 1970s mostly were opposed to 'matrics'–the matriculation exams that were mandatory for certain subjects and for which students had to cram for June in addition to their local teacher/school exam for the same subject. And, most teachers were as equally opposed to these provincial exams.

Recall why the students were opposed—because two exams had to be written! One exam was based on what the teacher taught and determined was important. The other, the provincial exam, the way the Education Department provided it. Now, one would ask, as did students, why they would have to write two exams for the same subject, and in June. Logically, to be followed up with a query as to why all teachers across the province did not teach the same subject the same way, and the response was because they disagreed with Fredericton and did not want to teach it that way...

In the major management, sales and other skills training organizations, those who collectively train millions globally, typically there are requirements to qualify to be a trainer/facilitator/instructor, including education/experience, professional designations, course completion, and so forth. Then, at the highest quality organizations, for each course or program or seminar, a certification process must be completed to a certain level, prior to being authorized to train or facilitate 'solo'. There are various approaches by the different companies to achieve this, and yet all have one key criteria in common: A trainer does not get in front of paying clients, internal employees or external contracts, unless they have been 'staged in' and reached the required level of competencies for knowledge and delivery.

One would expect that we have at a minimum a similar process for the final steps of certification for a teacher. Equipped with a university degree, a BED and a Teaching Certificate, until that person has taught each full subject, with appropriate observations by their principal and district subject support teacher, review of results from tests and exams, they really are Teacher-Candidates, not full Teacher certified. The private sector organizations also consider the student evaluations.

Fortunately, the primary and secondary education systems are providing more support and training for teachers beyond their BEd or MEd. And, the newer generation of teachers seemingly are open to team teaching, and other philosophies that have been introduced with the Middle School concept.

As reported by Business Insider, math teacher Paul Lockhart laments the pedagogy of math in today's schools. While one may agree with his essay, it would not be prudent for the Minister of Education, or the Assistant Deputy Minister, diving into another chaotic change in our school system. Neither can we tolerate the status quo. What we need is a strategic decision making process by the Department and the school system leaders to review first Language Education and then Math Education for the 21st century classroom, with recommendations by the Deputy Minister to the Minister within six months as to changes necessary for our students to reach our stated levels of competencies.

'Lockharts Lament Math Education is Wrong' begins with a story. "A musician wakes from a terrible nightmare. In his dream he finds himself in a society where music education has been made mandatory. "We are helping our students become more competitive in an increasingly sound-filled world." Educators, school systems, and the state are put in charge of this vital project. Studies are commissioned, committees are formed, and decisions are made— all without the advice or participation of a single working musician or composer."

"While it is important for students to work through a few basic problems at every level of mathematics they encounter, we live in an era when, once an understanding of the underlying concepts is mastered, one can turn to calculators or computer programs to do the mindless symbolic manipulations needed to get an answer. Pedagogy needs to move away from [only] finding the answer, and toward understanding **why** this is the answer and why we care about the answer." [21]

In 2010, Mark Zuckerberg, CEO and founder of Facebook, donated $100 million to the Newark Public Schools district. The goal was to not just completely transform Newark schools within five years, but to develop a model of education reform for all American cities. Five years have now passed, all of the money (which with a matching grant ended up totaling $200 million) has been spent and Newark schools are not much better off than when they started.

While the story of this failure, outlined in the book, 'The Prize: Who's in charge of America's Schools', is primarily about Newark, it also serves as a cautionary tale for us in Canada about monies spent, and America's failed approach to education reform. As in Health, Education with more funding, does not necessarily result in better outcomes.

A prepared Minister would be able to facilitate discussions around the issues that cause the most finger pointing to our students' outcomes: The trio of inclusion, bilingualism/immersion and classroom size. While none of these were issues 40 years ago, at least to the general public, and while New Brunswick was not at all near the bottom of the pack in those years, there is not necessarily a direct line between the two.

When it comes to comparative outcomes, it may be that we have not gained ground while other provinces have increased their outcomes. Some of it is attributable to areas where parents are of higher education and higher income and typically their children are higher performers at school. It also may be that as long as this province had a higher than national average rural citizenry with access to better paying forestry and mining jobs that did not require strong reading and arithmetic skills, students either slipped by in high school or slipped out without completing. And now they and we are in a situation of a shortage of 21st century workplace skillsets for the current working generation, and unfortunately it is being passed along generationally as well.

Class size is an ongoing aspect of discussion, disagreement and argument when it comes to anticipated outcomes of our students, along with our lacking in national and international testing comparisons. And, the inclusion policy factors into the same argument. And the (early) immersion issues. As

Finn Poschmann, CEO of APEC, wrote: "Make no mistake, the numbers of students per educator - class sizes, in other words - are falling. Across the Atlantic Provinces, over the past decade the number of primary and secondary school students has fallen by 18 per cent. However, the number of educators, meaning teachers plus administrators, has dropped by only two percent."

"In part the falling class sizes are demographically driven, in the sense that the school age population has been falling. But the decision to allow smaller class sizes to persist is a policy decision: a resource allocation decision."

"It is entirely understandable that teachers prefer the evolving status quo; it protects jobs and most will just plain prefer to have a smaller class, or fewer of them. And teachers are entirely right when they point to hefty classroom demands. We expect teachers to do well by special needs students, and to bring students from very different backgrounds and countries to a high performance standard. That takes time and so do testing, reporting and administrative duties. Smaller classes help with that."

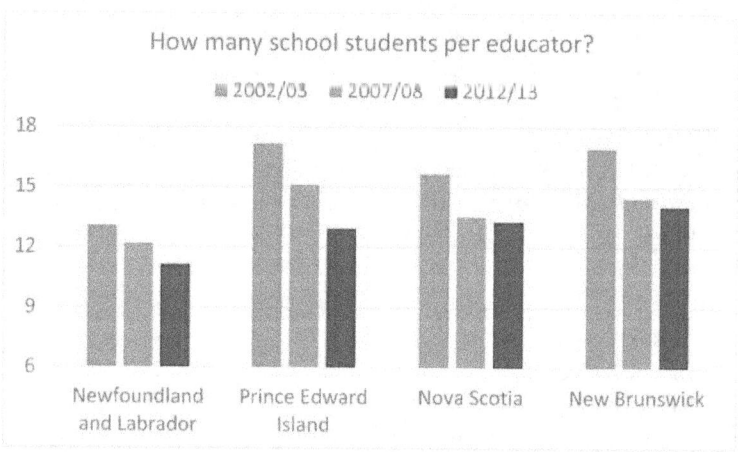

Source: Statistics Canada Elementary-Secondary Education Survey
Note: "Educators" refers to teachers and administrators. Part-time educators are pro-rated as one-fifth of a full-time equivalent.

"Meanwhile, parents too tend to prefer small class sizes: good for atmosphere, and we assume that it means some combination of better and more personalized teaching and better student performance. If this were true, however, we should be seeing steady improvement in student math and reading performance. With respect to most of the Atlantic Provinces, however, the Programme for International Student Assessment (PISA) shows nothing of the kind."

"And there is a reason for that. Parents and teachers are right about small class sizes being good for student performance, according to the empirical literature, up until about Grade 1. Not so much after that. After the earliest years, student performance seems to depend more on curriculum and the delivery of it, and testing, and in these regards smaller isn't better. But smaller classes consume more scarce resources per student." [22]

We cannot allow governments, or even different Ministers within the same government as they are reassigned portfolios, to make wholesale, disruptive changes to our students, and their teachers, without substantial evidence and best practice proven benefit. Still, we do need to change in a strategic and measured way to proven methodologies for our culture. Ours is not a culture where students will work all day and study all evening, unless we find a motivating reason otherwise, so we need to set targets that make sense.

A number of years ago there was a Chamber of Commerce in this province that experienced every President/Chair or two, a shift in the purpose of the Chamber, without the expressed consent, or consultation with the membership. While on occasion, a shake-up is certainly required in an association, there is a reason for being for that organization to exist. A Chamber of Commerce, a Rotary Club, or Realtors Association, each has a purpose for existing, and a new 'executive leader' may be given a mandate (an internal 'mission') for their incumbency. Rarely, are they given a mandate to completely change the organization.

It is not acceptable that a Minister of Education with a like or dislike for a particular philosophy (for example, 'streaming' and so change the year of entry for French Immersion) to foundationally disrupt a generally accepted method, holding back particularly gifted students, to align with their philosophical bias because they have the power.

If the entry level, or the graduation level, for language, math, or any other subject, is to be altered it ought to be evidenced based, for the benefit of the students and their education outcomes. Moreover, it ought to be changed in a transparent way, with stated reasons for the change and expected beneficial and positive outcomes. Preferences and philosophical feelings are not sufficient reasons for a Minister.

Early Childhood Education and Daycare need to be more adequately integrated from a systemic perspective. What is the 'hand-off' from the provincial system to the private daycare? What is expected in the daycare for reading and arithmetic usage as part of their certification and licensing?

Consideration should be given to Day Care as an Education and Development responsibility. Expectations would be a better streamlining and integration of the care of children and their early

childhood development. Daycare 'seats' or placements, sufficient for the children of this province, would be a provincial responsibility. A combination of private operators at their owner operator and not-for-profit sponsor sites, or private and public facilities in schools where the capacity is available.

At the post-secondary school level, community colleges are feeling the strains of infrastructure. The Province owns the buildings, and if it is going to continue with the traditional role of direct oversight, a different role than with universities, then it should retain ownership of the buildings or tender for P3 operators. Many of the structures are in need of maintenance and repair as anyone who has visited recently can notice upon entry, and sometimes without entry. If entire wings need to be demolished, it means that they are not being used and so should be demolished.

We need a continuous assessment of both NBCC and CCNB for this new century. Nova Scotia cycled through its transition of community colleges twenty years ago, and that may or may not be what we should adopt, at least in all aspects, but an evaluation of what this century holds for our state owned community college system would be appropriate.

The growth of private colleges, and their curriculums has been significant, and innovative, and in reply to customer demand. The community college system should exist to provide education and training where it is not already available. Maybe the entire curriculum, with an appropriate strategy executed with the assistance of a consulting company with expertise in education, should be privatized and the buildings demolished or sold with the land. (With proceeds applied to the provincial debt.)

A strategy with an execution plan that streamlines early childhood development, primary and secondary education, onward to a link with advanced education and training would integrate our children's education. Transparency of performance metrics and a system of national level benchmarks to attain, with continuous improvement may get us to 21st century achievements.

Justice and Public Safety NB

Significant changes in a province usually corresponds with legislation. The resulting workload on this Department may be more than it can expect to reasonably accomplish in the short time lines that are required. As with an earlier reference, this means supplemental assistance from private firms with relevant expertise will dispense with adding more staff while providing a developmental opportunity for those other lawyers. The contracts could be kept lower with this developmental opportunity consideration.

Policing (i.e., RCMP) contracts, aside from city forces, are managed centrally. Combined urban/rural police forces by Region, would mean contracts co-negotiated by the Ministry and the Regional Service Commission Boards with control and management residing in the latter.

One of the broader outcomes for this Ministry to aspire could be:

Value: A Safe Place to Live

Justice and Public Safety NB Key Indicator of Success:
   Protecting and providing a safe province, region and community for citizens and visitors through best practice services in Police, Fire, Emergency and Justice

On a creative note, New Brunswick should consider requesting a pilot program with Correctional Service Canada to use non-prison methods to deal with non-violent crimes such as theft, illegal drug possession, etc. House arrest with GPS-anklets, drug addict crimes with GPS anklets and mandatory detox/rehab paid by the province, is progressive.

Finance and Administration NB

The size, complexity, and level of expertise required of a full sized Ministry at Finance and Administration is at once indicative as to the reason for attracting at least some highly competent, seasoned business people to elected office, and ensuring that only the most competent are placed in the role.

Further, despite historical context being to the contrary, this role of Minister also is reason why a party leader should, at least on occasion, during the run-up to an election share with the public and his potential MLA mates, their preference for this position. The secrecy of Cabinet appointments is far overstated and overplayed. Undeniably, the individual would have to first be elected, but then so too does the Premier.

There is a wide range of important responsibilities in F&A and so it is one of the very few of the Ministries that may require more than one department, and certainly several direct reports. It also is a good

Ministry for a Secretary of the Legislature appointment, to a MLA with the commensurate capabilities. The specific role would be subject to significant issues of the day, including the agenda as electorally given to the Premier and Cabinet.

With the responsibilities of central procurement and supply systems in the Ministry, a government committed to the changes in the previous sections, would be well served by a Secretary of the Legislature with compatible skillsets to work with the Minister.

This wide ranging and wide reaching Ministry could have one of its key outcomes as:

Value: Governance and Civility

Finance and Administration NB Key Indicator of Success:
   Ensuring efficacy and fiscal responsibility in the provision of services of value and value for taxation

Established in 2010, The New Brunswick Internal Services Agency (NBISA), had a mandate to realign and deliver 'common services' – information management and technology, human resources, and financial and administrative services – within the Government of New Brunswick, using a shared-services delivery model, according to the website.

In other words, NBISA was a Department of Government Services, and is quite similar to the federal government and larger provinces equivalents. Services internal to government is a completely different operation than services to citizens and taxpayers. A review of the list of branches within the former NBISA would say that if anywhere, it should be a department reporting to the Ministry of Finance and Administration. An overview follows.

Corporate Services oversees all: Finance, Information Services Coordination, Records Management, Asset Management, Human Resources, Payroll and Benefits, Administration and Communications. It is also responsible for Algonquin Properties Limited and Algonquin Golf Limited.

Finance and Administrative Services is responsible for internal control and budget coordination, accounts payable, accounts receivable, chargebacks and the coordination of financial information for public accounts and budget estimates.

The Technology and Information / Records Management ensures that departmental program delivery is supported by effective use of technology. Staff provides technical support and advisory services and monitors and approves the acquisition of technology and related products to ensure compatibility with corporate standards.

Human Resources is responsible for staffing, training, labour relations, classifications and the administration of various Human Resources related programs.

The Communications Office serves as the first contact with the media, coordinating various media events, providing direction and support in the writing of various publications, speeches and news releases.

Containing all of these services 'under one roof' with the other financial and administration services, brings a critical mass of expertise and skills together. More productive workflows and workload sharing are possible, allowing movement to seasonal or situational peak demands. There even may be less positions required.

The primary role of most F&A services, those from NBISA and those already residing in Finance, is one of ensuring or being responsible for certain functions and services internal to government. A government of oversight would establish which of these would be a candidate for outsourcing, and determine which jurisdictions have been successful in that activity.

Operations and Systems would be a group of cross-functional and experienced high performers, knowledgeable in processes, systems and workflows, who could support and audit all areas of the civil service to ensure optimum effectiveness, efficiencies and staffing. This is a best practice function, existing in some of the top businesses, in major sectors including the finance industry. This is the group that would follow-up on Auditor General reported non-compliances. Also, it would provide guidance and expertise in six sigma, continuous improvement, and similar initiatives.

There may be services best placed within another Ministry. Information Technology is a vital infrastructure, and may be better managed within the Ministry of Infrastructure. Given the considerations previously, both Algonquin Properties Limited and Algonquin Golf Limited should be within Infrastructure NB. Consolidation of expertise and activity, within an accountability framework that is outcomes oriented and oversight driven, is more apt to provide value to the citizens of this Province.

Chapter 6

Righting Our Ship

and Moving Forward

Nearly three years ago, in a letter to the Editor of the Times&Transcript, I began, **"Only through major moves and revamps—a 're-set'—will we even have a chance of success in the no-turning-back challenge we face."**

What has become the standard by governments of increasing taxes is the easy way out. Companies must cut costs, increase quality control, and satisfy customers over competitive alternatives, which are intended to drive increases sales and gross profit. Governments collect income and other taxes which by definition may be revenues, but taxes are not sales whereby there is a direct exchange, and therefore cannot be gross profit. Worse still, taxes can be raised without increased value, quality, or user satisfaction; often either with or in place of cost cuts.

We need to re-set our attitudes to what we expect from and by government. But not one of lowering expectations, as that is one dimensional and scarcity thinking. It is taking responsibility seriously, making legitimate strategic decisions, and providing proper oversight of our services on our behalf. Governments have already tried to preserve and enhance our health, education and other services by increasing "revenues", our taxes; not value, but debt. It may be strategic to make cuts, but death by a thousand cuts is not only painful, the cuts are not a strategy.

If we are going to be righting our ship and moving forward, what I believe New Brunswick needs to do is what follows.

Approached with experience and knowledge, this requires a compelling vision, with a capacity and capability to communicate the vision, coalesce a focused group of nine other capable Ministers, set the strategy, consult and collaborate, then delegate the Ministers to execute with the Deputy Ministers and their professionals.

We need a real **New Brunswick re-set**, or we will accomplish no more than some tweaking with pain, still not prepared for the inevitable interest rate increases, always significantly dependent on federal government transfers and national changes in priorities. With resolve, competency, capacity building, and trust, we can be:

Sail Ready and Seaworthy

We can, within four years, say that:

We have restored hope, in harmony, community and opportunity
We are directing our future and by 2018 we will be re-building our Province for a 21st Century New Brunswick

We can say that we are:

A province of peoples living in peace, order and good government
—and by Righting Our Ship we will by 2017 be back in control with a zero deficit and be moving forward to better health, education, social services and community emancipation

We can be resolute and assert our principles of:

Respect ∼ Integrity ∼ Bilingualism
 Rights entrenched in our Constitution

We can as the times require refine the indicators of success that are reflective of what we mean by our Values of:

Dignity and Well-Being
A Safe Place to Live
Governance and Civility
Our Way of Life

We will know that we are moving forward if we:

Create a 21st century government for the people of New Brunswick

Create a transparency and openness of government, from strategy to actions to outcomes, including clear financial reporting

Transform the civil service to one of oversight and not doing

Emancipate the regions and unincorporated areas of this Province

Accept the stewardship of our lands and waters for living, recreation, economic benefits, and environmental conservation

New Brunswick citizens deserve a strategy that establishes an overarching purpose for the decisions we make with regard to services and to budgets, not just cuts and cutbacks, not succumbing to lower expectations, but renewed objectives to live up to our values. We need to start on day one as we:

Create a 21st century government for the people of New Brunswick

1-Modernize the Governance of New Brunswick with a Cabinet of ten, including the Premier. Redefine the role of Minister to be that as chair of a Ministry. Redefine the role of Deputy Minister to a Chief Operations Officer role that leads and manages the Department(s) within that Ministry.

2-Establish both protocol and process for a new-world order of Cabinet, management and meetings, delegation protocols to Ministers defined, and a consistency in chairing of Ministries and delegating to Departments. Ministers will be appointed for 18 month terms, with explicit expectations and monthly performance reporting to the Premier and Cabinet.

3-The Premier's Office will devolve Deputy Ministers and decision making to the respective Ministry, with explicit and implicit authorities from the Minister. The Premier's 'control' will be through effective chairing of Cabinet and delegation to Ministers; not the bypassing of authority with Deputy Ministers as direct reports to the Premier's Office. Best practice processes and professional training will be provided to guide and ensure Ministerial roles.

4-Provide a government of *Clarity and Truth* in the priorities presented to the voters as the same priorities of the government, honest when adjusting course when necessary, and without agendas hiding an underlying intent. *Accountability and Trust* will be upheld, and politicians and civil servants held to it.

Create a transparency and openness of government, from strategy to actions to outcomes, including clear financial reporting.

1-Communicate and share all Ministry outcomes, objectives, as well as quality and quantity metrics, reporting on a semi-annual basis a publicly released straightforward report card to ensure full disclosure. In essence, a Minister's full mandate and expected metrics will be known to the public, and their assessment will be obvious.

2-All Ministerial outcomes, 'report cards'—strategic, operational and financial—will be posted on the government website, in the same prescribed format, with all reports remaining accessible for six years before archiving to an site with access in perpetuity.

3-Institute *Openness* of government to remove the culture of secrecy. Create *Transparency* including sharing information and ensuring understanding of the workings of the people's government on their behalf. All information, data, reports—schools, hospitals, departments, and government funded or sponsored programs such as day care centers—will be posted, and no longer by exception; rather, the exception will be private, confidential and security related using an established and disclosed protocol.

Transform the civil service to one of oversight and not doing

1-Establish a framework of Deputy Ministers communicating and delegating expectations of outcomes, with professionals and support staff who are equipped to provide appropriate administrative oversight of the quality and quantity measurements necessary for those outcomes.

2-Work with experts within and without the civil service to reconstruct government, beginning with a full and complete strategic review to continue across the entire government for a 2016-17 zero deficit budget.

3. Rehabilitate our education and health services.

-Establish outcomes for healthcare and hospital services to reach Canadian median ranges.

-Establish outcomes for Grade 12/9/6/3 students so that they are prepared for each next step of their learning lives, at Canadian median ranges.

-Collaborate with the professionals in the implementation of changes necessary, and execution of processes to reach outcomes.

-Transparency and reporting of key data and results

-Professionals will focus on their professional outcomes, not buildings, vehicles or cleaning.

4-Rehabilitate government structure and operations for effectiveness and value for cost to the taxpayer.

-Freeze all salaries and wages to 2018-03-31. Reduce the number of civil service (proper) positions based on changes to what is required by the nouveau government. (Each 1000 employees equates to approximately $50-80million savings per year.)

-Freeze number of all health care employees, except physicians, nurses and deemed necessary specialist roles who will be replaced at attrition.

-Reduce the number of teachers and teacher support positions to a national benchmarked ratio

-Contract out all non-government-necessary positions, including bus drivers, cleaners, cafeteria workers, construction/maintenance workers.

5-Get our government out of the business of running businesses. Hire an expert to assist in privatizing NB Liquor to two or three wholesalers, and province wide private retailers, with a royalty stream of revenues. License fees to be collected similar to licensed beverage establishments. Establish a 'dealership' model of ServiceNB to Credit Unions and Caisse-Populaires. Property, capital and initial dealer fees proceeds to pay down provincial debt. Share all details of an updated review by a reputable expert of the NB Power sale with five fully outlined options and comparisons.

6- Establish a Province wide hotel levy night fee, $2.50 per $100 per room per night, collected by the hotels and remitted to the N.B. Finance. Monthly, 80% disbursed to the applicable RSC for the Regional Tourism Council, the remaining amount to the provincial Tourism & Hospitality promotional budget. Partner with the Regions, to manage Provincial Parks, within local recreation departments or private operators, with land ownership retained by the Province. Create joint weigh-station / auto toll booths for trucks at the current locations, while providing NB registered a special tax deduction.

7-Establish, based on best practices proven in other jurisdictions as well as this Province, protocols and contractual inclusions in outsourcing of services and goods. Transparent and open RFPs, with contracting to two or more providers for healthcare, IT, and laundry; primary highways maintenance and snow removal; hospital and school cafeterias; procurement of all other goods and services.

Emancipate the unincorporated areas and enable the Regions to enhance their communities

1-Consistent with legitimate *Representation and Consultation* as the new norms expected by citizens, by 2018 all incorporated areas will be facilitated to direct local representation; no longer will the all commanding 'mayor' of Local Service Districts be the Minister of Environment and Local Government.
-Beginning with a 'pilot' region, ready with the resources and willing with the know-how, there will be wide ranging information sessions, discussions and town halls, with meaningful data on costs and benefits.
--LSDs and adjacent towns and villages and cities will be part of the decision making in transforming to larger municipalities (targeting 3000+ and $300million tax base)
-In line with existing legislation, property tax rates will not be of a singular structure in each municipality; rather the rates will be reflective of services provided. Municipalities will comply. RSCs will mediate.
-Twelve regions, based on consultation and collaboration, will likely become a more equitable (population, geography, economic, resources) 8 or 9 regions
-With all residents residing in a municipality, by-elections for additional councilors to be held for balance of terms to 2020 spring elections.

2-The Province will work with the Regional Service Commissions, at the strategic and operational levels where real, meaningful change will transpire in services that are close to the citizens, and real savings will be derived from regional oversight and accountability to the Board of Mayors of the Region.
-District Engineer to move to the office of the RSC reporting to the Executive Director with responsibility to contract out all roads in the Region for maintenance and snow clearing, and the oversight of quality and quantity; exception will be the primary highways retained by the

Province. Budgets to be ascertained and funding transferred form the Province to the RSC. Savings to adjust the funding.

-Equalization grants to be replaced with a line on a new, detailed and transparent, Property Tax Assessment, indicating a (-) for receiving an equalization subsidy. No complicated 'secret' formulae, no politics or political intervention, full transparency.

-Infrastructure 10-year plan to be created by the Ministry of Infrastructure, in consultation with the RSC Boards, for regional and municipal infrastructure projects. Priority based decisions and annual budget commitments will replace uncertain unconditional grants.

-Regions will evolve, as contracts will permit and situations are relevant, to single Police forces with rural and municipal expertise.

-Fulltime and volunteer Fire Fighting Services will form a regional council to work together on services and procurement management for optimum pricing on equipment and sharing of resources.

(Savings could be in the range of $60million plus depending on final equalization 'subsidies' necessary for minimal service levels in identified communities.)

Accept the stewardship of our lands and waters for living, recreation, economic benefit, and environmental conservation

It is worth repeating: Stewardship of our resources is more than those issues related to environment and conservation. Good stewardship also is concerned with long term viability, such as harvesting and replanting our forests, or fish farming that is respectful of natural wildlife. Exploiting our minerals and gas and oil in environmentally safe methods and economically beneficial payback also is good stewardship.

1-Using the NB Crown Land Conservation Areas Map along with the RSC Regional maps, a full inventory of all recreation parcels and trails, conservation, and environmentally protected areas will be completed. All roads and industrial activity will be noted, and each future activity projected then actual will be noted on a corresponding map, that then the host site GeoNB, will allow an overlay.

2-There will be a review of all environmental approval procedures, Environmental Impact Assessment (EIA) processes, with a wide ranging committee of experts, and informed citizens from English, French, Mi'kmaq, Maliseet, rural and urban communities, as well as industry representatives, and civil servants, lasting no more than three months and completed by 2016-04-15.

3-The Sisson Mine project, and hydraulic fracturing of gas by Corridor Resources and SWM Resources projects, will be reviewed and if all completed assessments are compatible with the requirements of the Province New Brunswick, approval will be provided to proceed by 2015-05-15. (These are exceptional revenue streams, by New Brunswick standards, and good paying jobs.)

4-The Canada East oil pipeline project will be requested to proceed with completion of all assessments, followed by a direct request to Ottawa for this national project to proceed. The Irving Oil group will be asked to investigate, or complete their investigation, for an expanded refinery prior to export, for additional value add in Canada and jobs and tax revenues in New Brunswick.

5-Professional oversight by engineers with the requisite expertise, working with the Environment and Community NB Department, will ensure all projects to be in compliance with regulations, safety, security, operations as well as environmental impact. Full transparency and openness will be evident with all reports and inspections on the government website. The potential of an environmental mishap protection 'insurance policy', additional to the usual policies, with the Province as beneficiary, will be investigated to provide compensation above penalties.

As will be recalled, the chapters in this book provide further context, background, and details for these objectives and goals.

Principles are the bedrock of our society, and a Premier has to be the primary advocate. Where there is disagreement, if a case of misunderstanding then communicate for understanding; if one of conflict, then assertively press as to the realities of an advanced society; if situations of extreme that are contrary to our collective communities' good sense then facilitate to appropriateness.

Respect;
Integrity;
Bilingualism;
Rights entrenched in our Constitution
(by the Canadian Charter of Rights and Freedoms)

A Premier should collaborate with all an all-party committee of the Legislature, at the beginning of the term, and as an annual check throughout the term, as to how we our living up to our values as well as to the refining of the indicators of success of our values.

Dignity and Well-Being
~As a person, a group, a community, a people
~Be who you are, with respect and respectful
~Quality of life in health, education, work, recreation
~Accessibility and inclusion of all persons

A Safe Place to Live
~In our Communities
~On our roads and highways and byways and trails and waterways
~For family, as any of us may describe
~Through expression, of who we are individually and collectively
~Well-being protected and defended

Governance and Civility
~Competent, capable government, accountable and fiscally responsible
~Transparency and trust in policy, action and outcomes
~Talents and skills of our people respected and leveraged
~Resources optimization, environmentally, economically, socially
~Services of value and value for taxation

Our Way of Life
~Livable places for home, work and recreation
~Neighborly concern, support, respect, courtesy
~Opportunity for prosperity as each of us defines and lives
~Contributing to others in our province, country, world

Let's get sail ready and seaworthy. We can work this together, transcending parochial pursuits or competition amongst our own communities and regions. We have the opportunity to do **the 're-set' that we need by recreating government, rehabilitating services, emancipating our communities in a model of Regions, and accepting a full stewardship of New Brunswick.**
Ours is a Province of small population and without one of our larger population cities being significantly larger than the others to centralize major infrastructure within a substantial mass of population. Unique among provinces, we are absent a dominant city and metropolitan area, with the

singular important large airport and harbour, the major seat of universities, health centers, as well as the provincial government, arts center, and so on.

In New Brunswick, for a century now we have had three cities sharing what is concentrated in the one large city in the other provinces. A model of regions will enable more direct citizen control, allowing the province to focus on the significant services upon which we rely for our health, well-being and lifestyle. Ours is a richness of all that is New Brunswick and we should believe in our potential in a few years from now saying:

We have restored hope, in harmony, community and opportunity, we are a self-sustaining participant in Canada.

The Way It Is

There's a thread you follow. It goes among
things that change. But it doesn't change.
People wonder about what you are pursuing.
You have to explain about the thread.
But it is hard for others to see.
While you hold it you can't get lost.
Tragedies happen; people get hurt
or die; and you suffer and get old.
Nothing you do can stop time's unfolding.
You don't ever let go of the thread.

William Stafford, American Poet

We need to know our thread. Our thread is our core set of principles, our values and how we define them, our mission as a peoples living here in this Province, and our vision of who we are ultimately. Aspiring to the vision, we can decide that:

We have restored hope, in harmony, community and opportunity by Righting Our Ship and Re-creating a Nouveau New Brunswick.

End Notes

[1] Over the Cliff?: Acting Now to Avoid New Brunswick's Bankruptcy, by Richard Saillant

[2] "values-based, customer-centric, and sales-driven" © cfsteeves
"lead by those values as a base, their mission as a mandate, and their vision as an inspiration" © cfsteeves

[3] Why Change Programs Don't Produce Change HBR 1990Nov-Dec by Michael Beer, Russell A. Eisenstat, Bert Spector Mastering Change APR 1993 adapted from Rosabeth Moss Kanter's speech at a Utah State University symposium.

[4] © David Osborne and Ted Gaebler, 1992
My copy was obtained not long after the 1993 printing, and the book has been my recommendation to more than one government minister, provincial and federal. *cfs*

[5] The Cult of Efficiency, © 2001 Janice Gross Stein and the Canadian Broadcasting Corporation

[6] Over the Cliff?: Acting Now to Avoid New Brunswick's Bankruptcy, by Richard Saillant

[7] From https://www.gnb.ca/legis/publications/tradition/legtrad10-e.asp

[8] Said to Angelo Lombardo, Executive Director, Ontario Federation of Anglers and Hunters 2014-10-17

[9] "Reinventing Government" ©David Osborne and Ted Gaebler, 1993 Plume, Penguin Group

[10] From 'Boards that Make a Difference' © 1990 Jossey-Bass Inc, Publishers

[11] * From 'Bureaucratizing the Atlantic Revolution, Vol. XXXVIII, No. 1 Winter/Spring - Hiver/Printemps 2009, article https://journals.lib.unb.ca/index.php/acadiensis/article/view/12473/13396

[12] © David Osborne and Ted Gaebler, 1992 'Reinventing Government'

[13] Over the Cliff?:Acting Now to Avoid New Brunswick's Bankruptcy, by Richard Saillant

[14] © Jeffry D. Sachs, 2008 Published by The Penguin Press

[15]   https://www.linkedin.com/pulse/whats-more-important-business-good-idea-just-timing-chip-cutter?trk=li_tw_corp_goodidea&sf8106191=1

[16] William Watson, National Post 2015-08-25

[17] Excerpt from *Little Louis and the Giant KC* by John Edward Belliveau 1980 Lancelot Press

[18] Frank McKenna, to John Chilibeck Telegraph Journal 2014-10-24

[19] from his Commentary on CBC News NB 2014-08-27

[20] from a Commentary by Dr Ezekiel J. Emanuel, at https://t.co/zOrqzRflY5 #FortuneInsider 2015-11-11 Dr. Ezekiel, Reinventing American Health Care

[21] Read more at: http://www.businessinsider.com/lockharts-lament-math-education-is-wrong-2014-10#ixzz3HHFBFgqz

[22] Email from the desk of Finn Poschmann 2015-12-08
 President and CEO APEC|Atlantic Provinces Economic Council

I am grateful

For a trio of Grade 8 teachers who inspired me to think about society, politics, literature, and the world

For my friend Robert MacDiarmid for good thinking conversation and golf

For my sons Carl and David who think about the world about them and how to make it a better place

For my best friend and life partner Betty who shows me every day how to think and be generous toward others

cfs

Righting Our Ship
Re-creating a Nouveau New Brunswick

Righting Our Ship probes the essence of a small Canadian province that must do nothing short of a transformation by Re-creating a Nouveau New Brunswick. The author prescribes a leadership that discerns the principles, values and mission of the Province, and the capabilities required for a new kind of government to execute on a vision for 21st Century Direction, Expectations and Governance.

Righting our ship is the first stage to take control and have a self-determined destiny in New Brunswick. Re-creating a Nouveau New Brunswick is about New Brunswickers pressing for and supporting a transformation, without delay, to a province of self-control, with a renewed sense of destiny and a self-sufficiency—something not seen for far too many decades.

C F (Chuck) Steeves is a strategist and facilitator of thinking with purpose and performing for success. His Atlantic Canada focused business is complemented with frequent travels around the world to assist clients in mastering processes and skills in interaction and transaction to get results.

He and his life-partner and spouse Betty have two adult sons. He is located in South East New Brunswick when not traveling for work, learning and pleasure.

www.ingramcontent.com/pod-product-compliance
Lightning Source LLC
Chambersburg PA
CBHW072042280526
45788CB00006B/2154